The Web Startup Roadmap

Navigate Your Way to a Successful Online Business

JP STONESTREET

Copyright © 2013 Ripen Publishing

All rights reserved.

Cover Design by Budi Saputra (Omini on 99Designs.com)

Reproduction or translation of any part of this work beyond that permitted by Section 107 or 108 of the 1976 United States Copyright Act without permission of the copyright owner is unlawful. Requests for permission or further information should be addressed to The Ripen Group, LLC.

This publication is designed to provide accurate and authoritative information in regard to the subject matter covered. It is sold with the understanding that the author and publisher are not engaged in rendering legal, accounting, or other professional services. If legal advice or other expert assistance is required, the services of a competent professional should be sought.

ISBN-10:   0-61573-931-8
ISBN-13: 978-0-61573-931-1 (Ripen Publishing)

DEDICATION

This book is dedicated to my parents who have always supported me and told me I could achieve whatever I wanted in life. They've always been great parents and advisors.

JP Stonestreet

CONTENTS

DEDICATION 1
CONTENTS 3
Acknowledgements 7
Wait! Before You Read This Book... 9
Who is this guy? 11
Phase 1: Planning for Success 23
    Why Do a Web Startup? 23
    3 Common Traits of Successful Startups 25
    What's Your Goal? 28
    What to do... What to do... 29
    Your Viable Business Filter 31
    Business Models That Work On the Web 32
    Your Startup Log 36
    Defining Your Idea At a High Level 38
    [Your Idea]: Brick or Balloon? 40
    Seed Capital: Bootstrapping vs. Funding 53
    Writing Your Plan 63

Crafting Your Elevator Pitch 70

Off to the Races 77

Planning For Success Checklist 83

Phase 2: Starting Your Startup 85

Before You Turn the Key 85

Legal CYA 92

Create Your Identity 114

Finances 133

Manufacturers & Suppliers 138

Starting Your Startup Checklist 140

Phase 3: Building Your Website 141

The Importance of Quality 142

10 Things Every Website Needs 143

8 Optional Things Your Website Might Need 170

Defining Requirements 186

Website Development 194

Finding Talent 205

Interviewing 207

Managing Your Team 214

Testing Your Software 218

Deployment Time 221

Building Your Website Checklist 223

Phase 4: Marketing Your Website 224

Cost-Per-Acquisition (CPA) 225

Pay-Per-Click Advertising (PPC) 232

Affiliate Marketing 235

- Social Media Marketing ... 239
- Email & eNewsletters ... 250
- Postcards ... 252
- Telemarketing or Telesales ... 254
- Networking & Shoe Leather Marketing ... 255
- Content Marketing ... 255
- Search Engine Optimization (SEO) ... 257
- Marketing Your Website Checklist ... 270

Phase 5: Running Your Business ... 272
- Entrepreneurship Unplugged ... 272
- Reinvestment ... 274
- Growth Phase ... 275
- Exit Strategy ... 282
- The Good Life ... 288

Please Review! ... 291
About the Author ... 292
Resources ... 293
Index ... 297

JP Stonestreet

Acknowledgements

Even though I'm a closet writer and most people didn't know I was writing this book, they still had to deal with the invisible effects such as my absence from events and my irritation from writer's block. Thankfully, my family and friends were extremely supportive during this very difficult time. I hope this counts as an apology!

I would especially like to thank my parents for supporting me and my crazy dreams since I was just a little, starry eyed kid. Even on those rare occasions when I lost faith in myself, they never lost their faith in me. I couldn't ask for better parents.

Next, a huge thanks to Greg Ahern, my old business partner who worked tirelessly with me for years on several unsuccessful businesses before we figured out what we were doing.

Thank you also to my former wife, Stacey, for helping support me while I chased my entrepreneurial dreams. It is NOT easy being married to an entrepreneur! My daughter Sydney also deserves some credit for putting up with a dad who "works all the time," as she puts it.

Finally, a big thanks to all my friends: Amelia, Jen, Stephen, Cathie, Marc, Matt, Anna (aka Deanna), and everyone else who had to listen to me incessantly blather on about my business and my plans. You guys are the bee's knees!

JP Stonestreet

Wait! Before You Read This Book…

This book is intended to be a roadmap for starting and running your own online business. You can use it as a reference when you're doing various activities, but I highly recommend reading it from start to finish at least once so you'll have a clear picture of the entire roadmap before you leave on the trip.

This book is *not* intended to be a city guide…just a roadmap. My goal is to give you the outline with enough information to get started and ask good questions. If you want to delve deeper into any one section, for instance, legal entities or social media marketing, you can find entire books written on those subjects at the bookstore or library. I've also included a resources section at the end of this book with several recommendations for further reading broken out by topic.

The sections in the book are more or less chronological based on the order that you'll likely do things. You don't need to do everything in the order I've outlined; however, you'll find that most things flow naturally once you start.

Some of the concepts are difficult to grasp (at least they were for me). I'll do my best to describe them in layman's terms. Unlike many business books on the shelf, you won't need an MBA to understand this one.

Some free supporting materials are available for download at www.TheWebStartupRoadmap.com. Feel free to use and modify them to fit your business needs. You should double and triple check all the formulas in the spreadsheets to make sure they're accurate (they're offered without warrantees or guarantees). I once made a whole line of decisions based on an incorrect formula in one column of a spreadsheet. Trust me; you DON'T want to do that!

Aside from parenting, starting a business is the grandest adventure you'll ever undertake! Adapt and be flexible. Stay positive and enjoy the ride. But most importantly, be persistent! There will be bumps in the road and your first idea may not work, but if you stick with it and keep trying, you just might be able to retire early and taste the fruits of your labor while you're still young enough to enjoy them!

Follow the guidelines in this book and you'll be well on your way to freedom and financial independence. I wish you the very best. May victory be yours!

Who is this guy?

You may be wondering who the heck this guy is and what makes him qualified to write a book about web startups. Every time I read a book, the first question I ask myself is "Should I listen to this person and why?" Of course I'm much more skeptical than the average bear, but if you're like me, here's a little info about the author.

I'm actually a very normal person, just like you. Possibly the only significant difference is that I've launched several websites and sold two at the tender age 36 to a company near Silicon Valley in California. It was a long road to get there and many lessons, both painful and pleasant, were learned along the way. Please join me on my journey from lawn mowing in a small town in Kansas to selling a successful web startup.

Biz Kid

Like many entrepreneurs, I wasn't born into a rich family. My family was comfortably middle-class. My dad was a manager in a large corporation and my mom worked several jobs over the years, mostly office work and customer service. Contrary to what most people have believed over the years, I wasn't born with a silver spoon in my mouth.

For as long as I can remember, I've always wanted to own a business. Like most children, I tried the lemonade stand, but the cash flow on that venture was miserable and the margins were non-existent. I may not have used those exact words at the time, but I was smart enough to recognize the impact.

Once I was tall enough to see over the handle of a lawn mower, I found that mowing lawns was much more lucrative. At one point, I was mowing nearly every lawn you could see from my backyard.

I've often wondered if entrepreneurship is genetic. Several of my family members have owned businesses. My aunt owned several different restaurants over the years. My uncle owned a discount store similar to Big Lots. I'm told my great-grandparents owned a local grocery store. I think business ownership is in my blood, so it's no surprise to me that I've dreamed of it my whole life.

For a few weeks each summer WAY back in high school, I stayed with my grandpa in Texas. He was a retired executive and lived on a private lake and golf course called Lake Kiowa, outside Gainesville just north of Dallas. I didn't realize it at the time, but those summers would be some of the best educational experiences I would ever have.

Back in those days, I was quite the golfer and a "very polite young man" as my grandparents were often told. Since nearly everyone who lived in that secluded golf course community was retired, there weren't too many kids my age playing golf during the week, so I played with the retired folks. Sometimes I would play with grandpa and his friends; sometimes I'd just play with his friends while grandpa stayed home.

During their working careers, most of these men were either executives in large companies or they ran their own companies. If you've ever worked at a large company, these were the guys that everyone got nervous around when they walked through the building. And I played golf with them…when I was 16 years old…on a daily basis. What effect do you think that experience had on me?

Well, for one, I've never been nervous when someone like them walked through the building. In fact, more often than not, I walked with them and talked to them like they were real people, because that's exactly what they were.

When I was fresh out of college working my first job at a large corporation, I approached an executive who I admired for his intelligence and decision making abilities, and asked him to be my mentor. He was shocked that I asked, and more than happy to oblige my request.

We met officially on a weekly basis to talk about everything under the sun, but he liked me and would often talk to me in the halls and stop by my cube to check on me every once in a while. Needless-to-say, I quickly became known as the "suck-up" and the "teacher's pet" among my fellow co-workers, but it had nothing to do with that. I liked and admired him. I wanted to learn as much as I could from him. The attitude of my co-workers helps explain why they remained in the same position while I was promoted every 9 months, although I'm sure they thought it was because I was such a good suck-up.

Being an entrepreneur takes guts because you have to interact with people who have money and power. If you're too nervous to talk to them, or you think that talking to them means you're an ass kisser, you need to just get over yourself. They're people just like you. Get out of your head and be happy that you have the opportunity to learn from them.

Talking to people with money and power has always come naturally to me, but it took a long time for me to figure out why. It wasn't until many years later that I began to appreciate the value of those summers with grandpa on the golf course. Thankfully, I realized it before he passed away and I was able to tell him how much he meant to me and how much I learned from him and his golfing buddies during those hot Texas summers in my teenage years.

First Ventures

After I graduated from the University of Kansas with a Bachelor's in Communication Studies, I got my first job at a large corporation as an executive assistant. Still wanting to chase the dream of owning a company, I started my first venture with two friends from college.

We had the idea to launch a website called KansasCity.com. This was the fall of 1995 and the web was still in its infancy. We didn't know it then, but CitySearch was in the process of being launched a couple thousand miles away in Hollywood, California. KansasCity.com would have been a direct competitor.

Not having any true business experience what-so-ever, my friends and I had no idea what we were doing and no one wanted to follow anyone else. We all did what we thought needed to be done, which wasn't an effective strategy, because in the end, nothing was actually done that needed to be done. The venture was over almost as soon as it began.

While working my day job, I taught myself how to program so I could make my job easier. I spent 4 hours per day 10-keying data from network switches into an Excel spreadsheet for data analysis. This seemed like a total waste of time to me, which was motivation to spend the other 4 hours each day writing software to automate the entire process and eventually put myself out of a job.

Once that happened, my manager asked me to take over the analysis of the data I was collecting, and to automate anything else that could be automated. I quickly created reports the executives had never seen before and they used the information to make better business decisions.

When an executive who was responsible for a network expansion plan left the company, I took on additional workload to pick up where he left off. He had created a detailed financial model for the network expansion, but it was full of errors. Once I corrected the faulty formulas and updated it with accurate data, it changed the direction of the expansion plan and saved the company $24 million.

As a show of gratitude for saving them millions of dollars, I received a football signed by two of my executives (it wasn't signed by actual football players) and a gift check for $100. It was a nice gesture, but not commensurate to the value of my contribution. I thought about getting a t-shirt printed that read, "I saved the company $24 million and all I got was this lousy football" but I didn't think that would go over very well at work....

I still have that football in my office to remind myself why I'd rather own the company than work for one. I love to show people my "24 million dollar football" and tell them the story of how I got it.

One big company benefit that I utilized while working there was the education reimbursement program. That program foot the bill for my Master's degree from The University of Kansas in Organizational Communication. My degree focused on the interaction between communication and technology, which at the time was a relatively new phenomenon.

Part of my work involved a case study on the use of Happy Mail, which pre-dated Microsoft Outlook. The company I worked for used it as their email program and I gathered data on how people used it to communicate. We still used printed memos more than email back then, which made it very difficult to examine the social impact of communication technology in the workplace.

Unfortunately, I didn't find anything conclusive, and in retrospect, that's not surprising. We didn't know what the hell we were doing with communication technology back then. I mean seriously, our email program was called Happy Mail for crying out loud! What did you expect me find?!

Around that time, I also started my first consulting business on the side. It wasn't much of a success, but I did have a couple clients who contracted me to write software for them. I named the company "Informed Decisions" and my goal was to help small businesses make better decisions using data collection and analysis methodologies that I used in my day job. My thought was if they had some tools to analyze their customer habits, cash flow, and expenses, they could better manage their businesses and increase profitability in the same way big companies do.

However, it wasn't long before I realized just how little I knew about running a business. Doing the work was hard but at least I knew how to do it. It was the marketing, sales and finances that caused the most difficulty. After my first couple of projects, I closed up shop and started chasing a different rainbow.

Dotcom Days

Back in the early days of the dotcom boom, there was a lot of money to be made just working for someone else. There was little risk to accompany fat paychecks, foosball tables, pool tables, ping pong tables, game consoles, beer Friday's, great benefits and lots of vacation. Like heading west for the gold rush in the 1800's, I headed east to Washington, DC in search of my pot of gold (aka Stock Options).

The first company I worked for was a small consulting firm that wrote software for some big names. My first project was managing a team of thirteen developers and testers who were responsible for enhancing and maintaining the stockbroker certification, training and testing system used by NASD, the parent company of the NASDAQ Stock Exchange. My next project was managing a team that built a tracking system for the Associated Press, which allowed them to keep tabs on the rich, famous and powerful. I also worked on projects for Kinko's Corporate and for the Department of Housing and Urban Development (HUD). Going from a small town in Kansas to working in an office that was two blocks from the White House on projects for internationally recognized companies was quite the boost to my small town ego.

Then, one night while working late in the downtown DC office, I got a fateful instant message from my wife who was working in Reston, Virginia at the time. "Ba-ding" said AOL IM. The message was short, "I'm pregnant." And with those two little life changing words, I began the search for a job that was closer to my home in Vienna, Virginia so I could forego the hour long commute each direction every day.

That's when I went to work for a true startup that built websites for other true startups. The office was open air (there were no cubicles) and everyone could see everybody. It took some getting used to, but I grew to enjoy the openness. Plus the salary was great, my team of developers and testers were great and the perks were better. It was also less than two miles from my house. I went from an hour plus commute to a three minute commute.

Those were some fun times. Striking it rich was a common occurrence back then. I knew two people who worked at AOL when it went public. They celebrated with a night out in a limo, tickets to the Kennedy Center and dinner at the most expensive restaurant in DC. I personally had thousands of options from the dotcom where I worked. It was such an exciting time…while it lasted.

In the spring of 2001, the dotcom I worked for, as well as the one my wife worked for, went bankrupt just under a year after the dot-bomb hit. That's when my wife, daughter and I moved out west to Denver. And it's also when I started my first series of true dotcoms, with varying levels of success and failure.

MeteredWorks

My first venture was a website called MeteredWorks. I started it with a few guys I worked with at consulting companies in DC. Our concept was to offer a hosted service to any type of business that had to set appointments with their clients. Much like my first venture out of college, we had no clearly defined leadership and, in addition, we were geographically dispersed. We were also all developers and technical architects; we had no one with sales and marketing experience in our group.

Before we started development, I met with a potential alpha customer…a veterinarian and groomer. I used him to help hash out the requirements and wrote a very long document describing everything we needed to build. But once development was ready to begin, we all disagreed about how to do it and the partnership crumbled.

By this time, I was on the verge of giving up. I had tried several different things, learned a lot from each, but failed at all of them. I felt like I was getting closer and closer to a winning strategy each time, but couldn't quite get it to come together. One thing I decided was that I'd had enough with partnerships and committed to doing the next venture on my own.

PromoteWare

Falling back on what I knew, I launched a web consulting business. I knew I could build websites for a lot less than most of my competition, so I started creating my own framework for doing it. The framework would later be called PromoteWare, and it became the foundation of my consulting business, as well as the platform I used to build the next several dotcoms.

PromoteWare was a modular web-based development platform. I started building it two years before WordPress and it had similar functionality to WordPress (although PromoteWare wasn't nearly as easy to implement as WordPress is).

Once I had the foundational components built, I launched "Stonestreet Enterprises" and started attending local networking events to drum up business. Unlike my first consulting business, "Informed Decisions," I had numerous clients and launched several websites for local businesses. I certainly wasn't making a killing, but at $30K my first year, it was the most money I'd ever made from a business I owned.

At a networking event hosted by the Littleton Chamber of Commerce, I met a man named Greg Ahern. He was in the same business as me, only his focus was on website marketing. We agreed to send business each other's way and eventually started working together on projects. I built the sites and he marketed them for the clients. It was my first working partnership, and one of the keys to its success was having complimentary skill sets.

Home-Showing

With some experience under my belt and still wanting to start a true dotcom, I conceived and developed my first SAAS application: Home-Showing.net. After a painful experience looking for houses and trying to set showings, I spoke to my real estate agent about automating the entire process. My intent was to build a website that would allow agents to set showings online and retrieve lockbox combinations without the need to speak to anyone over the phone.

> ### Did you know...
>
> SAAS (pronounced sas, rhymes with gas) stands for Software As A Service. Unlike applications installed on a personal computer, SAAS applications are launched on the web or on an Intranet and made available through a thin client such as a browser like IE or Chrome.

Greg knew the owner of a brokerage office and he convinced them to beta test the site that I had built. They loved it, but it was missing a key ingredient: the listings. They didn't want to reenter the hundreds of listings they had; instead, they wanted the software to integrate with the local MLS Company. Sounds simple enough, right?

Wrong. MLS companies are monopolies in metro areas and they're very protective of their data. They perceived us as a potential threat so they refused us access to their database and killed the business before we had our first paying customer. Another failure!

Luckily, PromoteWare was doing fairly well. Greg and I formed an official partnership, which allowed us to pool our resources and gain some synergy. We were making a living, but nothing more. We both had much loftier goals, so we kept looking for another idea that would catapult us out of the drudgery of consulting.

TimeToParent

Being in a new city with a very young child and starting a company is hard on a marriage. There's a saying that every business is a family business because the whole family is involved whether they work directly for the company or not. The long hours and stress took its toll, and my wife and I filed for divorce.

During the process of getting divorced, I began to realize how hard it would be to coordinate all the activities involved with parenting. How would we keep track of the schedule? How would we coordinate pick-ups and drop-offs? Who do we call in case of an emergency? How can we avoid talking on the phone as much as possible? I thought to myself, "I've got it! I'll build a website to automate the process of parenting after divorce!" And thus, TimeToParent was born.

The site was designed mainly for single parents to communicate about their children and collaborate with their ex-spouses. My thought was that if I could provide a platform for separated or divorced parents to communicate, maybe I could take some of the emotion out of their interactions to help them get along better and the children would benefit as a result.

The concept was sound, but the model didn't work. There was a need, but no demand. It turned out that people would rather argue over the phone than use a system to help prevent it. After 18 months and fewer than 100 subscribers, we shut it down and it became yet another bone on the scrap pile of failures. "At least we have PromoteWare," became our mantra, and consulting continued paying the bills.

QuoteCatcher

Finally, in December of 2004, I went to the bookstore for a solid week. My goal: to figure out what business models work and pick one that's already been proven. I was tired of trying to change the world; I just wanted to start making some money!

During my week at the bookstore, I read every business related book I could find about the Internet and the most successful online companies. During my research, I created a list of business models that worked and grouped them into categories. That list generated a clear picture for me of the path we needed to take. I'm going to cover these categories later, but one in particular stood out.

Doing consulting, we used a service to generate sales leads for web development jobs. We weren't at all happy with the service and we knew we could do better. It just so happened that this business model fit very nicely into one of the main categories that I discovered worked best for online companies: the brokerage.

Some brokerages that you might have heard of are eBay, StubHub, ServiceMagic, and AngiesList. Any business that specializes in connecting two different parties is considered a brokerage. QuoteCatcher brokered sales leads. We connected people who needed services with companies that provided them.

During the last two weeks of December, 2004, I wrote the code on top of PromoteWare that became QuoteCatcher. We officially launched the site on January 2nd, 2005. During our first month, we generated $70 in revenue and our second month we generated $700. We continued to grow for over 3 years until we eventually sold QuoteCatcher and PromoteWare in October of 2008 to QuinStreet, Inc. in Foster City, CA.

As part of the sale contract, I agreed to work for QuinStreet to help them integrate QuoteCatcher, as well as other companies they had purchased, into their core technology platform. Once the integration was nearly complete and my knowledge had been transferred, I resigned to spend more time with my daughter, travel, volunteer, and do all the things I wanted to do but never had the time or money to do before.

SCORE

One of the first things I did (after a long vacation) was start volunteering at SCORE, the Service Corp of Retired Executives. I wanted to give back something to the community and I enjoy talking about business and helping people who've never owned one before.

One common theme that I've noticed among most of the people I mentor is that they think starting an online business is hard and they don't know where to begin. I'm *not* going to tell you it's easy, but with the secrets I'm going to share in this book, I'm convinced you'll be able to do it. It's not rocket science! With a little knowledge and perseverance, you'll be able to *navigate your way to a successful online business*, just like I did!

"By failing to prepare, you are preparing to fail."

~Benjamin Franklin

Phase 1: Planning for Success

The time has come! Maybe you've finally reached your limit at work or maybe you have a great idea and you can't find anything quite like it on the web, or maybe you've always wanted to start your own company and now's the time to do it.

Regardless of your motivations, you've reached the starting line, which is probably why you're reading this book. And now you're wondering what the next step on your journey should be. Well, you've come to the right place!

In this first section, I'll discuss the most important things you need to consider before you take the leap and quit your day job, such as common traits of successful startups, business models that work on the web; need vs. demand; staying optimistic yet realistic; and understanding monetization (aka making money). Plus a whole lot more.

This is the section that will help you get prepared to navigate your way to success. The planning phase is the step that most people skim over or skip entirely, but you're MUCH too smart for that. I know you're going to stick it out to the end and once you're finished with this section, you'll be ready to start your startup!

Why Do a Web Startup?

This book is about starting a web business. I'm obviously a big fan of this type of business for a couple of reasons.

First, compared to a traditional brick-and-mortar business like a restaurant or a retail store, a web business has relatively low startup costs. You can expect to pay tens of thousands or even several hundred thousand dollars to open a restaurant, depending on how nice it is. It requires a substantial amount of collateral and experience to get a loan for that much money, making it infeasible for most people.

Many websites, on the other hand, can be launched for under a thousand dollars. Even complex, custom websites will cost far less than a typical brick-and-mortar. That means owning a web business is well within reach for most people.

> **Did you know...**
>
> Brick-and-mortar is a term the tech world uses to describe businesses with physical locations, meaning they're not web-based. It mainly refers to businesses like restaurants, retail stores, spas, gyms, etc.

The second reason I'm such a huge fan of web-based companies is because of the risk/reward ratio. True, most websites don't make it. They close up shop before earning enough to cover their costs, but luckily, most websites are started with very minimal expenses. That means there's not much at stake if it doesn't succeed. In other words, the risk is very low, especially compared to the potential reward.

Facebook was started by one guy in a college dorm room and is now worth billions of dollars. Pinterest was started by three friends in an apartment and now has an estimated worth of over a billion dollars. Craigslist was started by one guy and is now worth billions. eBay was started by one guy in San Jose, CA. It now owns dozens of other sites, including PayPal, and has a market value of around $60 billion.

All of these sites and thousands more were started with very little money and a lot of sweat equity. That makes the risk very low compared to the potential reward if it's successful, and that's why so many people start web-based businesses.

3 Common Traits of Successful Startups

If there's one thing you should learn from me, it's the value of learning from others who have already been successful. There are countless reasons why one company succeeds when another fails, but I've noticed three common traits of the most successful companies that I think contributed to their success.

#1 – Good Idea and GREAT Execution

Having a good idea helps, but it's not nearly as important as the execution of the idea. QuoteCatcher wasn't a new idea. In fact, Greg and I used a similar service to get sales leads for our PromoteWare consulting business, and we were quite unhappy with the service and the quality of the leads. We decided we could build a better mousetrap and that's exactly what we did.

We targeted a smaller niche and offered better service and higher quality leads at a higher price. In our case, the idea wasn't anything special; it was the execution that made the difference. There are probably a dozen people doing something similar to your idea right now, but no one will ever hear about them because they'll fail to execute.

#2 – Target a Small Niche

The second trait of most successful startups is that they targeted a very small niche, at least in the beginning. This allowed them to focus their limited marketing budget on a much smaller audience. It also allowed them to provide very targeted products and services to make their customers happy.

When I talk to people about starting a business, one of my first questions is always, "Who's your target audience?" I can't tell you the number of times I've heard an exuberant, "Everyone is!" Well, everyone might be your target audience…someday…down the road, but if you ever hope to get that far down the road, you need to focus on a smaller niche to start.

When Amazon launched, they only sold books, Facebook was only for Harvard students, and eBay only sold collectibles. If the small niche strategy worked for them, there's a good chance it will work for you, too.

#3 – Powerful Customer Value Proposition

The third trait shared by most successful startups is a powerful customer value proposition. Your value proposition is what sets you apart from the competition and why someone would choose you over them.

I think the best way to explain this concept is to use an example. I'm big on examples, if you haven't noticed, and Facebook is a great example for showing the power of a good value proposition because they succeeded in knocking MySpace off the social media pedestal when no one thought it was possible.

Facebook had several value propositions that MySpace lacked when the takeover was occurring. I'm only going to talk about the four I think had the most influence in knocking MySpace off, but they certainly had a lot more.

First, Facebook capitalized on simplicity while MySpace was clunky and hard to use. Some of my friends had both audio and video on their profile pages, and both would play at the same time when the page loaded making a cacophony of unintelligible sound. Facebook simplified this by limiting the options users have on their profile setup, and by not playing audio and video by default when the page is loaded.

Second, Facebook was a lot faster than MySpace. I remember waiting sometimes two minutes for some of my friends' pages to load because they had filled them up with complex layouts, large graphics and videos.

Third, when Facebook started, it was exclusive to Harvard students, then to Ivy League schools, and then to all universities before it opened up to the rest of us old fogies. Exclusivity is a powerful value proposition because people who are lucky enough to be part of the chosen group feel very special, which translates into strong customer loyalty and fierce brand evangelism.

Finally, Facebook was highly adaptive. They were one of the first companies to provide an open API (Application Programmer Interface), which allowed outside companies to use their data. This gave rise to games like Farmville and MafiaWars, as well as social dating sites and a whole slew of other third party services.

Did you know...

API (Application Programmer Interface) is a term you'll hear a lot in the tech business. It's a fancy way of talking about a company's software and how other software interacts with it. An "open" API refers to software that's been made available to other companies. Most major websites have an open API these days, including Facebook, LinkedIn, eBay and Amazon. Their API's provide access to their user and product information.

By opening its API, Facebook allowed 3rd party companies to create tools and games that attracted more users to the site. These companies then began advertising their new games, which created an army of free marketers for Facebook.

The simplicity, speed, exclusivity and adaptability of Facebook combined to create a very powerful customer value proposition, one that MySpace hasn't been able to overcome.

You can learn from successful startups and model their traits. A good idea is important, but it's the execution that matters most. Targeting a small niche will help focus your energy, and providing a powerful value proposition will keep your users coming back.

What's Your Goal?

The first thing you need to do is define your goal because this has a big impact on your course of action. Why are you starting a business in the first place? To work for yourself instead of someone else? To retire early and enjoy your life while you're still young enough to do the fun stuff? To travel and use work as an excuse to travel, or at least be able to work *while* you travel? Is it to earn extra income so you can pay off bills and send your kids to college? Or is it just a hobby and if you make money doing it, even better?

It's very important to understand your goals and motivations. If you're hoping to retire early, that will take a different plan of action than if you're simply trying to earn some extra income. The same is true if you're trying to replace your job working for someone else with a job working for yourself.

If you want to retire early, you need to think bigger. You'll need a long-term vision and you may eventually need to hire employees. You'll need connections and partnerships/affiliations/joint ventures with other people or businesses. You'll need to reinvest most of what your company earns back into your growth plan, partially by paying yourself a small salary and saving your payday for a few years down the road.

However, if you'll be happy working a job where you're the boss and you aren't worried about retiring early, you can think much smaller. You may not need employees, but you may still need some strategic partnerships or contractors to help do the tasks you can't or don't want to do. You also won't need to reinvest everything into growth, allowing you to take more of what you earn home in your salary.

Before you continue reading, I encourage you to sit down and write out your personal goal for starting a web business. There is no wrong answer. It's purely based on what's important to you.

What to do... What to do...

> *"He who knows when he can fight and when he cannot will be victorious."*
>
> ~Sun Tzu

When I speak to people who want to start an online business, one of the most common questions I hear is: What should I do? This is a great question to ask yourself, even if you already have an idea in mind. My response to this question is always the same: What are you good at doing, what's your background and what do you enjoy doing?

Sometimes it's better to start with the "what should I do?" question than to start with a business idea. When your idea is outside your realm of experience and knowledge, you'll have a large learning curve to overcome, and that can get very expensive in terms of both time and money.

Malcolm Gladwell wrote a book on this topic called "Outliers." In it, he says it can take up to 10,000 hours to become a world-class expert in any given field. Luckily, you don't need to be a "world-class" expert to start a web business, but you do need to know more than the average person at whatever you decide to do. If you've never started a website before, you already have a lot of learning to do. If your website idea is in a field in which you're not already an expert, you've just doubled your learning curve.

If you have 20 years' experience building furniture, you'll have more success starting a website that somehow relates to furniture, such as an ecommerce site that sells it or a content site that discusses it or a lead generation site that connects consumers with builders.

On the other hand, if you want to start a website that targets restaurants or real estate and you don't have any or very little real world experience in the field, your likelihood of being competent enough to run a successful web business is very low. You simply won't have the knowledge to understand how to meet your clients' needs, nor the connections required to grow your business. Plus, you may find out you absolutely hate doing it, but how would you know if you've never done it before?

Having well established connections in your chosen area can help tremendously. Continuing the previous furniture example, if you already know dozens of other furniture builders from doing business with them, meeting at tradeshows, belonging to the same associations, etc., you've already got a built in client base. Why start from scratch if you don't have to?

This advice applies to any type of business, whether online or offline. I was lucky enough (or cursed enough, depending on how you look at it) to have my start in software and the web from very early. That's my area of expertise so that's what I've done with my career. Had I started off building furniture (and I almost did!), my expertise would have been much different and I would have started a different type of business.

My advice to you is to sit down right now and make a list of all the things you know better than the average person, the things you're good at, and the things you like to do. If people ask you questions because they know you'll have the answers, write those things down, too. I call this a personal "niche" list.

I'm not above my own advice. This is exactly what I did very recently. Since I sold my company, I've been trying to figure out what I want to be when I grow up. That prompted me to create my very own niche list. Here's what it looks like:

1. Parenting
2. Travel
3. Scuba diving
4. Business startups
5. Eating at nice restaurants
6. Self-help
7. Writing
8. Public speaking

9. Mentoring and coaching
10. Lead generation
11. Automation
12. Problem solving
13. Process improvement
14. Analysis
15. Social philosophy

You get the idea. Now, go create YOUR list!

Your Viable Business Filter

One of the things I do before I start a new business is run it through my viable business filter. If it doesn't measure up to what I've defined for myself as a viable business, I don't do it. Of course, sometimes an idea makes it through the filter and it still doesn't work, but that's another story!

Your viable business filter should contain things that are important to you and things that you feel will give you the best chance of success. Here's my filter to give you an idea of what I mean:

1. Simple as possible to start
2. Low start-up costs (I'm very frugal)
3. In my area of expertise
4. The market isn't saturated with competition
5. Scalable (meaning it can be automated)
6. Profitable
7. Independent of the economy (as much as possible)
8. It fills a real need AND demand that people or businesses have, and are willing to pay for
9. It provides real value to its customers
10. It's a win/win for all involved

This is my litmus test. If an idea doesn't pass enough or all of my rules, I don't do it. I've had many business ideas (a notebook full of them) that don't measure up to these requirements and they won't ever come to fruition.

Please feel free to use my list and modify it to reflect the things that are important to you. Be picky and don't jump on the first idea you have, unless it makes it through your viable business filter mostly unscathed.

Business Models That Work On the Web

As I mentioned earlier, before I built QuoteCatcher, I spent a week researching business models that work on the web. After creating a huge list of successful websites, I was able to group them into the following six main categories. If your idea doesn't fit into one of these categories, either you haven't classified it correctly, you've hit on something that has never been done before, or you're not likely to make any money at it.

Ecommerce or eTailing

These websites sell products and sometimes services. Some examples are Amazon, Zappos, Overstock and DrugStore.com. They make their money the old-fashioned way: buy wholesale and sell retail. Many of the suppliers that these big companies buy from will also sell to you, although for higher prices since you won't be buying in the same bulk sizes that they do.

It's getting harder and harder to compete with this business model because a few big companies are rapidly dominating the online landscape. You'll need to sell something that's unique and hard-to-find if you want to stand a chance. Otherwise, you run the risk of someone finding the product on your site and then going to Amazon to get a better deal, or because they're more comfortable buying from a well-known company with a clearly defined return policy.

One way to get around the challenges of ecommerce websites is to launch an Amazon or eBay store instead of building your own website. Your products will be listed right alongside theirs and the consumer won't know the difference (unless they pay close attention). Sometimes the best way to beat the big guys is to join 'em.

The Brokerage

This is my personal favorite category. It applies to any type of business that connects people or businesses, or acts as a middle man. Some good examples are eBay, StubHub, ServiceMagic, Angie's List, Craigslist, and Etsy. QuoteCatcher fits into this category as a sales lead generation site, connecting businesses that provide services with other businesses that need them.

Distributor sites that connect retailers and manufacturers such as ProductSourcing and WholesaleDistributorsNet are also considered brokers, as are transaction processors such as PayPal and Google Checkout. They connect consumers with credit card issuers like Visa and MasterCard.

Auctions that connect a buyer with a seller like eBay also fall into this category, but penny auction sites like Swoopo do not; they're ecommerce sites.

Brokerage websites make money by charging a fee either to the buyer, the seller or both for facilitating the transaction. At QuoteCatcher, we sold sales leads that ranged in price from $20 to $200 per lead, depending on the budget of the project.

The reason I like this category more than the others is because the broker doesn't have any inventory to manage. They simply facilitate the connection of two or more parties and then step out of the way. It's a relatively low cost business model, although advertising to two different audiences can get expensive.

Human Connections

Human connections websites specialize in connecting people. They're a subset of the brokerage category, but it's such a huge and specialized segment that I think it deserves its own label.

If you haven't heard of Facebook, you need to move out from

under your rock before starting a web business. However, you may *not* have heard of Ning, which allows you to create your own private social network.

In addition to social networks like Facebook and LinkedIn, Meetup, MeetIn and FourSquare also fit here, as well as dating sites like Match and eHarmony, and job search sites like CareerBuilder and Monster.

The trend now is in specialization; meaning the community makeup is becoming more and more granular. For instance, DeHood is a social network for neighborhoods and SpiceWorks is for IT managers.

How do these community sites make money? Good question. Facebook and Twitter didn't turn a profit until late in 2009 after posting several years of losses. Facebook makes most of its money from games like Mafia Wars and Farmville, as well as the ads you see on the site. Twitter makes its money from selling data to companies like Google and Microsoft's Bing search engine, plus some new pay-to-promote features.

Some communities charge a subscription to belong, but these are usually highly specialized, professional communities. Most make money from ads, and advertisers pay top dollar to place them on a website with a specialized community of professionals.

Medscape is one of these specialized social networks (owned by WebMd). You can bet pharmaceuticals and medical supply companies pay dearly to advertise to the thousands of doctors who belong to that community.

Content Creators and Aggregators

These are websites that either generate their own content, publish other people's content, or aggregate content from across the web. iVillage, AskMen, CNN, CNET and WebMD fall into this category. Newsletter services like UrbanDaddy also fit here, and all blog sites. Wikipedia also belongs in this category, along with YouTube. These types of websites make money in several ways, mainly from advertising, affiliate links, pay-per-view or subscriptions.

Pinterest caused quite a stir when it became public knowledge that the links people post on their pin boards have a SkimLinks affiliate ID appended to them. Affiliate links allow Pinterest to make money when people buy as a result of clicking a link.

Software Tools

There are several different types of software tools. WordPress, Posterous, Dropbox and Evernote fall into this category, as do business management systems like SalesForce, NetSuite and many others. Their purpose is to allow businesses to outsource their IT and to automate business functions.

There's a growing market for personal and small business utilities, such as MyFoodDiary, MapMyRun and OpenTable. Specialized search engines are also becoming more popular as the sheer volume of content on the web continues to grow exponentially.

Mint.com is a personal financial management application that helped kill Microsoft Money. It was founded in 2006 and sold 3 years later for $170 million to Intuit, the makers of Quicken and Quickbooks.

Sites that target consumers make most of their money through advertising, although some charge a monthly subscription fee. Business sites like OpenTable charge restaurants a fee to use the system and some charge licensing fees.

Games

Many of the most popular games now are community based, such as those found on Facebook. Farmville and MafiaWars are two of the most popular. They were created by Zynga, a company that was founded in January 2007 and is now worth nearly two billion dollars. Their revenue comes from game players who pay for virtual merchandise, which allows the players to level up or perform additional activities in the game.

SecondLife is a virtual world that's both a community and a game. Like Zynga's games, SecondLife charges for virtual merchandise. However, it also allows players to setup shop and sell their own goods, but you'll have to pay real money for the real estate under your virtual shop, just like a real store in the physical world.

Mobile games are quickly becoming a huge industry. Games like "Angry Birds" for the iPhone and Android are immensely popular, but there are now well over 100,000 of them. Many are free and make their money from little banner ads placed on the bottom of the game screen. Others charge a few dollars for the game and some have been purchased over 1 million times, making their creators millionaires.

Mobile gaming is the latest gold rush. The market is quickly becoming saturated and it's becoming more and more difficult to create unique games. With all the competition, it's also hard to get a new game noticed among the hundred thousand others.

Gambling sites also fit in the games category, although you should avoid starting one of these unless you have specialized experience due to all the legal restrictions.

Gaming is an extremely hard category because people get tired of playing games very quickly. That means you'll need to constantly be creating new games just to replace lost revenue from games that aren't being played as much anymore. It helps to build in some social and addictive elements that will keep your users coming back. I'm going to talk about that more later.

All websites fit mainly into one of these six categories, but the best ones have elements of more than one. For example, some content sites have a loyal community following, some social media sites have games, some brokers provide software tools, etc.

When you're defining your idea, knowing which category it fits into can bring clarity to your vision, and it can help you identify your competition.

Your Startup Log

You're taking a shower, enjoying your solitude, the drone of running water, drawing funny faces in the steam, when suddenly a light bulb goes off in your mind. "I could build a website that allows people to post pictures of their bathroom steam drawings and share them with the world! Brilliant!"

Whether or not this is a good idea, we'll save for later. The point here is that inspiration can strike at any time, especially if you're actively looking for it. I wake up in the middle of the night with new ideas all the time. Sometimes, I even dream about new ideas for websites or new features on one of my current sites. When this happens, I quickly write down the idea in my Startup Log so I don't forget it.

My Startup Log is a 3-ring binder with tabs that allow me to group my ideas into categories. Some ideas are related specifically to projects I'm currently working on; these ideas are logged under their own project tab. Other ideas are completely off-the-wall and unrelated to anything I'm doing right now; I have a general "Ideas" tab for those.

The method you use to log your ideas isn't important. What is important is that you have a method. Albert Einstein kept detailed manuscripts of his ideas that scientists and scholars still reference today. Do you think he took the time to write all of his thoughts down purely for posterity? Nope.

Einstein was a very private man and didn't like the idea of publishing his every thought. In fact, he wrote to his biographer, Carl Seelig, in 1953, "In the past, it never occurred to me that every casual remark of mine would be snatched up and recorded. Otherwise I would have crept further into my shell." He didn't write for everyone else; he wrote because even Albert Einstein had a limit to his memory.

Having a Startup Log or some other means of documenting your ideas is crucial. Don't assume you'll remember them. Write them down! It's the worst feeling to remember that you had a great idea, but you don't have any memory of what the idea was!

When I first have an idea, I recognize that it's not always a good time to execute it. I may be in the middle of another project or the market timing might be off. Once in a while, I review my entire notebook to refresh my memory and to decide if anything is ripe for picking.

This process also leads to the creation of new ideas or the combination of ideas. Sometimes during this process, the light bulbs start flashing like Christmas trees and I can't write them down fast enough!

Use your Startup Log to store all the information about your business. It will not only help you stay organized, it will also document your entrepreneurial history for future posterity and make your biographer's job much easier!

Logging your thoughts is so important that it's the first thing you need to learn if you want to succeed in your own online company. You can decide later if you want to pursue the idea, but only if you remember what it was.

Defining Your Idea At a High Level

In the next section, I'm going to talk about how to determine if your idea is worth doing, but before you can do that, you need to define your idea with enough detail to make an evaluation possible.

What Problem Are You Trying to Solve?

The first question you need to answer is, what problem are you trying to solve? This is often called the pain statement. Every idea has a reason for being and it usually owes its existence to some form of pain that you or someone you know endured.

Before Jeff Bezos decided to build Amazon, he researched the top 20 mail order businesses. He saw a similarity between the mail order business model of selling things from a *printed* catalog, and the ecommerce business model of selling things from a *virtual* catalog.

What he discovered was a big opportunity in the book mail order space because it was simply not feasible to create and mail a catalog containing the titles of every book ever written; however, the web was perfect for providing access to extremely large amounts of searchable data.

What was the problem that Jeff Bezos wanted to solve? What was his pain statement? Here's what I think it might have been: It's impossible to print the titles of all the books ever written in a mail order catalog. In fact, it's not possible to house them all in one physical library or even one physical card catalog. People deserve the right to have access to every available book and not just the ones that catalog editors or librarians deem worthy.

Now I don't know if that's exactly what Jeff Bezos thought, but there's a good chance it was something similar to that. He wanted to solve a real problem and make money doing it and I'm assuming you have the same goal. Before you move on to the next step, take a minute to define the problem you want to solve at a very high level, by answering the following questions:

1. What is the problem? (It's currently not possible to…)
2. Who is affected by this problem? (People who _____ …)
3. How is it done today? (The way this is done now…)
4. Why is the way it's done today wrong? (The way it's done today is inefficient/problematic/limited/etc. because…)

Don't define the solution in this step. We're going to talk about that next. Instead, focus specifically on the problem you want to solve.

How Are You Going to Solve the Problem?

This is the next question you need to ask yourself. This is often called the solution statement and it's the crux of your brilliant idea. The solution Bezos came up with for the book mail order dilemma was simple: Build a website with a searchable catalog of every available book.

Following his vision, Bezos moved from New York to Seattle with his wife so he would have easy access to Ingram (a large book publisher) and a sizable talent pool of software developers. He set up shop in a garage with three computers sitting on doors converted to tables and several months later, Amazon was born. Within two months of launching and with nothing but word of mouth advertising, Amazon was earning $20,000 per week in revenue.

Amazon solved a real problem for an obvious pain statement, and several members of his family are billionaires as a result. And it all started with a problem and a solution.

Now it's time to define your solution at a very high level, by answering the following questions:

1. What is your goal? (My goal is to enable…)
2. How are you going to achieve your goal? (My website will enable people to…)
3. How is your solution different from other websites or companies? (My solution is unique because…)

Notice that I said to define both your problem and solution at a "very high level?" The purpose of this exercise isn't to hash out all the details of your idea…it's to define your idea well enough so you can evaluate it before you spend much time and money on it. You're going to define your idea in more detail during the business plan section, but for now, you just need to understand it well enough to determine if you want to move forward.

[Your Idea]: Brick or Balloon?

Now that you've written down your idea and defined the problem and solution, you need to decide if it's a balloon that will fly or a brick that will sink you. In other words, does the idea have merit and do you have a reasonable chance of success if you start building it?

Competitive Research

Don't tell me there's nothing like your idea. I've heard that a hundred times and every time I've been able to find something similar. It may not be the same, but similar enough to draw some conclusions about the merits of your idea. Before you grab onto a balloon that won't fly, spend some time researching the competition.

With the millions of websites on the web, the odds that your idea is truly unique are very low. Facebook was a better version of MySpace, which was a better version of Friendster. Google was a better version of Yahoo!, which was a better version of AltaVista. Almost everything is derivative now, at least until a new field or technology is discovered.

That does NOT mean that everything has already been thought of. Charles H. Duell, the Commissioner of the US Patent Office in 1899, is famous (now) for saying that "Everything that can be invented has been invented." He could not have been more wrong then, and he'd still be wrong today. New ideas and new websites using new technologies and new ways of thinking are being invented every day and your idea may be one of them.

However, that doesn't mean your idea will have NO competition. It just means you may not have DIRECT one-to-one competitors. Meaning, you still need to spend time doing competitive research.

Competitor Intel: Keep Your Enemies Closer

Machiavelli is famous for saying, "Keep your friends close and your enemies closer." That's sage advice in war and in business, and gathering intel on your competitors is the only way to do it.

When I have a new idea, I spend a lot of time researching potential competitors. To demonstrate how important I think this step of the process is, I'm going to share with you how I do it using "online dating" as my case study.

Online dating is a good example because it's a well-established online business model with several large competitors, but there are still new dating sites popping up all the time that are gaining market share. If I was thinking about starting an online dating site, here's how I would research the competition.

Step 1: Search Keywords

The best way to start this process is to go to Google and type in keywords related to your business. For the online dating example, you can use the term "online dating" to get started, but this isn't the best choice for an industry with a large number of established competitors because it's too generic.

Using this search term will yield all the big names like Match, eHarmony and OkCupid. If you're just starting out in this field, are these your direct competitors? Not really. They have 50 million users and international recognition. There's no way you can compete with that.

Your main competitors are going to be other <u>new</u> online dating sites that launched within the last couple of years and that are doing well in terms of attracting users. They're using some new technology or methodology that's different than the big guys because they know that trying to compete head-on with a company that has 50 million users is tantamount to Don Quixote chasing after his windmills. Why would anyone use a site that's just like Match except with no users? They wouldn't, unless it's different in some important way.

Instead of searching for a generic term like "online dating," you'll be better off with more targeted terms like "new online dating websites." This search yields some much more interesting results. Have you heard of HowAboutWe, CoffeeMeetsBagle, TheComplete.me or Hitch.me? All of these sites were launched in the last two years (as of this writing) and they're doing a good job of capturing users. Each has their own customer value proposition and most target online daters who are tired of the way the big sites work.

Create a folder in your browser bookmarks called "competition" and bookmark every website that's even close to being a competitor so you can check back in on them periodically.

Step 2: Document Your Findings

Now that you have some direct competitors identified, it's time to dig deeper into how they work and who their target audience is. Here's a list of all the important data elements that I like to capture:

1. Domain name
2. Year founded
3. Tagline
4. Fees
5. Revenue stream(s)
6. Investor funding info
7. Niche market
8. Value proposition

I also like to do a SWOT analysis, which stands for Strengths, Weaknesses, Opportunities and Threats. As an example, here's the data I captured for HowAboutWe:

1. HowAboutWe.com
2. Founded 2010
3. Tagline: The offline dating site
4. Fees: $35/month or $18/month for 3 months
5. Revenue stream: Membership fees, restaurants who sponsor date ideas, advertising
6. Funding: $3.1M Series A, $15M Series B
7. Niche: City-based, experienced online daters, women seem to like it more than men (60% women), 30's+
8. Value proposition: Meet offline faster than other dating sites
9. Strengths: More fun, less formal, meet faster, activity based
10. Weaknesses: Several long profile questions, a lot of non-paying users making it hard to communicate with everyone, can't tell who is paying vs. non-paying
11. Opportunities: Simplify the profile and setup, allow people to read messages they receive even if they aren't paying members
12. Threats: Funded, established, big marketing budget

> **Did you know...**
>
> Finding a competitor who's been funded already is a good sign that your business idea has merit. Investors don't invest in bad ideas, but it does mean you won't be able to do the same exact thing. You'll need to *differentiate* yourself somehow.

As you can see, there's a large amount of data here and you may be wondering how I found all of it, but it's a lot easier than you might think.

First, I checked out the About Us page on their website and then signed up for their service. They share details about their business model in the marketing messages so I also read their ads both on their site and in their Google ads.

Information can be found simply by searching for their domain name on Google using both the "Search" and "News" tabs. When you search for a tech company on Google, one of the top results is for a website called CrunchBase, which has valuable data about most tech companies, including investor information, news and videos.

By doing this for your top five competitors, you can get a comprehensive view of the competitive landscape for your idea. Too many people skip this part of the startup process because they don't want to put the energy into it or maybe because they're afraid of what they might find that could squash their hopes and dreams. But even if you find a major competitor, it doesn't mean all hope is lost.

Competition Is Good

You're in the middle of your competitive research when you come across a website that's doing almost exactly the same thing you want to do. "Argh!!!" you scream in anguish, "My hopes have been dashed!" It's a sad moment, but don't get discouraged. This will probably happen, and it might be a good thing.

There are three reasons why having competition is good. First, they've already proven the business model for you, which means you don't need to worry about blazing a new trail. Second, they make it easier for you to set your pricing since they've already base-lined it for you. And finally, the best thing about having competition is that your target customers are already used to spending money on whatever it is you're selling. That means you won't have to spend your marketing dollars trying to convince people to spend money on something totally new.

Having <u>no</u> competition might actually be a bad thing. It could mean that the business model isn't profitable. In other words, there's no market or demand for your product or service. It could also mean that other companies may have tried and failed for valid reasons, and if you're brand new to the business, you might not see the pitfalls they fell into.

Many successful sites are copies (with minimal modifications) of other proven websites. Search engines had been around for years when Google was launched. Groupon has several copycats now, such as WeeklyPlus, Blissmo and LivingSocial (recently valued at $10 billion!). There are about 100 successful dating sites out there, some nearly exact copies of each other, such as Match, Chemistry and PlentyOfFish, and others that are more unique, like CoffeeMeetsBagle and HowAboutWe.

Some new websites are popping up that target very specific niche markets in a field dominated by a big player. Mimvi is an example of a specialized search engine and ThisNext is the Facebook of shopping.

If your competition is backed by Venture Capital (normally called VC...they invest in startups), this can be very good and very bad. First, it means that the VC's have confidence in the idea. They don't invest unless there's a good chance of success, which means your idea has merit. However, because your competition is backed by VC, it means they have deep pockets to fund their startup's overhead and advertising. If you're taking the bootstrapping approach (funding it yourself), you may have a hard time competing toe-to-toe with them.

What happens if you find a major competitor who is dominating the market? Should you throw in the towel? Take your ball and go home? Run away and live to fight another day? Ok, enough clichés already! The point I'm trying to make is, don't give up just yet.

Big competitors are like bomber airplanes. They can cause a lot of damage to a large area, but I wouldn't want to be in a bomber and see a fighter plane coming towards me. Bombers are slow moving and they don't change direction very easily. Fighters are much more agile and maneuverable. They can quickly change direction if they need to.

MySpace used to be a bomber circa 2007, but then the much more agile and maneuverable Facebook came along and blew them out of the sky when no one thought it was possible. Of course, what's happened now? Facebook has become the bomber and now a whole squadron of fighters has it in their crosshairs. Maybe you've heard of some of them: Path, Pair, FamilyLeaf, Bebo, FourSquare, Google+, MocoSpace, Pinterest, and many, many more.

These companies are providing what some argue are better features and services, while targeting a smaller niche to gain a foothold in the marketplace. It remains to be seen if any of these sites will succeed in knocking Facebook off the top of the social media pedestal. Everyone seems to think it's impossible, but that's exactly what they said about MySpace.

Competitive Advantage

Your competitive advantage is what sets you apart from your competition. It's how you differentiate yourself from them, and it's what makes customers spend money on your website, instead of theirs.

For example, if you're going to sell books, you'll need a very good competitive advantage to beat Amazon. Your competitive advantage will rarely be price, although that's what most first-time entrepreneurs think it will be. They assume that since their overhead is much lower, they'll be able to offer the products or services for a much lower price; however, the mistake they often make is underestimating their cost of doing business and the value of buying in bulk.

Amazon has years of experience and millions of dollars of

infrastructure that allows them to be highly efficient, which reduces their operating costs. Sure, their overhead is much higher in terms of sheer dollars, but proportionate to revenue, it's probably about the same as yours or even less. That means you can't assume you'll be able to beat them on price. Plus, they can afford to take huge losses to capture market share if they need to. If they see you as a threat, they'll just lower their price until you can't compete at all.

The Amazon Kindle is a good example of this. Some people think the largest cost for a real, physical book is in the cover, paper, ink and manufacturing process. Wrong. Most of the cost of a book goes to the publisher for royalties. The natural resources required to print a book accounts for a much smaller percentage of the book's cost, usually less than 20%.

When I starting pricing out the cost of self-publishing this book, I found that I could have it printed for around $4 per book, but if it sells through Amazon, they will take about $6 in royalty fees. If I sell this book for $20, 20% will go toward the cost of printing and 30% will go to royalties.

Big name publishers take even more, though. Publishers will take around 75% of the sale price for their royalty, leaving you about 10% after the cost of production. That means, for a typical printed and published book that sells for $25, the publisher is expecting to get around $18 in royalties.

If your idea of buying in bulk is ordering 100 books from a publisher, think again. Amazon's orders are ten or a hundred times bigger than that, and the larger the order, the better deal you get from the supplier. This means Amazon will be paying far less for the books than you will, which increases their profit margin per book.

Instead of fighting your competition on their home field, choose a small niche and offer products or services that they don't or can't offer. For the book example, you might only sell books that fit in a single category such as sci-fi or mystery, and then provide an interactive "book club" community where users can communicate and share the reading experience with each other. You would still need to offer a competitive price or perhaps require a purchase to gain access to the community.

These are just a couple ideas off the top of my head for one type of ecommerce website. The message you should be hearing is to thoroughly evaluate your competition and then figure out how you're going to set yourself apart from them in a way other than price. This difference will be part of your competitive advantage and if you can't come up with something meaningful and substantial, you need to take a trip back to the drawing board.

Monetization Plan

We're still in the section that's meant to help you determine if your idea is a good one, so the next thing I'm going to cover is your plan to generate revenue. Monetization is a term you'll hear a lot in the tech business, especially if and when the time comes to sell your company. It refers to how your business makes money, and you need a plan for it. In other words, you need to sell a product or service that people are willing to pay for.

Your competitive research can help here by showing you how the competition does it. If you're planning to charge a subscription fee to users, but your competition offers the same type of service for free, you're going to have an uphill battle. You would need to offer something highly specialized and hard to find if you're going to get the same target audience to start paying for something that they're used to getting for free.

My business partner and I needed income to support our families, which is why we chose a business model with a short-term monetization strategy. We monetized QuoteCatcher by charging setup fees to vendors and per lead fees when they bought a lead. We also monetized the service by selling advertising on the site, and by selling extra leads to affiliates. We even sold the unwanted leads (leads that didn't pass our qualification criteria) for a steep discount to vendors who didn't care about quality. Viable businesses have several monetization strategies; they don't put all their eggs in one basket.

If you don't need the money in the short-term and you can afford to wait for a long-term payoff, your monetization strategy in the beginning isn't as important. Facebook, Instagram and Twitter fell into this category. They didn't have a monetization strategy until several years after their creation. That's because with sites like those, it takes a lot of users to generate revenue and there's no point in worrying about generating revenue until you have critical mass.

> ## Did you know…
>
> Critical Mass is a physics term that refers to the amount of fissionable material needed to maintain a nuclear chain reaction. The tech world has borrowed this term to describe the number of users a website needs to continue its growth with minimal support. Facebook and Amazon are examples of websites that have reached critical mass.

One more point I'd like to make on this topic is that selling advertising space on your site is not a short-term monetization strategy. You need many thousands of unique users per month to make any kind of revenue from advertising, and it can take a long time to do that. If you have a low traffic volume site with ads from Google AdSense, you can expect to earn less than $20/month. This is not a monetization strategy, unless you have a thousand of these sites.

Some people I talk to about this topic tell me their plan is to sell ad space to local businesses. First, most local businesses don't understand online advertising very well, but they will understand the cost of marketing. They won't pay very much unless you can guarantee a return on their investment, which you can't do without a high volume of traffic on your site.

Second, if the local business IS online marketing savvy, they're going to ask what your CPM is, which stands for cost-per-thousand impressions. They'll expect to pay only a couple cents per impression, or even less! That means if you show their ad to a thousand people in a month, you can expect to make less than $20! I don't know about you, but I can't support my family on $20 per month.

If that isn't enough bad news about selling ad space to generate revenue, here's one more piece for you: until you have a large volume of traffic on your site, advertisers won't waste their precious time talking to you about your ad space. Bottom line, it takes tens of thousands of users per month to make any kind of money from selling ad space, which makes this a very poor monetization strategy for new websites.

Changing the World vs. Making Money

Mark Zuckerberg of Facebook and Jeff Bezos of Amazon are true success stories. Looking back now, it's obvious that they've changed our world. And while both probably always had big dreams, they both started small.

Facebook only allowed Harvard students to register when it first launched. It later expanded to Stanford, Columbia and Yale. Then to all the Ivy League schools and finally to most schools in the US and Canada.

When Amazon launched, it only sold books. That's it. Nothing else. I still remember the day I first learned about Amazon. My college professor in my graduate program told me about it in 1996. She was quite the bibliophile, so having books available for her to purchase at any time of the day or night was worthy news. At the time, I would never have dreamed that Amazon would go on to sell everything under the sun and be the largest online retailer in the world.

Perhaps Zuckerberg and Bezos knew what they were doing when they launched. Maybe they *did* set out to change the world. Whether that was their original intent or not, neither tried to do it on day number one.

Had Bezos decided to sell everything from books to clothes when Amazon launched, he would have exhausted his capital on inventory and had nothing left for marketing. Amazon would have also been branded "just another ecommerce site." Instead, his site became known as the book site; the place to go when you need a book you can't find anywhere else. That made people talk about it, like my professor did to me. Then when Amazon started selling other things, they were able to build upon their already established image and reputation.

Had Zuckerberg promoted his site to everyone in the world when he launched, Facebook would probably be an insignificant footnote in the history of the web. Instead, he limited membership, creating an exclusive "club" atmosphere, and people felt an urge to be part of it. His exclusive club spread like a virus from campus to campus until it crossed the school barrier into the real world and now infects the lives of over 1 billion people!

Unless you have deep pockets (meaning a large operating budget), you need to figure out how to make money first and then worry about changing the world later once you can afford it. Starting small is the best way to begin unless you're extremely well-funded. It's been proven over and over.

Need vs. Demand: The Story of TimeToParent

Several years ago, Greg and I launched a social networking website called TimeToParent.com. As discussed earlier, the site was designed mainly for single parents to communicate about their children and collaborate with their ex-spouses. My thought was that if I could provide a platform for separated or divorced parents to communicate, maybe I could take some of the emotion out of their interactions so they would get along better and the children would benefit as a result.

Before I built the site, I conducted an informal survey among friends and family, as well as at local networking events through several chambers of commerce. Everyone I spoke to was in love with the idea and agreed there was a large "need" for a service like it. Doing my competitive research, I found only one site doing something similar, and they lacked many of the community and collaboration features I had in mind.

With my brilliant idea in tow, I set off creating the site with all the bells and whistles I could conceive. It ended up being an entire parent's collaboration portal, with private discussion boards (aka news feeds), shared address books (aka friend lists), calendars (aka events), and much more. Everyone I showed it to absolutely loved it. They all agreed that it would improve the lives of children from divorced homes. But only a hand-full of people used it. Leaving me bewildered and asking, why?

To research this conundrum, I spoke with several people who said they loved the idea and would use the service, but never signed up. I also called the women who registered (no men registered) and spoke to them. The most common response to my question, "Why aren't you using the site?" was, "My ex won't use it simply because I asked him to." Reading between the lines, what these women were saying was, "We would rather argue over the phone than use a tool to help prevent it."

After 18 months and fewer than 100 registered users, we shut the site down. I was curious how our competitor, who is still in business, was able to succeed in this space and what I found was very disheartening. They worked with the courts to get their service mandated. In other words, they were forcing people to use their website. While an effective strategy, this doesn't seem right to me. Using the justice system to force people to do something against their will doesn't seem very just to me and I have a hard time being hypocritical.

The lesson I learned from this experience was that despite how much something is "needed," if there's no "demand" for it, no one will buy it. Someone once told me that if you have a choice of selling antibiotics or vitamins, sell antibiotics because there will always be a demand for them regardless of what's going on in the world. There may be a need for vitamins, but when times are tough, they're one of the first things to get axed from the discretionary spending budget.

As a side note, the term "social network" wasn't a popular term when I built TimeToParent so I didn't realize that's what I'd created and therefore, didn't realize the potential it had for a broader audience. The platform I built for TimeToParent is what I later used as the foundation for PromoteWare. Had I realized the broader application of the features I built, I could have easily used the platform and tweaked it to be one of the first true social networks. Sometimes, bad ideas lead to good things and sometimes all a bad idea needs is a little tweaking to become a good thing, but only if you recognize it....

Good Idea or Not?

"Don't let people tell you your ideas are stupid – if you're really passionate about something, find a way to build it."

~Dennis Crowley, Foursquare Co-Founder

By now, you've defined your idea, researched the competition, determined if and how you can make money with it, and analyzed it six ways to Sunday. Now it's time to make a decision. Either the idea is worth doing or it's not. Only you can make that decision and hopefully you can make it objectively before you spend too much of your time and hard-earned money on it.

Speaking of money, you're going to need some to start, and that's the topic of the next section.

Seed Capital: Bootstrapping vs. Funding

Every business needs money to start and this startup funding is called seed capital. Depending on the complexity of your idea, this can be as little as a few hundred dollars to as much as a million dollars or more.

This is an important element of the planning stage because if your idea will require $50,000 to build a custom website and you don't have the money to pay for it, you either need to find the money somewhere else, reduce your idea to a more affordable website, or do something different. When you're looking for seed capital, you have two options: Bootstrapping or External Funding.

Bootstrapping

Bootstrapping means paying for everything yourself. It's the way many online entrepreneurs started and it's the way I started. The good thing about this approach is that you own the entire company. All earnings from operations or from selling the business go to you. There's no one to answer to or tell you how to run the business. It's your baby.

The downside to the bootstrapping approach is that it can take a lot longer to grow. You'll be slowly building and inching your way along, reinvesting your earnings into better software, new features, more marketing, employees, etc. This can take a while, which can test your patience.

You also won't be paying yourself anything in the beginning, and then not much for quite some time. Your business will be growing in value, but you won't have much in the way of liquid assets to show for it.

If you don't have a large amount of cash sitting in the bank, then where do you get it? One option is to use credit cards. This was the primary source of funding for my business in the beginning. Banks won't loan money to an unproven web business without consistent cash flow, but most anyone can get a personal credit card and use that to pay bills.

After we sold QuoteCatcher, one of the developers who worked at QuinStreet asked me how we funded our business. When I told him we used credit cards, he nearly fell on the floor. He didn't think people actually did that. I told him that living in Silicon Valley (aka The Echo Chamber) has tainted his view of entrepreneurship.

In the valley, the value of a company is based on the amount of venture capital it can raise. Out here in the real world, the value of a company is based on how well it can turn one dollar into two dollars. If that means you have to fund it with a credit card, then that's what you do.

Another option for funding is a home equity line of credit (HELOC). Of course, with the current state of the housing industry, you may find you no longer have equity in your home, and even if you do, the bank may not loan you money for it. It's worth investigating, just don't get your hopes too high or pin your entire business strategy on obtaining a HELOC.

If you're set on bootstrapping and you don't have much in the way of cash, credit card limits or HELOC's, try to pick an idea that doesn't cost much to start. There are lots of them.

This is actually a great way to get your feet wet with little risk. If you can start selling products successfully through Amazon or eBay, or if you create a successful blog or affiliate website, you'll learn lessons that will help you launch bigger ideas while earning some income that you can use to fund them.

You don't have to swing for the bleachers on your first time at bat. Entrepreneurship is a life long journey that starts with a single step, and sometimes a simple idea.

External Funding

If you need external funding to start your business, you may want to think of a different business idea. I'm not saying you can't get funding for your idea, but it doesn't happen very often.

In the beginning, you'll need to convince friends and family to fund you. Hopefully, they'll believe in you and your idea enough to do it. Investors who don't know you personally will require much more than an idea to open their wallets.

If your idea is capable of attracting investors, you have several different options for external funding, but none will be easy to come by if you're a one or two person shop starting out of your house. The general rule is that you can only borrow money if you don't need it. With that said, here's a review of the options you might investigate.

Friends and Family

Your friends and family are perhaps your most likely source of funding. If they believe in your idea, they may want to invest in it (and you) in exchange for shares of the business or interest on the loan. Draw up a legal contract either way specifying how the money is to be repaid.

If it's a loan, you'll have to repay it with a fair interest rate, regardless of how the business does. If they're investing in exchange for shares of the company, they'll lose their money if the business goes under, but they'll also make a killing if it does well. Several of Jeff Bezos's family members are billionaires thanks to their early round investments in Amazon.

It's essential to treat this as a professional business deal and not a favor. You don't want to leave any room for confusion or you could end up in court battling your friends and family. Legally document all of your agreements, even for your parents.

Bank Loans

Banks aren't really worth mentioning because they won't loan money to a web startup unless you already have a healthy cash flow, which means you're no longer in the seed capital phase. The reasons banks don't like web startups is because they have no collateral. You need money to pay for software and marketing, but those two things have no intrinsic value (like real estate or inventory does) so if you default on the loan, there's nothing for them to take back.

When I opened my new business bank account, I was told that my business would need three years of tax returns with qualifying income before they would even consider it for a business loan.

Microlenders

After the credit crisis of 2008, microlenders experienced a boom because they lend money when banks won't. Microlenders get money from various sources to fund loans, such as the Small Business Administration (SBA); other federal, state and local government agencies; and some philanthropies. Most loans are between $5,000 and $35,000 and interest rates are only slightly higher than a typical bank loan.

Whether a microlender will loan you money for your web-based business is uncertain. They typically specialize in loaning money to brick-and-mortars who have collateral to back the loan, or to companies with decent cash flow that can be used to make the loan payments. However, this is a much more viable option than a bank loan. Give one or two of them in your area a call and ask about their qualifications.

Crowdfunding

Your next option for seed capital is from crowdfunding. Personally, I think this term is far too broad, which is why I've broken it out into its three distinct types: Crowdlending, Crowddonations and Crowdinvesting.

Crowdlending

LendingClub.com and Prosper.com are both websites that facilitate what's called crowd, or peer-to-peer lending. Some people register on sites like these to lend money, while others register to borrow money.

The websites facilitate the loan by checking your credit rating and by assigning an interest rate based on your credit score. You can expect to pay in the neighborhood of 5% to 15% on the loan amount, and you can borrow money for anything from a new swimming pool in your backyard to a business loan for your new website. It's technically not a business loan, however, because the loan is solely based on your personal credit score and not your business value.

Crowddonation

Remember the stories about the "bullied bus monitor" incident that happened in June of 2012? In case you don't remember, some middle school students on the bus were making fun of the bus monitor and the whole thing was recorded with a video camera. It made national news.

In response to this terrible incident, a fundraising project was posted on Indigogo.com to raise money for this woman to take a vacation. When the campaign closed, $703,123 had been donated to the cause and this bus monitor took one hell of a vacation.

You may be wondering what this has to do with seed capital, and rightly so. Sites like Indigogo and Kickstarter.com are crowddonation websites, but they're not limited to noble causes, such as funding a bullied bus monitor's vacation.

On Indigogo, anyone can post a project for just about anything and get people to donate money. Kickstarter is specifically for business donations and in return, all they ask is that you offer some sort of "perk" that's commensurate with the amount of the donation. For example, you might give away a free product once it's developed, free advertising on your website, dinner with the founder, or anything else you can think of. The sites take a percentage of the donations, which is how they make their money.

The beautiful thing about crowddonations is that you don't have to repay the money. It's not a loan and it's not in exchange for a percentage of your company…it's a donation. People who donate understand they will not get their money back. The only real challenge is creating a compelling project profile that will resonate with people and persuade them to donate.

Did you know…

Kickstarter no longer allows "e-commerce sites, web businesses, or social networking sites" to be posted as donation projects. They now require your project to be a "creative" endeavor that has a clear end point and doesn't require ongoing maintenance.

Crowdinvesting

This is a new type of crowdfunding that's legal as of January 2013. Several websites have already been created to facilitate crowdinvesting, such as CrowdFunder.com and WeFunder.com.

Crowdinvesting is a cross between the crowddonation sites like Kickstarter and the crowdlending sites like LendingClub. People register on crowdinvesting sites who want to invest small amounts of money in startup companies in exchange for shares of ownership.

If you're looking for seed capital, you can register on a site like CrowdFunder to raise money for your startup, but you'll have lots of SEC hoops to jump through, making this the most challenging of the three crowdfunding sources.

Angels

No, I'm not referring to the ones with wings. Angel Investors are people with money who like to gamble on…I mean…invest in startups just for the fun of it. There's no guarantee any angel investor will like your idea or your team enough to invest, but if you find one who does, he can bring a lot more than money to the table.

Most angels prefer to invest in business models that they already know and understand, which means they'll have valuable expertise and contacts in your industry, and that could help launch your business.

Angels usually invest less than a million dollars, although there are exceptions. As for what angels want in return, the easy answer is a good return on their investment. The hard answer is anything else under the sun. Clearly define in a legal contract what they expect and by when.

If you don't know any angels, you can submit your business plan on several different websites that will connect you with them, such as GoBigNetwork.com and the Angel Investment Network.

Venture Capital

Also commonly referred to as VC, these are professional startup lenders. Unlike *banks*, they're comfortable with higher risk and they're looking for a huge return on their investment. Unlike *angels*, they're often a large company with a huge amount of capital, and they sponsor many projects at a time.

VC's have some major downsides, though. First, they only invest in ideas that have a very large potential of being worth many millions of dollars in a short period of time, usually less than 5 years.

Second, they'll want a large piece of your company pie. This amount can be negotiated, but if you're hurting for money, they'll make you pay dearly for it in the form of shares.

Finally, if the deal isn't structured correctly and they don't like you or they don't care for what you're doing with the company, they can bring in their own management team and kick you out! They can force you to take a buyout based on the current value of the company, which may be nothing compared to its potential.

Before you enter into any agreement with a VC, hire the best legal support you can afford. Don't let their lawyers represent you. You need your own representation to ensure someone is looking out for your best interest. You certainly don't want to have your company pulled out from under you.

VC's aren't usually a good source of seed capital because they want to see *something* before they invest. That means you'll need a prototype at a minimum…cash flow and/or user signups are even better. If you already have users and cash flow, you're past the seed round, which means VC investments would be for growth funding instead of seed capital.

Plus, most VC companies are only interested in investing millions of dollars. Some won't even talk to you unless you need more than $10 million. If you're still in the idea or prototype phase, you wouldn't even know how to spend $10 million! At least not on your business….

If you think you're going to need VC funding at some point and you don't know any VC investors, you need to start the process of finding them now. They invest in people they know and trust, and it can take months or years to build that kind of rapport.

Most major cities have a venture club that meets regularly. For example, The Rocky Mountain Venture Club in Colorado meets monthly to listen to pitches from entrepreneurs. They also offer classes on various investor and business related topics, such as how to pitch your idea to investors and how to start a business.

Find the venture club in your area and attend their classes and events on a regular basis. Introduce yourself to everyone you meet and learn as much as you can from them. When it comes time for a VC round of investments, you'll know them, and more importantly, they'll know you.

There are literally entire books written about startup funding and if you're considering it, you need to read several of them. My personal recommendation is to bootstrap if at all possible, even if it means putting your big idea on the back burner for a while until you do a trial run with a smaller idea. In the end, this may be your only option anyway if you're an unproven entrepreneur without deep pockets or connections.

Job vs. Business

There is a difference between a job and a business. I've spoken to several would-be entrepreneurs with an idea for a job and a need for funding to do it. Investors fund businesses, not jobs. If your idea has you working by yourself out of your home earning a modest salary with little or no growth potential, you've created yourself a job.

This may be all you want to do and there's nothing wrong with that. You'll be self-employed and not working for someone else. But if your "job" requires funding, you're going to be disappointed. If you want to have any chance of obtaining funding from investors, your idea needs to be for a viable business with substantial growth potential that can survive without you behind the wheel.

Intellectual Property

Intellectual Property, also commonly referred to as IP, is what investors love most. If your idea involves valuable IP, you have a much better chance of getting funded early on, but IP isn't easy to come by.

I'm often asked by people with an idea for a web-based business if they should patent their concept or website. I usually respond by telling them that I'm not a patent attorney and they should speak to one before investing too much time or money trying to patent their idea because website patents are extremely expensive and hard to obtain.

Now, if they have some unique component of the business or a tangible product that gives them a strategic advantage in the marketplace, they may be able to patent the idea, but you don't need a patent to have Intellectual Property.

In fact, it may be in your best interest NOT to apply for a patent. Google's most valuable IP is their search algorithm. Kentucky Fried Chicken's is their 11 herbs and spices recipe. Coca Cola's is the list of ingredients for their syrup. Are any of these priceless trade secrets patented? Nope. The main reason is because in order to obtain a patent, you have to document and make public the details of your trade secret, which kind of violates the whole concept of a "secret."

The patent protects you from having your idea stolen. Actually, that's not totally accurate. The patent gives you the right to sue someone who violates the patent by substantially copying it. These types of lawsuits can be very lucrative, but they're time consuming and expensive to fight. While you're busy suing someone, your business and finances suffer.

Notice how I said "substantially copying it" earlier? That's an important distinction. If a business looks at your patent, and then develops their own way of doing the same thing that's "substantially" different than your way of doing it, they might not be violating your patent. The problem here is that "substantially" is a subjective term that's open to interpretation by the judges and jurors deciding your case. If your opponent has deep pockets and can afford a high-priced patent attorney, your low budget attorney might not present a compelling enough case for a judge or jury to decide in your favor. Patents are great, but only if you have the money to defend them.

The good news is that IP is much broader than patents, and can include things like trademarks, names, copyrights, phrases, symbols, designs, inventions, discoveries, etc. Anything that you have and other people don't have that can be used to generate revenue and set you apart from the competition may be considered IP by potential investors.

IP has to have real, tangible and quantifiable value. You may love your domain name, but that doesn't make it worth a million dollars. However, if you develop your business and your domain name becomes synonymous with the product or service you're offering (think "Googling"), you have some very valuable IP. Unfortunately, that can take years to develop and if you need money to get started, you won't be able to count on that form of IP.

Several people have come to me with ideas for new types of search engines. Obviously, you can't patent or claim ownership of the "search engine" concept since the web already contains hundreds of them. However, you may have a brand new idea for a specific type of ranking algorithm or a new way to crawl the web and index data that's a 100 times faster or more accurate than current methods. Assuming your ideas are truly unique and powerful, investors may consider them IP with tangible value.

This is just one example and only you (and possibly a qualified patent attorney) will know for sure if your web-based business contains enough IP to attract early-stage investors. If it does, you're ahead of the game, but don't give up if you don't have IP. You may not be able to attract investors, but you may still have a viable business with growth and income potential.

Writing Your Plan

> "Reduce your plan to writing. The moment you complete this, you will have definitely given concrete form to the intangible desire."
>
> ~Napoleon Hill, "Think and Grow Rich"

If you decide to seek investors, one of the first things you'll hear from them is "show me your business plan," but investors are not the only reason to have a written plan. Some people will tell you not to spend your time writing a business plan unless you need it for investors, but I disagree. The person the plan benefits the most is *you*.

Whether you're seeking funding or not, the act of writing the plan will help you hash out and solidify your ideas. Writing the plan is an invaluable exercise, even if you're the only one who reads it.

When you're writing your plan, you have two options. The first is a traditional business plan that investors will want to see. The second is a simple business plan that you can use to organize your thoughts and focus your energy.

Traditional Business Plan

The traditional business plan includes all the nitty-gritty details about your business, including a financial plan and a marketing plan. In my opinion, this plan isn't nearly as valuable to a web startup as it is to a traditional business for a few reasons.

First, it's very easy to change direction in a web business. That means if you spend a week or two writing a traditional business plan, your entire business may have changed direction two or three times during that time span. It's not like a brick-and-mortar in that regard.

When you're ready to break ground on your brand new retail location, you better know what the plan is; that you're going to make money doing it; and that your target audience frequents that location. On the web, your target audience is everywhere; you can make money doing almost anything; and your plan can change daily if you need it to.

The second reason why I'm not a fan of traditional business plans is because there are far too many unknown variables in your assumptions. All those unknowns make it impossible to predict things like revenue growth, especially if you haven't launched and you don't have any users yet.

Third, if you're in the very early stages of your startup and you're not seeking outside investors yet, your time will be better spent working on tasks that have a higher return on investment, such as creating your MVP (Minimum Viable Product), surveying potential customers, and marketing your website.

> ## Did you know...
>
> MVP or Minimum Viable Product is a common term used in the web startup world. It refers to the absolute basic product you can launch that will allow you to gauge interest and draw some conclusions about your business model. It also allows you to get some feedback from customers and alter your course if need be, before you're too far down the road. I'll cover this concept in more detail later in the book when it's time to document your requirements.

The number one reason websites fail isn't because they're lacking a good plan or because they're missing features, it's because they lack enough users to generate a profit. Spending a week or a month writing your plan isn't going to help you avoid this common pitfall.

Before we launched QuoteCatcher, I spent two weeks writing a full-blown business plan. Greg told me I was wasting time that could be better spent writing code or working on building the business, but I was convinced we needed a detailed plan in writing.

After we sold the business and were cleaning out the office, we stumbled across my original business plan. We may not have used it much while we owned the business, but it was good for a laugh after we sold it. My growth projections were so far out in left field that it was obvious I had no idea what to expect before we launched. We also quickly realized after launch that the marketing strategy I outlined for attracting vendors to buy our leads didn't work.

In retrospect, Greg was right. I spent two weeks writing a plan based on my unrealistic and overly optimistic view of future events that were impossible to predict. My goal of having our plan in writing could have been achieved without spending two weeks on it, simply by documenting the most important things that we already knew and the things that were easy to find.

And that's why I think a simple business plan is a much better use of your time. In the next section, I'll explain the most important things to include in your plan that will allow you to maximize your results while minimizing your effort.

If you're seeking outside investors, your simple plan won't satisfy them. That means you'll need to write a traditional business plan with all the nitty-gritty details and your pie-in-the-sky vision for your company. If you go to the bookstore or library, you'll find entire books written on this subject. SCORE teaches a day-long class about writing business plans, as do other business support organizations. Some universities offer a semester long course on this topic! If you decide you need this type of business plan, check out one of these sources for help. I've also included a couple of suggested readings in the "Resources" section at the end of this book. However, if a simple plan will suffice, continue reading....

Simple Business Plan

Your simple business plan needs to address these main sections: overview, target audience, competition, monetization plan, marketing plan, and startup expenses. You can write this plan in a day of focused effort (especially if you're already done your competitive research), and it will provide you with all the clarity and direction you need.

Overview

The first section defines your idea, the problem you're trying to solve, your solution to the problem and your value proposition. It needs to bring clarity to your vision so it's easier to explain what you're building. If you have a business partner, discussing your vision and writing it down will help you both navigate from the same map.

Write a summary of your business idea. Include the problem and how you plan to solve it. Here's a list of questions to answer in this section:

- ❑ What problem are you trying to solve?
- ❑ What products or services will you provide that will solve the problem?

- What is your value proposition?
- What void in the market or special niche are you filling?
- Why is there a need and demand for it? Why will people use it?
- What benefit will the users get from your website? Discounts? Hard to find products? Premium services? Community?

Target Audience

The next section of your plan needs to define your target audience. Be as specific as possible here. "Everyone" is not your target audience, at least not in the beginning. Here are some questions to answer:

- Who is your target audience for the products and services you're selling? Women? Men? Under 20? Over 30? Over 50? Local? National? International? Middle income? High income? Buyers of XYZ product? Users of XYZ website? People who exercise? People who don't exercise? People who don't exercise but want to? Etc.
- Approximately how big is your target audience?
- How big is the market in terms of annual spending?

Competition

The next section of your plan needs to analyze your competition. That means you need to clearly understand who your target audience is and who your competition is. It also means you need to know what your customers want and what will make them buy what you're selling instead of what your competition is selling. Here are some questions to answer:

- Who are your closest competitors?
- Who is their target audience?
- How are you different from them?
- Why would a customer choose your site over theirs?

You need to answer these questions for each of your main competitors. If you populated the Competitor Intel Log discussed earlier in the book, you can include it here or reference it.

Monetization Plan

Your plan needs to define your monetization strategy at a high level. Explain how you're going to make money on the site. Here are some questions to answer:

- ❏ How does your competition generate revenue?
- ❏ How will you generate revenue? Markups? Subscriptions? Fees? Ads? Affiliates? Etc.
- ❏ How much will your markup be on products and services?
- ❏ What's your expected profit margin?

Marketing Plan

The next section defines your initial marketing plan. Once you launch, you need to attract users to your site, and this is how you "think" you'll do it. You may also decide to change your marketing plan (and your monetization plan) after you're officially in business, but at least you'll have a place to start when it's time to launch. Here are some of your options:

- ❏ Pay-per-click ads
- ❏ Pay-per-impression ads
- ❏ Social media marketing
- ❏ Affiliate marketing
- ❏ Email marketing
- ❏ Telemarketing
- ❏ Shoe leather marketing
- ❏ Information marketing

You'll learn more about marketing later in the book, so you may want to wait until you read that section before your write this part of your plan.

Startup Expenses

The final section of your plan defines your startup costs. These costs include things like website development, graphic design, marketing, business cards, etc. If you have a business partner, knowing your expected costs upfront will ensure you're both on the same page. If one of you expects to pay $10,000 for website development and the other is expecting to pay $1,000, you could avoid a very uncomfortable conversation by discussing it before you start.

Your startup expenses might look something like the example I've included here in Figure 1.

Startup Expenses

Expenses	
Legal	$2,000
Business Cards	$200
Website Development	$3,000
Insurance	$500
Rent	$0
Marketing	$30,000
Expensed Equipment	$0
Other	$0
Total Expenses	**$35,700**

Figure 1

Did you notice that the marketing budget is $30,000? I chose that number to make a point. Most people completely underestimate the cost of marketing when they're starting their business. Your website is NOT the field of dreams. If you build it, they will only come if you market the hell out of it.

Crafting Your Elevator Pitch

"I would have written a shorter letter,
but I did not have the time."

~Blaise Pascal

Once you have your business plan finished, it's a good time to craft your Elevator Pitch. All the benefits of your business will be fresh in your mind, so writing your pitch should be simple. Yeah, right....

The elevator pitch is the thing most entrepreneurs have the hardest time doing well. We love our business idea, we think about it all the time, and we see it from every angle, which makes it hard to distill it down into a 30 second (or less) pitch.

I meet people all the time who pitch their ideas to me, and it's excruciatingly painful when the "pitcher" is so buried in the details that I have no idea what their business idea is. What that tells me (and everyone else who hears it) is that they haven't taken the time to think through their idea and to organize their thoughts.

Your goal is NOT to get your listener to understand your business as well as you do. Your goal IS to help them understand what your business does and why they should be interested enough to listen to you.

When you hear people talk about an elevator pitch, they're usually referring to the 30 second to 2 minute speech that explains your business idea to investors. I'm going to talk about that pitch in a minute, but before I do that, I want to first cover what I call the Greeting Pitch and the Follow-up Pitch.

Greeting Pitch

Picture yourself at a networking event. Maybe you're at the weekly Chamber of Commerce meeting or you decided to checkout a

Meetup group. What happens when you arrive? You start mingling, of course. And what does everyone ask everyone else? Right after you exchange names, one of you says, "What do you do?" Do you think these people want to hear your 2 minute investor pitch? Not a chance. That's why you need a Greeting Pitch to compliment your Elevator Pitch.

Some people refer to the Greeting Pitch as an "intro," but I think it's much more than that. Intros tell people what you do. For example, "I'm a Startup Coach" or "I'm a Real Estate Agent." But intros don't say why the other person should be interested in talking to you. You want them to know more than *what* you do; you want them to be *interested* in what you do. That means your pitch needs to be more than your profession…it also needs to be persuasive.

The Greeting Pitch is short and to the point. Don't waste your time stating the problem, just give them a one sentence (two at the most) answer that explains the most important benefit or overriding purpose of your business. You don't even need to include your profession in your Greeting Pitch. If you've crafted your pitch correctly, your profession should be obvious.

The pitch should be 8 seconds or less because that's the average attention span of someone at a networking event. Your main goal is to weed out people who have no interest in what you're doing and anyone who has no potential to add value to what you're doing.

Let's use my coaching and training business, JPStonestreet.com, as an example of a Greeting Pitch:

```
"I train and coach people who want to start
 their own online business."
```

This pitch takes less than 4 seconds to say, and it says exactly what I do. It alludes to my profession, which is a trainer and a coach, and it explains who my target audience is. If the person I'm talking to is thinking about starting an online business, or they know someone who's thinking about it, they'll be curious enough to ask more questions.

Here's another example for you. If your website sells sales leads like QuoteCatcher does, your pitch might sound something like this:

> "I connect people who need business services with companies that provide the services."

This takes about 5 seconds. After hearing this pitch, if the person you're speaking to needs sales leads, they'll be interested enough to ask a follow-up question.

Follow-up Pitch

After I say my Greeting Pitch, sometimes I hear, "Oh, you're a business coach?" That's a great question because it gives me the opportunity to respond with my Follow-up Pitch, which is:

> "Actually, I'm a speaker, trainer and author. I've launched several of my own websites and now I help other people save time and money by avoiding some of the painful mistakes I made."

A Follow-up Pitch is your response to a question about what you do. Like the Greeting Pitch, it needs to be 8 seconds or less and it needs to be both informational and persuasive. If you read my Follow-up Pitch out loud in a conversational style, it takes 8 seconds to say. I had to practice it and fine tune it to get it down to 8 seconds, and I succeeded without losing any meaning or value.

To continue the sales lead example above, you might hear in response to your Greeting Pitch, "How do you do that?" This is a great opportunity to expound on what your niche market is with a response like:

> "People who need services like web design or advertising submit a form on our website with details about their project and then we match them up with vendors who can help them."

Prepare your Greeting Pitch and your Follow-up Pitch ahead of time, and practice them until they're fluid and conversational…and 8 seconds or less.

Elevator Pitch

If you have an opportunity to give a short pitch in front of a group, or to investors, the Elevator Pitch is what you'll use. Sometimes you'll have a couple minutes to pitch your idea, especially if you're presenting to a group (or you're in the elevator of a really tall building). Other times, you'll have 30 seconds at the most. Therefore, you need a couple versions of your Elevator Pitch: one clocking in at 30 seconds and the other somewhere between 1 and 2 minutes.

Unlike the Greeting Pitch, which focused exclusively on the main purpose of your business, your Elevator Pitch needs to explain two things: the pain statement and the value proposition. Together, they describe the *problem* you're trying to solve and *how* you're going to solve it.

When you're crafting your Elevator Pitch, apply the following four rules. First, it needs to be focused on the problem and the benefits of your solution. Leave out the administrative and operational details that apply to every business. No one cares if you're incorporated in Delaware or you're launching out of your mom's basement. In fact, too much information can be harmful, especially if it's irrelevant.

Second, it needs to be easy to understand so leave out the tech jargon, the acronyms and the $2 words. If your audience asks technical questions, you better have the answers, but don't assume they understand or even care about the technical details.

Third, if you're pitching to investors, your pitch needs to explain how you're going to make money, and more importantly, how *they're* going to make money by investing in you. Tell them how much people spend on your industry niche each year, how much you plan to charge for your products or services and how much revenue you expect to generate in the first year. If you're pitching to non-investor types, leave out this section. You don't want other people getting ideas about launching their own competing business, especially if the numbers are compelling.

Finally, your pitch needs to be irrefutable. That means everything you say in your pitch needs to be accurate and bullet proof. I met a woman in 2010 who spent 10 minutes pitching her website idea to me. Once I finally figured out what she was talking about, I asked her if she'd heard of the website "Friendster.com," which was launched back in the 90's and was almost exactly the same as her idea. I explained how that site works and how hard it's been for them to make money and compete with Facebook. Her reply was, "Well, they must not be marketing themselves very well because I've never heard of them."

I suggested that if she was set on this idea, she should pick a small niche and create a very special offering around their interests. She didn't see the value in that and was convinced everyone would love her website. She wasn't very happy with me or my advice, and I haven't heard from her since.

There are two lessons to be learned from this story. The first is to be prepared and do your research. A simple search on Google for "friend websites" returns "Friendster" and several other similar websites. If you can't do a basic search to find your competition before you pitch your idea, and your audience knows more than you do, I promise you're not going to be happy with the outcome and you're going to feel like a putz.

The second lesson you should learn from this story is to listen to the advice from people who know more than you. You don't have to follow their advice, but you should at least listen to it and ask questions. This woman completely disregarded my ideas and left in a huff. She wasted an opportunity to learn from someone who's been there and done that. I was more than happy to help her fine-tune her idea into something that might work, but her ego got in the way. Don't be *that* person…you know…the one who would rather be *right* than *successful*.

To recap the four rules for your Elevator Pitch, it should be:

1. Focused

2. Simple
3. Financially compelling
4. Bullet proof

There's nothing like an example to drive home the lesson. Here is my 30 Second Pitch and my Under 2 Minute Pitch.

30 Second Pitch

"Starting an online business is really hard. The path is full of trap doors and I've fallen in most of 'em. I had to learn the lessons the hard way, but my goal is to help other people avoid some of this painful lessons.

A lot of people have great ideas but no clue what to do with them. I sold a web startup so I know the path to success. I've walked it. It's hard. But it's doable if you know how.

My training and coaching program will teach you how to be successful so you can launch your own online business and hopefully avoid the 7 failures most entrepreneurs rack up before they succeed."

Under 2 Minute Pitch

"Starting an online business is really hard. The path is full of trap doors and I've fallen in most of 'em. The average entrepreneur fails 7 times before they're successful and that's exactly the number of failures I racked up before I learned how to do it the right way.

I read lots of books and lots of articles about starting a business along the way, and they were definitely helpful. But there's just no substitute for having a real person by your side who's both failed and succeeded. They can point out the trap doors before you fall in 'em. I regret not having a support system on my journey. I had to learn all the lessons the hard way.

And that's why I launched JPStonestreet.com. I absolutely love the web startup world. It's the only type of business that you can start for a few hundred bucks, and turn it into billions of dollars within a few short years. It's the modern day gold rush.

A web business is very easy to start…IF you have a good idea. The idea is the hard part. A lot of people have great ideas but no clue how to take the idea from dream to reality.

That's where I come in. I've launched several websites and I sold a successful web startup so I know the path to success. I've walked it. It's hard. But it's doable if you know how.

My ideal client has some basic computer skills and they use the Internet on a daily basis. They don't need to have an idea in mind, but it helps if they at least have an area of expertise that we can use as a launching pad to generate ideas.

My goal is to help people who have good ideas but not a lot of connections and no technical background. My training and coaching program will teach you how to be successful so you can launch your own online business and hopefully

avoid the 7 failures most entrepreneurs rack up
before they succeed."

My 30 Second Pitch clocks in at exactly 30 seconds and my Under 2 Minute Pitch clocks in at 1 minute 37 seconds. I wrote the long one first and then trimmed it back until I hit the 30 second mark for the shorter one.

Notice how the tone is very conversational? You don't want this to *sound* like a memorized speech, even though you're going to memorize it. The subtext of a conversational tone says that you know your business inside, outside and upside down. Plus, your audience will zone out if you sound like a robot. That means you need to practice it until it sounds fluid and conversational.

Don't take this step of the planning phase for granted. Spend some time to craft each pitch and practice, practice, practice it.

Off to the Races

I'm going to close our discussion of Planning for Success with some advice and general observations from nearly 15 years of entrepreneurship and over 10 years of starting and/or working for dotcoms. First…

Control Your Excitement!!!!

You have an idea and you've been thinking about it non-stop for the past three weeks. It's taken on a life of its own. You're picturing a big house, fancy cars, and trips around the world. It's your ticket out of the rat race! Yippee!

Hold on just a minute, though. Excitement is a valuable driving force, but it can cloud your judgment if you're not careful. Remaining objective is easier said than done, but it's absolutely critical. Run your concept past a few people you trust, or contact your local SCORE office. Have them sign an NDA (Nondisclosure Agreement) if it makes you feel better. But here is the most important part… Listen to what they say. Ask questions. Get suggestions. And don't blindly follow your excitement over a cliff!

Don't Quit Your Day Job

My next piece of advice is don't quit your day job unless you have a second income source and can afford to live for up to two years without earning any money from your new website. Everyone thinks their idea will skyrocket (even I do), but that seldom happens.

The reality is that it could take a year or two, or even longer to start generating enough revenue to pay yourself a decent salary. If you have an equal business partner, it could take twice as long.

It's best to continue working until your website's revenue is steadily increasing and your business model has been proven on the battlefield. Quitting your job could put extra stress on you, which may force you to make desperate business decisions that you wouldn't make if you weren't strapped for money in your personal life.

It's a Family Business

"Nice college boy, didn't want to get mixed up in the family business."

Sonny says to Michael Corleone in "The Godfather"

Michael learned, just like you will, that the family can't stay out of the business. Even if they don't work directly for the business, they are affected by it and the decisions you make in it. If you're married, it's especially difficult.

When I was first starting out, I worked 16 hours a day. After my wife went to work in the morning, I would start coding (aka writing software) and that would last all day. After a break for dinner, I would go back to coding. When she went to bed, I would code until one or two in the morning. Then I would get up and start the whole thing over again. I did take a little time off on weekends, but not much.

If I was making better money back then, it would have been easier to justify it. But I wasn't. The mantra in our house soon became, "You need to earn more and work less!"

After a few years of this, it eventually took its toll and my marriage ended. The business ended the family (at least it was partially responsible for it ending).

I remember having a conversation with my former wife while we were still dating. I told her that I was an entrepreneur at heart and that someday I would run my own company. I went on to tell her that it would be a long road and there would be some hard times at first, but it would eventually pay off. She said she was ok with me being an entrepreneur and making short-term sacrifices…. One of us was right….

Before you strike off on your own, your family needs to be 110% in support of it because *they* will be stressed to the limit right along with *you*.

You're So Lucky!

It's true, I am lucky. I've always been that way. But that's not why I've been successful in business. At least that's not the ONLY reason.

Thomas Edison once stated that "Genius is one percent inspiration and ninety-nine percent perspiration." I mostly agree with this, but I'd like to add a couple percentage points in there for luck.

Some people don't believe in luck. They say "luck is where opportunity meets preparation." This is true much of the time, but some people are just lucky, and some are just unlucky.

In his book, "Think Big and Kick Ass," Donald Trump tells a story about a friend who's always hurting himself and losing at ventures. He describes an incident when the guy was on his way home from the hospital after being treated for a broken collarbone when a light pole falls across the road and hits his car, sending him back to the hospital. Now that's just bad luck!

Hopefully you're not unlucky like this guy, but even if you are, you have the ability to nudge the Universe in a better direction. By keeping a positive attitude and believing good things will happen, you can actually improve your chances that they will. You can call it the Law of Attraction, but I prefer to look at it as birds of a feather flock together. Being positive and talking about your success is very appealing to other people who are positive and successful, and they often bring their success with them to share.

While luck does play some role in the outcome of events, the largest contributing factor to your success is how hard you work. Pour your heart and soul into it and your odds of success are very good.

Ready, Fire, Aim

Many people have an idea for a business and want to start one, but they never take the leap. They think they need to read just one more book or attend just one more seminar. They're convinced that they don't know enough and they want everything to be just perfect before they start.

While I am a proponent of starting with a plan and thinking things through, you eventually need to pull the trigger and start moving forward. A term I've heard before and one I use quite often with procrastinators and people who lack the self-confidence to get started is "ready, fire, aim." This term essentially means that once you're ready, go for it. You can always adjust your aim and direction once you're underway, but if you never leave the starting gate, you'll never get to where you're going.

Don't let yourself get paralyzed by analysis. Aristotle once said, "That we must learn before we do, we learn by doing." It's ok if you don't know every little thing. You'll have plenty of time to learn along the way. What's important is that you get started and make some progress toward your goals. Ready, fire, aim!

Perseverance

"Success is going from failure to failure
without loss of enthusiasm."

~Sir Winston Churchill

When I talk with someone for the first time about starting an online company, I always end the discussion with a speech about perseverance.

The hard truth is that many businesses fail. I've had several of my own that failed miserably. If that happens to you, get up, brush yourself off, and get right back to work on the next idea. If you learn from your mistakes and stick with it, you're much more likely to eventually succeed.

Jim McCann owned several flower shops in the New York City metro area when he decided to start selling flowers nationally. He approached a company with a very memorable phone number and acquired them for $2 million, only to find out later they had $7 million of debt. The purchase nearly bankrupted the flower chain and it was on the verge of closing, but McCann wouldn't give up. 1-800-Flowers was one of the first online retailers and is now a household name worth several hundred million dollars.

When interviewed on CNBC's, "How I Made My Millions," McCann was asked what the largest factor was in his success. His response? "Perseverance."

Starting any type of business is hard and full of turmoil; starting a web business is no exception. You're going to have ups and downs along the way. One day you'll feel great about some small success; the next, you'll feel terrible about some minor setback. Just try to keep everything in perspective and don't let minor setbacks kill your momentum. Sometimes, the most important component of success is perseverance, or, put another way, how long you can keep going.

That about covers the Planning for Success phase. The next chapter is about Starting Your Startup and it covers all the little things you need to think about while you're preparing to leave the starting gate. Unfortunately, it has very little to do with the actual website, but it's a necessary step in the process that will help you hash out your idea's operational details and better understand what it will take to do it.

Planning For Success Checklist

- ☐ Create a notebook for ideas and plans
- ☐ List your strengths, likes and areas of expertise
- ☐ Create your Viable Business Filter
- ☐ Think of a brilliant idea!
- ☐ Assign a business model category?
- ☐ Determine if there's a need AND a demand
- ☐ Do some competitive research
- ☐ Document your competitive analysis
- ☐ Define your target niche market
- ☐ Develop your monetization plan
- ☐ Locate your seed capital (aka startup funding)
- ☐ Write your Business Plan
- ☐ Talk to your family and get their support and approval
- ☐ Keep your day job or identify income or savings to support you for at least 2 years
- ☐ Control your excitement
- ☐ Ready, fire, aim
- ☐ Dig deep for your perseverance

"Start where you are.
Use what you have.
Do what you can."

~Arthur Ashe

Phase 2: Starting Your Startup

In this section, I'm going to cover all the little things that are required to get your startup started. This phase is the time to form your legal business entity to protect your personal assets from any bad things that might happen to the business.

Forming an official business will also allow you to realize the tax benefits of owning a company. Once you learn about all the things you can write off and how much it saves you in taxes, you'll never again be caught alone in the dark alley of the IRS without your business by your side.

Protecting yourself legally, creating your identity, managing your finances and more! There's lots to discuss here so let's get started!

Before You Turn the Key

Before we jump into the nuts and bolts of starting your company, I want to share a couple strategies and tactics that will help during all phases of the web startup process. The first is....

Finding Focus

This book has been written with the assumption that you're not rolling in cash or funded from the deep pockets of Venture Capital or Angels. In fact, if you took my advice from the last section, you're planning to keep your day job while you start your new company. If that's the case, your time and money are very limited, which means it's even more important to stay focused.

Energy Focus

There are three different types of focus that I'm referring to. The first one is "energy focus." Since you're starting this by yourself (or maybe with a business partner), time is your most precious commodity.

There will always be more things on your list of to-do's than there will be time to do them. You'll be wearing several hats, from accountant to marketer, and each requires some amount of your energy on a regular basis. Spend too much time wearing one hat and another role suffers. That means you need to protect your time from the drains that are sucking it away.

The best way to do this is to use lists. Back in the late 1990's, I worked at a consulting firm in Washington, DC, about two blocks from the White House. I was a technical project manager with a large team of developers and testers reporting to me. Once a week, we had a manager's meeting with the owner of the firm and he would conclude every meeting with a simple phrase: "Don't forget: Make lists. Check things off." When you have more things to do than time to do them, this simple advice will help you maintain focus on the things that are most important.

The temptation to do the fun things will be tremendous. I suffer from this regularly. Sales is the part of business ownership that I enjoy the least. It's hard for me, but I dedicate time to it because I won't have any customers or a business if I don't.

It works best to commit a certain amount of time each day to your various responsibilities. If a particular task doesn't require daily attention, such as accounting, set aside time one day a week for it. If you don't have anything pressing to do at any given moment, you can use the time to review and reprioritize what's on the list.

You may find that a weekly schedule works well for you. You can use a calendar application or Excel to prioritize every hour of each day during the week. Block times for each of the hats you have to wear and then commit to following the schedule.

An accountability partner or startup coach can help you stay on track. Consider asking your business partner, a friend or coach to hold you accountable. You can even ask them to create a schedule for themselves, and then you can help each other stick to it.

Product Focus

The second type of focus is "product focus." Since you're operating with limited resources, start with a small niche first. Don't try to be everything to everyone on your first day of business.

Let's say you're starting an ecommerce site to sell writing instruments. You'll have a better chance of attracting repeat customers if you focus on one area, such as calligraphy, instead of offering everything from Bic 12 packs to Meisterstück Montblanc Diamond Pens.

Product focus will also reduce your inventory costs. If you offer a few, targeted products, you'll be able to buy larger quantities of them from suppliers, which will reduce your wholesale purchase price. This means you'll make more profit on each item you sell.

It's also more likely that people will remember you when they need what you sell. If I need a new battery for my digital camera, I don't think about Wal-Mart; I think about Batteries Plus. With product focus, it's easier to get picked out of a crowd, and the web is a crowded place.

Service Focus

The third type of focus is "service focus." If your website offers a service, focusing on a small niche to start can help create very loyal users and a good cash flow.

As I discussed earlier, Facebook only allowed Harvard students to register when it first launched. They created a very loyal and active following with this feeling of exclusivity. eBay only sold collectibles when it first launched and it became very popular with people who like to collect rare items. If a collector wanted something, he knew to look on eBay.

When we launched QuoteCatcher, we focused most of our energy on services relating to advertising, such as website designers, advertising agencies and PR firms. We did this for two reasons. First, it's what Greg and I understood the best from our own personal experience. And second, it was the most lucrative focus area we could choose at the time, based on the search volume for our key terms.

Service focus also applies to the features you want developed for your website. A few years ago, I met someone who was building a specialized search engine. He had a list of requirements a mile long and wanted advice on managing developers because they were months behind schedule. The first thing I told him was to strip out all the bells and whistles. He didn't need all of the "extras" to launch the service and start getting users. They were nice-to-haves and they were bogging down development.

My advice to him and to you is to stay focused on your goal. Your goal should be to create your MVP, start your online company and start generating revenue. Your goal should NOT be to provide everything to everybody on your first day.

Whether you're launching a product or service business, maintaining focus allows you to better target your marketing dollars. It costs a lot of money to market to everyone, but if you can whittle down your audience, it could save you thousands of dollars in advertising expenses. Then, once you've established a good position in the market with a healthy cash flow, you can broaden your target audience with new products and services. This was the model for Amazon and eBay, and it works very well.

Focus will also greatly improve your search engine ranking. Search engines such as Google and Bing reward websites for relevancy. If someone types in a search term for "calligraphy pens" and your entire site is focused on that topic, you'll be rewarded over time with high ranking, assuming your products and content are good. I'll discuss this more in the next phase when I cover SEO.

> **Did you know...**
>
> SEO stands for Search Engine Optimization. It refers to the process of making your website more attractive to search engines so it shows up higher in search results. The main component of SEO is good, relevant content, but there are several other factors that play a role in how well your website ranks, which I'll discuss in "Phase 4: Marketing Your Website."

A focused (or specialized) web business costs less to start and operate, and it will generally lead to more loyal, repeat customers and better search engine ranking. Then, once you have a strong foothold in your niche, you can expand into other areas.

Be SMARTER

You might be saying to yourself right now, "Yeah, focus is a great thing. But how do I get it?" Well, I'm glad you asked!

There's a saying in project management circles: "Be SMART." This phrase has a double meaning. The first is obvious: don't do anything stupid. The second is a mnemonic that stands for Specific, Measureable, Attainable, Relevant and Time-bound. In recent years, two more letters have been added to make it "Be SMARTER." The additional letters stand for Evaluate and Revise.

This is a good tool to help you stay focused. Each idea, feature, product and service should be filtered through this mnemonic before you prioritize it and especially before you take action. Let's look at an example for how to do this.

What's your reason for buying this book? My guess is you want to build an online business. You're not trying to learn how to fly or get elected to public office. You want to build a website and make money from it. We've defined your "Specific" goal.

How will you know when you've succeeded? This is a little subjective and is based on what you consider successful. You can break this down into several milestones, such as starting development, launching the website, getting your first sale, generating $1,000 of revenue in a month, and generating enough revenue to quit your day job. Each one of these goals is "Measurable." You'll know when you've achieved them, but you'll also need to assign a due date to make them fully measurable.

How likely is your goal to be achieved? If you've set a due date of next week to have your first sale when you haven't purchased a product to sell or launched the website to sell it, your goal isn't very realistic and it's going to be discouraging when you fail to meet it. It's important to set goals and timeframes that are "Attainable," which makes it easier to succeed and feel a sense of accomplishment.

Does your goal apply to what you're doing? Setting a goal to spend more time with your family may be important to maintaining balance in your life, but it doesn't have anything to do with starting an online business. You may want to create a different set of SMARTER goals for your personal life, but for the purposes of your business, keep them "Relevant" to your "Specific" goal.

When are you going to deliver? If you don't set a due date, you'll wander around in a lackadaisical manner and never finish. Do some analysis and figure out how long your goal should take, and then set a date that will challenge you a little. Let's say you've done your financial projections and you should reach $1,000 in monthly sales within 6 months. You can set that as your due date, or you can challenge yourself and set 4 months as your due date. This will motivate you to expend more energy to drive traffic to your site and increase the conversion rate. Every goal you set should be "Time-bound."

You're half way to your due date…are you half way to your goal? You should be constantly monitoring your progress toward your goals and "Evaluate" how likely you are to meet them within the allotted time. If you're falling behind, it's time to "Revise" your approach to try to get back on schedule. If you're ahead of where you thought you'd be, maybe you should move up the due date and set another goal.

One of my favorite sayings that I tell myself almost every day is "work smarter not harder." Using SMARTER goals helps me do just that.

KISS It!

Keep It Simple Stupid is a popular phrase in the software development world. It basically means, don't develop a complex solution to a simple problem; a mistake made by many rookie (and some veteran) developers.

Sometimes it's hard to keep it simple. We have complex brains with complex thoughts and a limited number of tools to solve problems. When confronted with a challenge, we use whatever means we have at our disposal to solve it, and those means may not be the most effective.

Finding a simple solution can also require more time. Blaise Pascal, a famous mathematician, once said in a letter to a colleague, "I have made this letter longer than usual because I lack the time to make it shorter." Pascal's point was that keeping it simple would take too much time and he just needed to get it done. It's a tough balance between doing the *right* thing and being *productive*, but it's one you should strive to achieve.

You may have a great idea for a website, but if it's not in your realm of expertise, it may be too complicated for you to be successful. I met a photographer who operated his own photography studio last year. He had a great idea for a web-based service targeting travelers and restaurants in airports. Unfortunately, he had never worked in a restaurant, he didn't have any contacts in the restaurant business or in airports, and the startup capital required would have been tremendous.

The idea was simply out of his reach given its complexity and cost. It wasn't simple enough for his current expertise and talents. In order to help him think of other options, I asked him to tell me about his photography business. We brainstormed some ideas for a web-based business relating to photography since he was an expert in that field. He also had numerous contacts with customers, photographers, service providers and suppliers. If his goal was to start a web-based business, focusing it on photography was going to be a much simpler approach, and much more likely to be successful.

When you're evaluating your business ideas, try to keep them as simple as possible by picking an area where you already have some experience and contacts. A large component of a business' success involves the network of people that support it and you. If you're new to the industry and don't speak their language, you're making life a lot harder for yourself and decreasing the likelihood of your success.

Welcome to company headquarters. Sorry the bed's not made…

The last thing I want to discuss *before* you start the engine for your online business, is *where* you're going to start the engine for your online business. Some people just starting out are tempted to blow their startup wad on office space. Think long and hard before you do this. Remember, your goal is to KISS it.

You can save money by starting out of your house; money that you can use on software and marketing. Set aside a guest room or part of the basement. When I first started, I turned a dining room into my office (much to the wife's chagrin). It was a little inconvenient when we had guests over, but it saved a lot of money on rent, phones, insurance, office furniture, etc.

It's best if you can close the door, though. You'll be tempted to work incessantly if your office is always in sight. Plus, interruptions can be a constant distraction. Being able to close the door from both the inside and the outside can make your home office much more effective.

When it's time to move out of the house and into an office, it will be easily recognizable. I'll talk more about this in the "Running Your Business" section to follow.

Legal CYA

Now it's time to discuss the nuts and bolts of all the little things that are required to start your business. In this first section, I'm going to cover all the legal things that will protect you and your personal assets from evil people who will want what you have. This part of the process isn't very fun, but there are a few things you absolutely have to do. Just accept it, do them, and move on.

Shhhh! Don't Tell Anyone About This!

Even though most ideas are derivative these days, that doesn't mean you shouldn't protect yours. You may have a new take on something or a way of doing it that's unique, and you don't want people copying it. Enter the NDA, or Nondisclosure Agreement.

An NDA is a legally binding document that prevents people from talking about or stealing your idea. You can find many samples of these on the web that can be tailored to your specific needs and I've included one with the downloadable material.

I won't go into much detail about what the NDA should include, but at a minimum, it needs to contain your name and the person or company who's signing it and a description of what needs to remain confidential, such as any intellectual property, customer lists, etc. This can be an uncomfortable step to take, but don't let that dissuade you from doing it. If you're going to own a business, you'll often encounter uncomfortable situations so get used to it.

Most investors won't sign an NDA because they work with many different people, and signing your NDA may prevent them from talking to other people in the same field. It's simply too much risk for them. Besides, they know most ideas aren't that revolutionary anyway, and they understand it's the execution that makes the most difference.

Operating Agreement

An operating agreement provides a level of protection that separates your personal assets from your business assets. Many states require an operating agreement that identifies who owns the company and what percentage each person owns. It also includes the basis of each member, which is the amount of money each member put into the company from their own personal or business accounts.

And it explains what role each member/owner plays in the company.

Some states require this document when you register your legal entity and you'll need it if you want to borrow money, but even if you don't need it for either of these reasons, it's still a good document to have on record for legal purposes. You can find example operating agreements online and tailor them to fit your specific needs, or have your business attorney create one for you. I've also included one in the downloadable material.

LLP, LLC, S Corp, C Corp, Sole Proprietor… Eni Mini Miny Mo….

Choosing a legal entity for your business is a very important decision…don't leave it to chance. I can't give you legal advice on this, but I can at least share a few of the more important aspects of each to help you be better equipped to make a decision or ask a lawyer the right questions. You should definitely consult an experienced business attorney if you have any doubts about which type of business entity is right for you.

Sole Proprietorship

This is the easiest legal entity to do. Hang a shingle outside your door and you're in business, figuratively speaking. Income from the business is reported on your personal income tax statement. Easy peasy.

Now for the bad part: If you get sued, you could lose everything you own. Your personal property is in no way shielded from your business. Let's say you launch a specialized job search site. You're going along really well and revenue has increased enough to quit your day job.

Then your competition finally notices you, and they own a patent on the way you're collecting resumes, which happens to be the secret to your success. Not only do they force you to stop using their patented method, but they also sue you for damages that are far more than your net worth, especially now that your website has to be retooled. As part of the settlement, you have to sell your car, your house, your jewelry, your first born child…you get the idea.

Some people choose this entity because it's easy and they don't want to go through the hassle of filing paperwork required for the other entities. Don't fall into this trap or you could literally lose everything.

LLP

This is a Limited Liability Partnership. If you'll be starting your company with one or more partners, you may want to consider this type of business entity. However, every state and country has its own laws governing LLP's. Be sure you understand them thoroughly before you file the paperwork.

The main advantage to this option is that each partner is protected from the actions of the other partners. If one partner gets sued, the others won't be liable for damages. Again, the rules vary considerably so be careful with this one.

Some laws say you must be a professional such as an accountant or lawyer to use this entity. Since you're starting a website, you may not qualify. If you're considering this option, consult an attorney first.

LLC

This is a Limited Liability Company and the type of entity I've formed for all of my businesses. The main advantage for this option is that your personal assets are separate from the business assets. That means if you get sued, you won't lose your house. The LLC is the most popular entity for startups because it's easy, flexible and protects the owners' personal assets.

This entity is also very easy to create. In my state of Colorado, the Secretary of State website allows you to file the paperwork electronically. You'll need an Articles of Organization stating your business name and address, and registered agent names (you and your business partners). It takes about 10 minutes to fill out this form online and costs $50 (as of 2012). Each state is different so check your state's website for instructions and prices.

If your website name is different than your business name, you'll need to file a Trade Name document. In Colorado, this costs $1 and takes about 5 minutes to complete online.

You'll also need to file an Annual Report every year. In Colorado, this is a simple online form stating you're still in business and costs $10 to submit. It also allows you to update the contact information.

An LLC is a very flexible entity. If you want to make a change to your business, just do it. You don't need to get a board consensus to add a new feature or sign a new supplier. With a C Corp and S Corp, the rules are different, as I'll explain below.

Another advantage of the LLC relates to your taxes. An LLC is considered a pass-through entity, meaning any income made by the business flows down to the owners' personal income taxes. The business itself isn't taxed. In addition, you can file your taxes as an S Corp, which has additional tax advantages. You'll need to file a K1 Form with your taxes reporting your company's profit and loss.

The laws are changing constantly and the S Corp status is under attack so get help from a good business accountant to prevent mistakes. You can expect to pay them $300 to $500 to file your tax forms, but a good one can save you more in taxes than their fees cost.

What's the downside to an LLC? If you commit fraud or misrepresent your business, a court could rule that the limited liability doesn't apply to you, thereby declaring open season on your personal assets. Hopefully you're an honest person and treat your customers and suppliers well, so this shouldn't be a problem.

Also, the income and loss that gets reported on your personal income tax return may not reflect your amount of ownership in the company. If you're only a 25% stakeholder, you could end up paying much more than 25% of the taxes; another advantage to filing taxes as an S Corp.

Finally, if your business is making good money, but you're pumping that back in for growth, you could potentially owe taxes on money that never touched your personal bank account. If you're reinvesting most of your profit, you may want to consider filing as a C Corp. At QuoteCatcher, we issued ourselves a distribution when taxes were due to cover the portion of the tax bill that was directly related to the company's profit.

S Corp

The S Corp is very similar to an LLC. In fact, from a tax perspective, if you file your LLC taxes as an S Corp, they're identical.

What's the main benefit of the S Corp? If you're planning to give most of the profits from the business as dividends to the shareholders (meaning you and your partners), you could save thousands of dollars in taxes by registering as an S Corp. That's because some dividends are taxed at the Capital Gains rate, currently 15%, instead of the ordinary income tax rate, which can be as high as 35% (and likely higher in coming years once the Bush tax credits expire). You still have to pay yourself a normal salary comparable to other people in your industry or the IRS may say you're evading taxes, and that's a can of worms you don't want to open.

There are some limits to the S Corp status, though. For example, you can't have more than 100 shareholders; all shareholders must be individuals and not a business; and all shareholders must be United States citizens. Check with a business lawyer for other restrictions.

C Corp

The C Corp is the ultimate in owner protection. The business can get sued (and most are at some point), but the owner's personal assets cannot be touched. That doesn't mean you can't be held personally liable in cases of fraud or deceptions (just ask Bernie Madoff or the president of Enron). However, if the business gets sued for patent infringement, or by a disgruntled employee, or a supplier you never paid, you won't lose your house.

C Corps are taxed as a separate entity and must file their own tax forms. They also have their own tax brackets, which may be less than your individual income tax bracket and that could save you money in taxes.

Unlike the S Corp, there's no limit to the number of shareholders and you can also have different classes of stock with different rules relating to profits and losses.

If you're seeking funding, especially Venture Capital, you'll need to create a C Corp. Outside investors want the protection that accompanies this entity and it's much easier to create shares they can own in exchange for their investment.

Why not just create a C Corp instead of an LLC? Because C Corps are a pain in the rear to maintain. You need a board of directors that meets regularly. You need to keep minutes of your meetings for reporting purposes. You need to file separate tax returns, which can get expensive. And you need board approval for many business decisions, which can bring your business to a grinding halt.

A C Corp may be the right decision for your situation. However, if you're starting a business in your spare time out of your house, the LLC is probably the best choice for you. And there's no reason you can't change your legal entity down the road. If you create an LLC now but your business grows to a point where you need it to be a C Corp for whatever reason, just change it by filing the proper paperwork.

With that said, here's my legal disclaimer about this entire section. PLEASE SEEK LEGAL ADVICE FROM A PROFESSIONAL before you make a decision. These descriptions are for informational purposes only and should NOT be considered legal advice.

Piercing the Veil

Regardless of the legal entity you adopt, it's extremely important that you keep your personal finances separate from your business finances. There's a term used in the legal world called "piercing the veil" and you don't want to be on the receiving end of that statement.

Again, I'm not an attorney and I'm not qualified to give legal advice, but I'm familiar with business law enough to share some things I've learned. As always, you should speak to a qualified legal professional if you have questions.

With the exception of the sole proprietorship, the business entities described above come with a certain level of personal protection. If someone sues your business, for whatever reason, your personal assets are protected…unless you haven't treated it as a true business as determined by a court of law. If that happens, your personal assets are not protected and they could be included in the compensation if a legal judgment is made against your business.

The best way to avoid this situation is to treat your business as a real business from day one. That means:

1. File the appropriate registration documents with your state.
2. Use the appropriate legal entity abbreviation (LLC, LLP, Inc.) in your business name and on all correspondence, business cards, letterhead, websites, etc.
3. Get a separate bank account under your business name.
4. Get a PO Box or mailbox that's different from your personal mailing address.
5. Dedicate one or more credit cards to your business and don't use them for anything else; if you have to charge something business related on a personal card, expense it and reimburse yourself from the business bank account just like you would if you worked at someone else's company.
6. File your business taxes each year and pay quarterly estimated taxes if you're earning a profit.

You can probably think of other ways to treat your business like a business, and a qualified attorney can think of even more. The bottom line is, keep your personal and business finances COMPLETELY separate and you'll hopefully never hear the term "piercing the veil" uttered from a judge's mouth.

Contracts

The next topic under Legal CYA is for vendor and customer contracts. I'm going to cover each of these individually because there are different reasons for having both.

Vendor Contracts

Most vendors, such as web designers or product suppliers, will have a contract and they'll want you to sign it. This is to protect them and you in case something goes wrong. Contracts are great as long as they're not too self-serving in the vendor's favor. If you're unsure of the terminology, have a lawyer review it before you sign it.

If the vendor doesn't have a contract, use one of your own. There are many free samples that you can find online, or you can pay a lawyer to create one.

Some small web designers don't use contracts, but you should use one even if they don't. Contracts are designed to set expectations and protect both parties in the event of a disagreement. It's a business and you need to treat it like one by protecting it with legal documents.

Customer Contracts

Getting your customers to sign a contract to use your services might not be an option for your business. Amazon obviously can't get their customers to agree only to buy books on Amazon so a customer contract won't work for them. However, if you're selling products or services to other businesses, customer contracts might be an option.

The first type of customer contract is a Purchase Agreement. In this type of agreement, your customer agrees to buy a certain number of things for a certain price for a certain period of time (or any combination of these). The nice thing about this type of agreement is that it allows you to better predict your revenue, which can help you better manage your budget. In order to get a customer to sign such an agreement, you'll need to offer a big incentive in the form of a discount or special service, but having guaranteed income is a beautiful thing.

The buyer of QuoteCatcher uses purchase agreements with its clients. For a steep discount off the regular price of their sales leads, their clients agree to purchase a set number of leads per month at a specific price. This allows them to more accurately budget the amount of marketing dollars they can spend to get the sales leads they need to sell to that client. It's a brilliant strategy and one I wish I would have thought of at QuoteCatcher.

The next type of customer contract is an Exclusivity Agreement. It's extremely difficult to get a customer to sign one of these and it will take a very good incentive for them to even consider it. But if you succeed, it not only helps your business, but it deals a blow to your competition.

The Exclusivity Agreement isn't a strategy that will work early on in your business because your customers won't have enough experience with you to trust that you'll be able to deliver on the promise. However, once you've been in business for a while and developed a strong rapport with your customers, they may consider it...with a good enough incentive.

Vendor contracts and customer contracts protect and benefit both parties: you and them. Do a search on Google for the type of contract you need if you don't have one (e.g. "web design contract example" or "customer purchase agreement sample"). Then tailor it to fit your business.

Partnerships: The Good, The Bad and The Ugly

It seems like nearly every tech startup involves a partnership containing at least two people, if not more. Usually, one partner brings the technical skills to build the technology, and the other brings the marketing skills to sell it.

These partnerships often begin with two friends talking about a problem they encountered and one has a solution to fix it. After hours or days of tossing the idea back and forth, they decide to do something about it, and a partnership is born.

If you're considering a partnership for your web company, you have several things to consider. A partnership can be the difference between success and failure, but it can also be the difference between friend and enemy.

A partnership is a lot like a marriage: compatibility may be the reason you're together, but the legal and financial elements are the ties that bind. That's why I'm going to talk about partnerships here in the Legal CYA section because you need to protect yourself, your partners and the business in case your compatibility runs its course before your exit strategy does.

Can't We All Just Get Along?

Like I said, a partnership is like a marriage, only you'll spend more time with your business partner than your spouse, so you'd better be absolutely positive that you can get along. If your personalities are exactly alike, there's a good chance you'll butt heads often.

If you're both high strung, ADHD types, all that energy has the potential of exploding and you may also have a hard time focusing the energy in a positive direction. On the other hand, if you're both laid back, easy going types, you may lack the energy to stimulate the business. However, if one of you brings the energy and the other brings the patience, you'll be constantly moving forward and you won't kill each other along the way.

I've had four different partnerships over the years, but the QuoteCatcher partnership with Greg was the only successful one. I'm a high strung individual, easily riled and very impatient. I'm also extremely focused and goal oriented. Luckily, Greg was very laid back and easy going. I never remember him getting upset about anything (even though he probably was a few times). I always told him that if he was like me, the partnership would have never worked.

There are several different personality types with various combinations of traits and talents. I happen to be a hyper focused and goal oriented ADHD type. Some people, like Greg, are ambitious and driven, yet laid back. It's a rare combination to find seemingly opposing traits in the same person, but many highly successful people fit that bill. And when you get two of them together in a partnership, they're virtually unstoppable.

Homogeny Is Bad

My first two partnerships were comprised of all technical people with similar skill sets. This was (and is) a recipe for disaster. If everyone brings the same skills to the table, there's no synergy. A business requires several different talents and you're much better off when you have complementary skills.

For instance, in my partnership with Greg, I brought the technical and operational talent to the startup. I wrote the software, managed the technology and handled customer service when we first started. Greg was a sales and marketing guy. He handled the cold calling, new customer signups and the pay-per-click marketing campaigns. He was also a great idea guy, while I was more of an implementer who took both of our feature ideas and brought them into reality.

We also had very different ways of looking at the world. Sometimes this caused some tension, but it always led to the best possible outcome. Since we each looked at problems differently, we each saw different possibilities and the best solution was usually a combination of the two views.

The best, most successful partnerships have members with complimentary skill sets. If the partners are all developers or all marketers, you're going to have a hard time defining roles and responsibilities, which can lead to conflict. Plus, if you're both working on the same tasks because that's what each of you knows how to do, the other things are going to fall through the cracks. Homogeny, or having everyone the same, is bad for partnerships.

Take Me To Your Leader

Your partnership needs a clearly defined leader. That doesn't mean this person will make all the decisions and tell you what to do, but he will help organize the tasks and provide the tie breaking vote when needed.

The leader will also be the "face" of the business to the outside world. He might be the primary contact for large accounts (when you're first starting), he may also be the liaison for partnerships with other businesses, and if you're lucky enough to attract media attention, he'll be the one to do the interviews.

Decisions should be made by consensus as much as possible. In my partnership with Greg, all decisions were made by consensus. If we couldn't agree on something, we didn't do it or we did something completely different. Sometimes when we didn't agree, we would choose one option and try it with the understanding that if it didn't work within a certain amount of time, we'd try the other option.

There are dozens of famous partnerships, especially in the tech world, but probably the most famous partnership was Apple's Steve Jobs and Steve Wozniak. This is a great example of complimentary skill sets in a very successful partnership. They both had technical talents, but Jobs was the obvious point man while Woz was the technical guru. Together, they built what is arguably the most successful company in the world.

Sometimes, partnerships can cause tension, especially when one of you is the designated leader. No one wants to start a company and feel like they're working for someone else, but if you have clearly defined roles and responsibilities, this isn't likely to happen. When everyone knows what areas they're responsible for, there's no debate about who has to do what and who gets the final say on a particular topic.

Partnership Agreements

Hopefully, your partnership is successful and you'll never have a legal need for a partnership agreement, but I cannot stress this enough: SIGN A PARTNERSHIP AGREEMENT! You can find free versions on the web that can be tweaked for your partnership so there's no reason not to have one. I've also included one in the downloadable material.

A partnership agreement, agreed upon before you start the business, can save friendships, legal fees and total disintegration of your business down the road.

Here's a list of several things you need to cover in your agreement:

- State the name of the business, each partner's name and the percentage of the business each partner owns (I'll cover equity splitting in the next section).
- How will each of you be compensated? Will you all be paid the same salary? What will the salaries be for each of you?
- How will you give raises? Does each partner get the same raise at the same time or is it based on a performance metric?
- Will you have paid vacation and how much? If not immediately, what criteria needs to be met for paid vacation to start?
- Are you allowed to work other jobs or should all available work time be devoted to the business?
- If one or some of you will work at the company full time while you're building it, and the rest will continue your day jobs, how will everyone be compensated? Who will be allowed to quit their jobs, in what order and when?
- What happens if you're not generating enough revenue to pay a large enough salary to support your families? Will one or more of you be allowed to get a job so the rest can get paid a larger salary? Who will go and who will stay? At what point can they come back? How will you agree on the salary of those staying at the company?
- Will you keep track of hours worked and how?
- How will you handle maternity/paternity leave? Is it paid and for how long? (I know of a woman whose business partner was pregnant and wanted to take a 3 month paid maternity leave. However, the business wasn't profitable enough to pay for the leave AND hire someone to replace her while she was out. The woman didn't have enough money to buy the partner out and they were on the verge of taking it to court. If they had a partnership agreement with maternity leave clearly defined, they could have avoided this nightmare.)
- What will you do with the profits (after you pay your salaries)? Will you reinvest it for growth or distribute it

among the partners? Maybe a percentage will be reinvested and the remainder distributed. Agree on this now.
- ❑ What happens if one partner wants a distribution that you had agreed to reinvest? Is this allowed? What are the rules for it? How do you decide whether to do it or not?
- ❑ How will you handle expenses such as phones, internet and mileage? If you're starting your business out of your homes and one of you lives 30 miles from town where all the sales take place, will mileage be compensated from the partner's house to the client's office or from the city limit to the client's office? At 51 cents per mile (the 2011 reimbursement rate), that amounts to $30 per round trip. If sales visits happen 4 times a week, that's $480 per month in mileage expenses for that partner. When you're just starting, that can be a large cost to the business for the partner's personal decision to live such a long way from the action.
- ❑ What happens if one partner wants to move away? It's a common thing for spouses to get transferred. Will the partner be allowed to continue or will they be required to sell their share in the business?
- ❑ When it's time to move out of your house and into an office, how will you decide where to lease or buy space? It's best to agree on a general area now so personal plans and decisions can take the location into account.
- ❑ What's your exit strategy? I'll discuss this in detail later in the book, but you'll need to agree on that now. If one of you plans to own the company and work at it forever, while the other is planning to sell it, you could be in for conflict when someone shows up with an offer to buy your company.
- ❑ Are the partners allowed to engage in extreme sports such as skydiving, paragliding and heli-skiing? Your lives are professionally and financially intertwined. That means the decisions each of you makes, whether personal or professional, affect the business. If your partner is seriously injured or killed doing an extreme sport, what impact will that

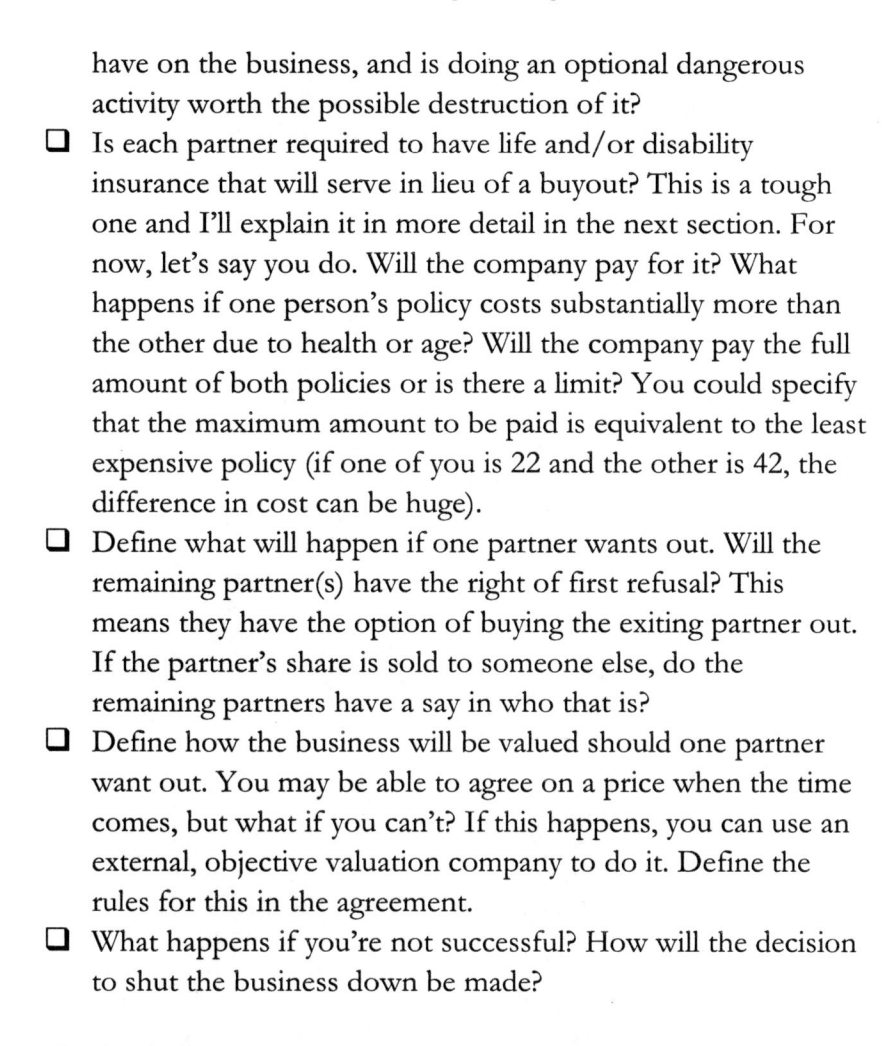

have on the business, and is doing an optional dangerous activity worth the possible destruction of it?
- Is each partner required to have life and/or disability insurance that will serve in lieu of a buyout? This is a tough one and I'll explain it in more detail in the next section. For now, let's say you do. Will the company pay for it? What happens if one person's policy costs substantially more than the other due to health or age? Will the company pay the full amount of both policies or is there a limit? You could specify that the maximum amount to be paid is equivalent to the least expensive policy (if one of you is 22 and the other is 42, the difference in cost can be huge).
- Define what will happen if one partner wants out. Will the remaining partner(s) have the right of first refusal? This means they have the option of buying the exiting partner out. If the partner's share is sold to someone else, do the remaining partners have a say in who that is?
- Define how the business will be valued should one partner want out. You may be able to agree on a price when the time comes, but what if you can't? If this happens, you can use an external, objective valuation company to do it. Define the rules for this in the agreement.
- What happens if you're not successful? How will the decision to shut the business down be made?

Think of a business partnership agreement as equivalent to a marriage prenuptial agreement. It's not fun to discuss, but it's absolutely critical that you do it to protect everyone's best interest and, luckily, there's usually no emotional love involved to complicate it.

When you're just starting out, everything is hunky dory. You're all excited about the potential of your idea and the prospect of becoming rich off of it. But now is the time to make the tough decisions about your partnership. If you wait until something bad happens, you could lose your friends over it and end up in an expensive legal battle. Do yourself a favor and spend two or three hours writing everything down <u>now</u> while everyone's in a good mood.

Life Insurance

When you have a partnership, each partner is usually critical to the success of the company. What happens if a partner's parachute fails to open when he's skydiving? Who will perform his work functions? Will you be able to afford a replacement? You need to plan for this.

When my business partner and I first started our company, we weren't making enough to cover the salary of an equivalent replacement. If he died or became disabled, I wouldn't have time to do the sales and marketing (and it wasn't my strong suit anyway back then). If I died or became disabled, he couldn't write the software. The business wasn't making enough revenue to hire someone with equivalent talent to fill the void, which meant it would have gone under.

To prevent this from happening, we each bought a substantial life insurance policy. Part of the policy was directed to the business; enough to cover the salary of a replacement employee for two years. The remainder of the policy went to our respective families as compensation for the buyout.

In other words, if I died, my wife and daughter would have received a substantial payout from the insurance policy, which was essentially my partner's way of buying my interest in the business. My family would then have no further interaction with the business or my partner. The remainder of the payout went to the business, to be spent on a replacement employee.

We included in our partnership agreement a requirement to purchase life insurance and specified that the business would pay for it. Once we sold the company, we each transferred the policies to ourselves and the beneficiaries to our families. Of course, we each have to pay for the policy out of our own pockets now, but it's unlikely that an individual would qualify for the amount of our policies without the business value to justify it.

Speak to a qualified business insurance agent to get policy quotes if you decide to go this route. This isn't something you need to do before you launch, since your business won't be worth anything at that time. However, once you're generating enough revenue to affect the value of the company, but not enough revenue to hire a replacement employee at the market rate, you should consider key-man life insurance.

Partner Equity Split

Most partnerships between two people start out as a 50/50 split, meaning each person owns half the company. This is because everyone wants an equal share, no one wants to devalue someone else's contribution, and it "seems" more fair. In reality, an equal partnership is almost never fair to one of the partners because someone usually contributes or sacrifices more in terms of time or resources.

Telling someone you think he deserves less ownership than you is never an easy conversation (unless it was his idea to begin with), but it's one you absolutely need to have very early in the partnership. If you don't, it could destroy the business. Here's how…

Let's say the original idea for the web business was yours and because of your current work schedule, you're able to devote 30 hours per week to working on it. You've also agreed to take on the CEO role because your talents are better suited for being the point man for the company. Furthermore, you're donating one of your laptops to be the development machine that your business partner is going to use to write the code for the website.

Your business partner is a programmer and brings a very valuable skill set to the partnership, but he can only work 10 to 15 hours per week, and that's the limit to his contribution. Does he deserve a full 50% share of the business?

To illustrate the point I'm trying to make, let's say 50/50 is what you agree to. Now, fast forward a month. The code still isn't written because he's only been able to devote 8 hours per week to your new venture. Meanwhile, you've spent time setting up the business, defining requirements, meeting with potential beta customers, setting up social media and online advertising accounts, etc.

You're so excited that you've spent 35 hours per week on your business. That's more than four times the effort your business partner has put into it. How does that make you feel? If you're like most people, you'll start feeling some resentment for your partner. If you're not good at expressing your feelings, that resentment will eventually build up until you explode, and your partner may not even know why!

The last thing your new business needs is resentment and animosity between its partners due to a perceived injustice. If you wrote your partnership agreement correctly, contribution expectations should have been defined up front and if a partner can't meet them, there needs to be a consequence. But even if your partner is meeting the expectations, if the level of agreed upon contribution is substantially different between the two of you, then the equity split should reflect it.

That means you're going to need to have an uncomfortable conversation, and sooner is better than later. While there's nothing I can do to take all the pain and discomfort away from this conversation, I might be able to help by making it a little more objective.

Here's a tool that I created for one of my partnerships that had an obvious disparity in the level of contribution between the two of us. We used this tool to divide the equity in a more equitable way. I call this model the Equity Splitter, and Figure 2 on the next page is an example of it.

Equity Splitter	Me	You	
Starting Shares	100	100	
CEO	20	0	
Original Idea	30	0	
Tangible Assets	10	0	
Time Commitment	100	25	
Prior Experience w/ Startup	0	50	Total
Total Starting Shares	260	175	435
Ownership %	**60%**	**40%**	

Figure 2

In this scenario, each partner is given 100 Starting Shares of the company. These are just made up amounts and don't reflect real, legal shares. It's just a way to establish a baseline for division.

The next several rows are used to add additional shares based on special contributions each partner will make to the company. For example, occupying the CEO role is worth 20 shares and having the original idea is worth 30 shares.

The time commitment refers to how much time each partner can commit to the business, based on a 40 hour work week. For this example, 100 shares is equivalent to a full time job while 25 shares equates to working 10 hours per week or a quarter time job.

Every value in this model is an assumption that the partners can discuss and agree upon. You can add rows that are missing or remove ones that don't make sense for your partnership. The important thing is to have the conversation, and using a model like my Equity Splitter can make it much more objective and much less emotional. I've included this tool in the downloadable material.

If both of you are mature and open minded, you shouldn't have any problem with this discussion. If you're not, it may be a sign that your partnership has rough waters ahead. And if that's the case, be glad you're finding it out now before you're legally and financially tied to each other.

One last thing I want to mention here is the need for a vesting schedule. Vesting means that ownership becomes official over time, instead of immediately. Most investors recommend a 5 year vesting schedule, which means 20% of your ownership in the company will vest (or become yours) each year.

For the example above, if my equity is 60%, that means 12% of my shares (or ownership) will vest each year. After two years, I'll officially own 24% of the company, and so on. There are a couple of important reasons for doing this.

First, if your partner decides to leave the company after six months or a year, does he deserve his full share in the company? Probably not, especially if you're responsible for buying him out. If you agree the company isn't worth anything at the time he leaves because you're not generating revenue, but neglect to officially terminate the partnership in writing, that old partner could come back a few years down the road when you have a buyout offer and ask for his share. If his shares only vested while he was working at the company, you won't have to deal with this unfortunate situation.

Second, and most importantly, if you decide to seek investors in a year or two, they'll want a share of your company. If ownership is fully vested already because you didn't have a vesting schedule, that means each partner will need to give up some of their shares for the investors. If one of the partners is no longer at the company, you could have a hard time convincing them to relinquish their shares, especially if they left on unpleasant terms and/or they aren't going to get a fat payout from it.

In this situation, most investors will just walk away and tell you to come back when everything is all straightened out. They have dozens of deals they're considering and if yours is full of headaches for them, they'll move on to another one.

Vesting your shares over time benefits everyone and it's the fairest thing to do. The ideal period is five years, but you and your partners can agree on a different vesting period if you want to.

Partnership Termination Agreement

No one wants to start out thinking about the need to terminate their brand new partnership, so feel free to skip this section now and come back to it later if you need to.

A partnership termination agreement is like a divorce decree. It states that the partnership is over and defines how you're going to divide the assets and ownership. If you spent an adequate amount of time on the original partnership agreement, this should already be defined. You can find examples of this type of agreement online and customize it to fit your situation.

Document the reason the partner is leaving, the effective date, how the assets are going to be divided, and how much ownership the partner will retain in the company, if any. If there's going to be a buyout, state the amount of the buyout and indicate that the partner will no longer have any involvement in the company and they are forfeiting all of their future rights relating to the company and the remaining partners. Then, once the partners agree to the content of the termination agreement, all partners need to sign it in front a of a notary public.

If your partnership ends, you need to document it...legally. If you need to get a lawyer to assist in the separation, or if each of you needs a lawyer to represent you, do it. Like I've said a of couple times now, a business partnership is like a marriage and the business is your child. If your goal is for the child to survive the divorce, the termination agreement needs to ensure that it does.

Licensing

You may need a business license for your web company. This is a difficult topic because it varies a lot between city, county and state. You can figure this out for your physical location by searching Google with "business license" appended to your location (e.g. Colorado Business License, Denver CO Business License, Denver County Business License, etc.).

Disclaimer: The following is in no way legal advice. If you're unsure whether you need a business license, contact a qualified legal professional in your area.

My home state of Colorado is very web-friendly (barring the recent affiliate sales tax debacle that has cost our state's residents millions of dollars in income). Colorado doesn't require a business license for a web business. Neither does the City of Denver nor Denver County.

Arapahoe County, where my home office is located, doesn't require a business license either, but if my home was a few blocks west of its current location, I'd be in the city of Greenwood Village, which does require a business license. It's called an Occupational Privilege Tax license and requires employers to pay $4 per month per employee, including the owners. That means even if you're working by yourself, you'd need to obtain this license and pay it monthly.

If you're selling products from your website to residents of your state, you'll probably need a sales tax license and you'll need to pay the sales tax to your state. However, if you're selling intangible items or services, you might not need to collect sales tax.

This is such a complicated, variable and constantly changing gray area that your best course of action is to contact a business lawyer in your city and ask them what you should do now, and ask them to keep you informed if anything changes in the future.

We've finally reached the end of the Legal CYA section. The next section in the Starting Your Startup phase is a lot more fun. It's time to....

Create Your Identity

Your identity is how your business looks to the rest of the world. There are many things that go into creating your identity and that's what this section is all about.

Company Name vs. Domain Name

When you're deciding on your business name, you can either use your domain name or come up with something different. My advice is to use something different than your domain name for your legal entity business name for several reasons.

First, since you need to file the legal entity paperwork to register your business very early in the process, you may change your mind about the domain name before you launch your website. If you've registered your business name as the domain name, then it wouldn't match the new domain. To rectify this, you would either need to re-register your business or you'd need to file a Trade Name document (sometimes called Doing Business As or DBA) to associate the new domain with the old one. That's not very clean.

Second, you may decide down the road to launch a new website targeting a different niche market. Let's say your first website is called FancyPens and your new website is called CheapPens. If FancyPens is your business name, now it will also be doing business as CheapPens. That just seems wrong.

A real world example of this scenario is a company called Spark Networks. Most people have never heard of them, but most people have heard of JDate and ChristianMingle. Spark Networks owns both of these dating sites and several others. If their company name was ChristianMingle, would it make sense (or be good business) for a Christian dating site to own a Jewish dating site? Not really.

Instead of using your domain name as your legal business name, pick a name that's unrelated or loosely related to your website. For example, the parent company of QuoteCatcher.com was Colorado Innovations, LLC. Under that umbrella, we also operated PromoteWare.com and several other sites. Each time we launched a new site, all we needed to do was file the Trade Name document, pay $1 and we were good to go.

Before you register your business name, you'll need to check its availability in the state where you're filing the legal documents. However, you should also make sure it's not being used in any other states. A web company knows no boundaries and you don't want to infringe on anyone's trademarks whether they're in your state or another one.

It's also a good idea to register the domain name for your parent company, even if you don't launch a website for it. This will offer you a little more protection and help safeguard your business name.

Master of Your Domain

A domain name is the official term for a website address. Think of it like the phone number for your website, only it's the name you type in a browser's address bar. You'll need a domain name for your website and now's the time to think of one.

Your domain name is FAR more important than your company name because it's what everyone will know and use. Your first choice may not be the best choice, much less available. It's getting harder and harder to find good domain names these days, thanks mainly to cyber-squatters who buy domain names in bulk and then try to sell them for a profit. Some of these "premium" domain names sell for thousands of dollars. If you're low on seed capital, spending all your money on a domain name isn't a very good use of funds.

Cyber-squatters aren't the only ones to blame for the lack of available domain names. Since domains are incredibly cheap and easy to buy, some individuals who get an idea for a business will register their domain name before they do anything else. Then, most never do anything with the domain, but it's still locked up until they let the lease expire. Searching for a domain name can be a very frustrating process…prepare yourself for disappointments.

How to Get Started on the Domain Name Quest

Before I spend much time searching for domains, I find it helpful to list out the main benefits of my website. Benefits are different than features. Features are things a user can do on the site; benefits are the reasons they'll use your site instead of someone else's.

Sit down and brainstorm a list of at least three to five major benefits. Write them down and then underline the keywords in the list. This will give you a good starting point for your domain name quest.

What Makes a Good Domain Name?

Over the years, I've done a lot of research on what makes a good domain name. What I found is mostly common sense. The best domain names are short and easy (e.g. Google, Twitter, Facebook, Yahoo, etc.). 80% of the top 500 domain names have one or two words and fewer than eight characters. Try to keep yours simple, easy to pronounce, relevant to what your site is about, and spelled correctly, if at all possible.

Spelling a word in the domain name incorrectly for effect (e.g. BriteGoldJewelry.com) might make it look neat, but people will type it in wrong (or right, depending on your point of view) and go to someone else's website. Don't try to be too clever or you could lose customers.

You should avoid hyphens in your domain name, such as Bright-Gold-Jewelry.com. Some people don't know what a hyphen is and it can be hard to explain. It's also hard to say! "What's your website address?" "It's Fine Hyphen Gold Hyphen Jewelry.com." See what a pain that is?! You don't want to force users to overcome obstacles in order to find your website, and a hyphen is an obstacle.

From a search engine perspective, your domain will rank higher if it's relevant to the content of your site. For example, if you're selling jewelry, it's better from an SEO perspective if your domain name has the word jewelry or a related term in it. BrightGoldJewelry.com will rank better than ThingsThatShine.com when people are searching for jewelry.

Getting Creative

The next thing to think about is your top level domain, or TLD. A TLD refers to the extension after the domain name. Most domains use the ".com" TLD, and this is the best choice because that's what people are used to seeing and typing. Most non-profit organizations use the ".org" TLD.

Avoid ".net" or ".biz" because people won't remember that when they're typing your web address. If your domain is FancyPens.net and someone else owns the FancyPens.com TLD, most people will go there instead. Plus, if the website is live and actively selling the same types of things you are, you'll be in violation of their trademark. You need a different name.

While using a ".com" TLD is the best choice, you may not find anything that works well using it. In that case, you have some other options if you want to think WAY outside the box. I said earlier that spelling the words in the name correctly is important; however, if your perfect name isn't available, you can get creative with the spelling.

For example, Fiverr, Flickr, Digg and Tumblr all use misspellings for their domains. When Fiverr launched , Fiver.com wasn't available so they just added an extra "r" to keep their name short and still relevant. They since bought the correct spelling, Fiver.com, for $80,000. Flickr and Tumblr also bought their correctly spelled ".com" domains for a healthy sum. Tumblr went to court over ownership of Tumbler.com and won. Digg is the only one of these examples that probably won't ever own the correct spelling of their domain. Dig.com is owned by Disney, which uses it for their Disney Interactive Media Group website.

Another creative option you have is to use the TLD as part of the name. In addition to the TLD's most people know, like ".com" and ".org," there are several others that most people don't know. Del.icio.us, Circl.es and theComplete.me use three of these rarely known TLD's.

Each country has its own TLD and some of them can be used to end words. Here's a list of several that you can register if you live in the United States: .com .org .net .biz .info .xxx .mobi .tv .am .fm .us .es .me .be .co .de .gs .tc .la .ms .vg .ws .bz .ly. There are dozens more available, but for most of them, you need to reside in the country to register a domain using their TLD.

Searching for a Domain

Registrars provide domain name search and recommendation tools that you can use to research and register your domain name. Registrars are companies that maintain the giant list of domain names. Think of them like a Yellow Pages for websites. GoDaddy is the most recognizable registrar, but there are dozens of others to choose from, including most webhosts.

Don't get discouraged if your first one or two or ten names aren't available. That's an unfortunate reality of domain names these days. Most of the best domains are taken, which means you'll need to try several different combinations of words, and maybe even think outside the box for some new ideas. This process is both fun and frustrating so try to stay positive.

Most registrars offer recommendation tools that will give you a list of alternate domains using some of the keywords in the domain you're searching for. These can be very helpful in your brainstorming efforts.

If you're not making any progress on your domain search, or you just want some fresh ideas, one website that might help is DomainNameSoup.com. They have many different tools for domain searches and recommendations. My personal favorite is called "Domain Name Mangle." It will give you other ways of spelling a word. For example, "flicker" becomes "flickr."

As you're conducting your search, take the time to document all the domains you've thought of and searched for. I use an Excel spreadsheet called the Domain Research Log for this process to store the domain name, the status (Available, Taken or Premium), and comments for anything important that I might want to remember about the domain. Figure 3 is an example with a few dating website domain names that I looked up:

Domain	Status	Comments
DateFunnel.com	Available	
DateFilter.com	Taken	
HoneyNet.com	Taken	Ad site
SimpleMesh.com	Taken	Dead
GoAfter.com	Premium	Auction for $4,000

Figure 3

Recording your findings will save you a lot of time, especially if your search spans several days. If you try to rely on your memory, you could waste time searching for the same domain names multiple times. Plus, looking over what you've already thought of might spark some new ideas. You might even change your mind about one you previously rejected.

The domain log for one of my business ideas has 723 domain names in the list. Hopefully, yours won't be that large or take as long to compile. I've included the Domain Research Log in the downloadable content.

Everybody Has an Opinion

Once you have your list narrowed down to one or a few domain names, ask some of your friends what they think of them. Getting feedback can help you spot things like unintentional misspellings, hard to say words or alternate meanings.

For example, you might totally love the domain FineJewelry.com, but when you run it by your best friend, she might say, "Is it FINE or FIND?" This may not be a deal breaker, especially if you can register both domains. However, if you can't get both domains, you could lose business to a competitor who owns FindJewelry.com.

Here are a few examples of domains that were not very well thought out. ExpertsExchange.com is a popular developer forum. Software developers use it to get answers to coding questions, but it's kind of a joke in the developer community because by changing the capital letters a bit, you get ExpertSexChange.com.

TherapistFinder.com is another example. They changed their domain to CouncelingCalifornia.com because the original domain also spells TheRapistFinder.com. GoTahoe.com now uses GoTahoeNorth.com as their primary domain because the original domain can also be spelled GotAHoe.com. My final example, SpeedOfArt.com is no longer in business. Is it because their domain also spells SpeedoFart.com? Maybe....

QuoteCatcher.com seemed like an easy enough name when we chose it. It was relevant to what we were selling (requests for quotes) and it was relatively short. However, it was hard to pronounce and understand over the phone. I can't tell you how many times I called a client or prospective client and the response was, "You're from

GoatCatcher?" Now, before I settle on a domain, I pick my favorites and ask several people to provide feedback. Someone more objective may be able to spot a flaw that I missed, and prevent me from saying a million times, "No...QUOTECatcher. Not GOATCatcher."

You can also ask your friends the next day if they remember the name(s) to gauge memorability. Liking the name isn't very important, but being memorable is.

The reason why it's important to choose a good name first is because it's not a good idea to change it once your site is launched. Search engines start ranking your site as soon as it's live on the web. If you decide to change your domain name in three months because of something you missed, you'll lose most or all of your search engine positioning, and you'll have to continue to maintain the old domain name indefinitely.

In the end, it's your decision. Spend some time on it and don't make your decision rashly, but don't spend so much time that everything else comes to a screeching halt.

Registering Your Domain

You've chosen a domain name and you've run it past a few people and they like it. Now it's time to buy it, but not just the primary name. You want to buy the related names, too. For the FineJewelry.com example above, you'd also want FindJewelry.com, with a "d."

You can buy the ".net" and ".biz" TLD's to protect them from being snatched up by someone else, but it's not necessary unless you have a specific reason for it. Personally, I think both of those extensions are revenue generators for registrar's more than useful domain extensions. If you own FineJewelry.com and someone launches a jewelry site called FineJewelry.net, you can send them a "cease and desist" letter for trademark infringement. Besides, it doesn't make sense for a legitimate business to use a domain name that's the same as an existing business that already uses the ".com" TLD. They would consistently lose business to your ".com" domain because that's what people are used to typing.

You should also consider registering versions that are spelled incorrectly, such as FineJewlry.com and FineJewlery.com (notice jewelry is misspelled). You can point these to your primary domain name, but when someone types the name incorrectly in the browser, it will still go to your site. In fact, unless you have a reason not to, all the related domains you purchase should be pointed to your primary domain name. Once your website is launched, your webhost can do this for you. I'll discuss webhosts in more detail later.

Most people refer to this process as "buying" a domain name; however, you're actually "leasing" a domain name from the registrar and the lease must be renewed every year, or at the end of your term. A one year "lease" on a domain will usually run you around $10.

When you go through the purchase process, you'll be prompted to buy a bunch of other services for the domain, such as Private Registrations or International Domain Names. In my opinion, you don't need these for a new website unless you have a specific reason for them. To keep your costs down, you can opt out of these additional services, at least for the first year.

You can choose to lease the domain for multiple years, which will sometimes give you a discount, but will cost you more upfront. If you're on a tight budget, lease the domains for one year to start and see how it goes. You may decide after three months to toss the idea and do something different, or you may think of an even better name. It would be a waste of money to spend $40 on a 5 year lease when you could have spent $10 for one year. Multiply that by 2 or 4 domains and you could save $120 or more.

My last piece of advice on this topic is to register your own domain name! Don't let your web developer or webhost do it for you, because then it will be registered to them. If you decide to part ways, they could give you a difficult time transferring the domain into your name, or worse, they could charge you a hefty sum for it. Registering a domain name is a simple process. Don't delegate that responsibility.

Parking the Domain

Once you have your domain, you can choose to "park" it with the registrar. This makes the domain available on the web, but it won't have a website behind it.

Some registrars allow you to put up a single page that can be found by search engines. You can add some relevant keywords to your "coming soon" message that will start the process of getting your search engine ranking, even before your site is launched. Then when the website is finished, your domain will already be known to the search engines.

Choosing an Email Address

Most Registrars supply one email account for free with your domain name. This can be used as a temporary account until your site is launched. You can use it for a generic catch-all email address for marketing or advertising, such as sales@yourdomain.com, or you can create a personal email using your name.

If you want to seem like a larger company than you are, consider using your first name and last name in the address, such as jp.stonestreet@yourdomain.com. However, if you're creating a content site as a subject matter expert, your first name is much more personal, such as jp@yourdomain.com.

If you're planning to start selling your services before the site is launched, this email address is how potential customers will contact you. For example, if you're starting a lead generation service, you'll want to conduct some market research and start the sales process as soon as possible so you're ready to go when the site is finished. Depending on what you're selling and to whom, it can take one to six months to close a sale. You don't want to wait until the site is launched to start this process, which makes having a functional email address very useful.

As you can see, there's a lot that goes into selecting a domain name. It's a time consuming process and often, inspiration will strike from out of nowhere. Be patient and diligent, but avoid analysis paralysis. In the end, you may just have to pick one and move on.

Choosing Your Color Palette

The next topic under your identity creation is about choosing your color palette. When you're thinking about colors for your site, your goal should be simplicity and pleasantness. Choosing a color palette for your website is a lot like choosing one for a room in your house. Choose a primary color and one to three accent colors that all go well together, plus black and white.

Go to some popular websites and look at their color choices. On Facebook, the primary color is blue-gray while the accent colors are lighter versions of that. The header bar and links are all the same darker color. The navigation bar and buttons are the slightly lighter version. And the main content areas make use of two lighter, dusty gray/blue colors. It's very soft, clean and all the colors go well together.

Now take a look at Twitter. They went with more of an aqua blue color palette, but they still have a primary color and a few accent colors that are soft and clean. Flickr uses bright blue, fuchsia and gray.

Some websites use relevant colors for the site's main purpose. If your site is related to the environment, money or finances, then cool green tones might work well. Mint.com is a personal financial management site that uses green for its color palette. This is a very relevant color to the double meaning of their name: the mint leaf and minting money.

If you have a women's issues site, consider using pink tones. The Susan G. Komen website is a breast cancer awareness and fund raising website that uses several shades of pink. Visit Komen.org to see their color choices.

If you want people to stay on your site and recommend it to others, you want them to "feel" good about it. And one way to do that is with a well-chosen color pallet. Also, use white liberally. It's easier to read black text on white than any other color, which will further reduce eye strain and keep people reading your content longer.

Now that you've seen some good examples of color schemes, let's look at a bad one: HistorianOfTheFuture.com. Go there now so you'll better understand what I'm describing here.

Using black (or any color that's not a shade of white or gray) as a background makes the text very difficult to read. You might be tempted to use a dark color for your background because you think it looks "cool," but remember the purpose of your site is NOT to look "cool." The purpose is to get people to use it. If you do decide a dark background is what you want, use content boxes with a lighter background to make the content easier to read.

Note the use of yellow and turquoise font colors. Many people have difficulty focusing on yellow. Plus, if the contrast is too high between foreground and background, the text appears blurry and it's hard to read. This site is simply trying to be too clever and needs to tone down the graphics and color scheme, A LOT.

The lesson I hope you're learning here is to keep it simple. Don't try to get too clever and overly complicate your site's colors. Less is almost always more.

Why Is the Web So Blue?

You'll notice while surfing the web that many sites use blue tones. This is not a coincidence. Blue is a soothing color that's easy on the eyes and it helps to relieve eye strain, as well as stress, but there are even more powerful reasons for using blue.

First, most people around the world say blue is their favorite color. If you want someone to have a good feeling about your website, using their favorite color is one way to do that.

Second, and most importantly, people are more likely to trust a blue website, which translates into more sales. In a study conducted at Eastern Illinois University titled "Color and Store Choice In Electronic Commerce: The Explanatory Role of Trust," the researchers found a significant correlation between website colors and purchase trends. According to their findings, "a blue environment led to more simulated purchases, fewer purchase postponements, a stronger inclination to shop and browse than a red environment."

When you're designing your site, keep your target audience in mind. Very few men say purple is their favorite color. If your site is targeting men, would purple be a good color choice? Nope. Purple or yellow or red might be YOUR favorite color, but the purpose of your website is <u>not</u> to make YOU happy, it's to make your customers buy what you're selling. You're not building your website for *you*, you're building it for *them*!

Next time you're surfing the web, pay attention to the color choices on various websites and make a mental note of how many use blue tones and which ones you like the most. Big companies have spent millions of dollars researching what sells best and that's why the web is so blue. Luckily, you don't need to spend millions of dollars to learn from them.

Creating Your Logo

The next topic under identity creation is dedicated to your logo. You have about 3 seconds to capture someone's attention when they come to your site and the logo is the first thing they see. You want to make a good impression, which means it needs to be high quality.

Hire a Professional

If you're not a graphic designer, pay a professional to create your logo. I've used Fiverr before and had good luck with it. For $5, you can have 20 graphic designers create a logo and only spend $100. Then pick the best one and you're done.

For my training and coaching business, I used DesignCrowd.com for my logo design. My logo contest received 119 designs from 29 different designers and cost me $370. My project cost was a little higher than normal because I opted to give a second place prize to entice more designers to submit their concepts. The user interface on the website is a little clunky, but I'm very happy with the designs that I received. It was extremely difficult to pick my favorite.

99Designs.com is another site that I like. In fact, I used it to design the cover of the book you're reading right now. My book cover contest received 61 designs from 7 designers at a cost of $299. With this site, you post the guidelines for your logo or design project, and multiple graphic artists submit their ideas. You have the option of paying more than $299, which will get more designers to participate. Once I had the designs narrowed down to four, I posted a poll to my friends and had them vote on their favorite. It was a great overall experience that I'm happy to recommend.

Craigslist is also an option if you prefer to work with a local designer, which means you can sit down together and talk about your logo. Most logo designers can also do graphic design for your website so you may be able to find one person to do both. This option will often cost more and you'll only get concepts from a single designer, but there's something to be said for meeting in person.

The Mark

When you're visualizing your logo, you need to decide if it'll have a "mark." The mark is the graphical representation of your business. Instagram's mark is the old-style camera to the left of their name. Theirs is a stand-alone mark that's separate from the company name.

Amazon.com uses a mark that's part of their name. They use the orange arrow that connects the letters A and Z in their name to tell us they sell everything from A to Z. It also looks like a "smile," which they now refer to as the "only company with a smile on the box."

Facebook actually has two logos. The logo they use on the website doesn't contain a mark. Their color and font choice is the mark. However, they do use a small square logo with a lowercase "f" for other things like share buttons and when space is limited.

A mark isn't required. If you can't think of anything that's completely relevant to your business, it's ok to go without it. This is the age of simple. Less has never been more than it is today.

The Colors

The same rules apply to logo colors that apply to website colors. I covered that in detail previously. Refer back to that section if you need a refresher.

Your most important consideration when you're deciding on a color palette for your logo is consistency with your website's color palette. They need to match and look good together.

Also, the web isn't the only place your logo needs to look good. If you print business cards or do any sort of print advertising, it needs to look good there, too. Sometimes, the print will be in black and white. If your logo doesn't look right or make sense without color, you won't be able to print it in black and white. Again, keep it simple.

The Text

The name in your logo needs to match your domain name. This is important for a couple of reasons.

First, if your domain name is different than your web business name, it means your users will need to remember two different names. When they're telling their friends about your site, which name should they use? You don't want there to be any confusion about your name, and you don't want people to remember which one will get them to your website.

Imagine if Amazon.com used "Big Book Store" as the name of their web business, and therefore, the text in their logo. It sounds crazy, but you'd be surprised how many people consider using a different name in their logo than their domain name. I mentioned HistorianOfTheFuture.com in the previous color choice example. The logo on the site is "Evolution," which doesn't match the domain name. Personally, I think the content of this site is fascinating, but the presentation needs some help.

The second reason it's important to use the same text in your logo as your domain name is for branding purposes. Your brand is how you distinguish your business from other businesses, and brand*ing* is the process of making your image recognizable to people. If your domain name and web business name are different, you'll have to brand both of them, which is expensive and ineffective.

Think of your website like it's a real business in the real world. For example, IKEA is the name of the business and its the name on the signs in front of the stores. How absurd would it be if the signs in front of the stores read IKEA, but their business name and logo was Swedish Furniture House? Since they use their logo in all of their advertisements, people would have to remember to look for the IKEA sign when they want to shop at the Swedish Furniture House. That's just crazy talk!

The sign is how people find a business in the real world, just like the domain name is how people find your website in the virtual world. Consistency is the first step to brand awareness and a simple message is the second. If your domain name doesn't match your business name, your message is neither consistent nor simple.

The Font

There are literally hundreds of fonts to choose from and you can even pay to have your very own custom font created. This is completely a personal choice, but try to choose one that makes sense with your business.

If your website is about something elegant, you might want an elaborate font like the one Instagram chose. However, if your site is about simplicity, you might want a very simple font like the one Facebook uses.

If you decide to use an elegant or intricate font, make sure it prints well and also ask a few people their opinions about it, especially older people. It should be easy to read, especially to your target audience.

Crafting Your Tagline

"You have to really be courageous about your instincts and your ideas. Otherwise you'll just knuckle under, and things that might have been memorable will be lost."

~Francis Ford Coppola

A tagline tells people what your site does. Most big, popular websites don't use a tagline anymore because everyone knows what they do already. But for your new website, a tagline can be very helpful.

Your tagline should convey your site's most important benefit. For example, the tagline for Angie's List is "Reviews you can trust." This is the main benefit of their site, and a message they use in most of their marketing materials.

Instagram's tagline is "Fast beautiful photo sharing." Their tagline tells us that you can share photos with other people, and it alludes to your ability to make your photos beautiful, which is how Instagram is different from other photo sharing sites like Flickr.

Did you know…

Flickr and some other photo sharing sites (and even Twitter) are now adding photo manipulation features similar to Instagram's. Copying functionality is commonplace on the web, but being first has its advantages. If you can patent your concept, it's easier to protect your position, but it's not always possible.

My daughter plays an online game called Poptropica.com. She likes the game because she has to gather clues and solve puzzles. Their tagline is "Explore Collect Compete." Three word taglines can be very powerful and I'm a big fan of them, but this one could be better. It says what the game is, but if you've never played it before, you wouldn't understand what it means. Your tagline should be used to educate and persuade potential customers to use your site. That means it should be geared to people who don't already know what your site does.

Your tagline can be incorporated into your logo, or you can put it above, below or next to your logo. Whatever makes the most sense.

You have some leeway with your tagline, but don't write a paragraph. Keep it short and sweet. Consider using humor, rhymes, puns or an alliteration to make it more memorable and catchy. Be a little edgy if it will appeal to your target audience.

> **Did you know...**
>
> An alliteration is a grammatical construct that refers to the use of the same or similar sounds in multiple words. They've been used for centuries in every language to help people remember things. For example, "Peter Piper picked a peck of pickled peppers" is an alliteration because of the repeating P's. Using alliterations in your tagline can help people remember it, and your business.

Phone and Address

The final thing I want to mention under the topic of identity is your phone and address. You might not think these have anything to do with your company's identity, but they do.

Thank You for Calling

You don't need a fancy phone system or service to start. Just get a dedicated line, an answering machine or voicemail, record a simple message, and tell your kids never to answer that phone.

If you're in the office and the phone rings, answer it. In the beginning, it will be mostly wrong numbers and telemarketers, but over time, your existing and potential customers will be calling and you want to be comfortable answering it.

Develop a standard script that you say when you answer the phone to make your business sound professional, such as "Thank you for calling [Company Name], this is JP. How can I help you?" This is one way your phone relates to your identity. How you and your employees represent your company over the phone says a lot about your business, whether good or bad.

You might want a toll free (800) number for your web business. After all, the web knows no physical boundaries and you could have customers anywhere in the world. If your target audience is local, you don't need one, but if your customers are national, a toll free number sends a message that you're a legitimate and reputable business.

Toll free numbers are cheap and easy to get. Grasshopper.com and FreedomVoice.com both offer plans starting at $10/month plus 5 to 6 cents per minute. There are other websites and companies that provide this service as well. Most offer a dedicated local phone number along with the toll free number, allowing local customers to call the local number instead.

A separate phone is tax deductible and it's a good place to start on the road to separating your personal expenses from your business expenses. It's also crucial for creating a professional image for your business and you'll need it for your business cards and other forms of correspondence.

Mailing Address

You might be tempted to use your home mailing address for your business address, but resist the temptation. When you register your website domains, you'll be required to provide a physical address which can be viewed on the Internet. The last thing you want is someone showing up at your door to sell you something or to complain in person. This is especially true if you have children.

Protect your home and family by getting a mail box at a mail facility near your house. A PO Box at your local post office is the least expensive option, but some businesses such as UPS and FedEx won't deliver to PO Boxes.

A more expensive but useful solution is to rent a box at a mail center such as a UPS store, Mailboxes Etc., or a similar location. These services allow you to have a physical address with a "suite" number instead of a PO Box number. The "suite" is just the number to your box, but the outside world doesn't need to know that. And best of all, UPS and FedEx will deliver to these locations. The clerk at the desk will sign for packages and let you know one has been delivered via email.

Like the phone, your address sends a message about your company. Some people will look for an address on your site because they want to know where you're located. If it looks like a home address, it makes your company look amateur. It doesn't cost much to have some peace of mind and an address that makes your business look professional.

You'll need an address for your business cards, domain registration, business name registration and bank accounts. You don't want to change this address unless you absolutely have to, so pick a location that works well for you and has easy access. You'll need to check the box at least once per week and you don't want to drive across town to do it.

That brings us to the end of the Create Your Identity section. You learned about how to choose your company name and domain name, color palette, logo, tagline, phone and address. Those make up the majority of your company's identity. In the next section, I'm going to talk about....

Finances

Most people don't like this part of owning a business, especially tracking expenses. We entrepreneurs started our businesses to do what we love, and unless that's being an accountant, managing finances is not it.

In this section, I'm going to cover the basics. There are a few things that you have to do to protect yourself and your company and I've figured out how to do the bare minimum in the most efficient way, so here we go....

Get a Tax ID (EIN)

You need a federal tax identification number from the IRS, also called an employer identification number or EIN. It's free to obtain and takes about 10 minutes on the IRS.gov website. Have your Articles of Organization or Articles of Incorporation handy when you start the process. If you're idle for more than 10 minutes while you're looking for information, it cancels your request and you have to start over.

Most banks require a Tax ID to open a business bank account, and you'll need one to report wages you pay to employees or contractors. It's free and easy, so there's no reason not to get one.

Take It to the Bank

Once you've selected a business name and obtained your EIN, it's time to open a business checking account. You can shop around for the best deal, or you can go to the bank where you have your personal accounts, or you can go to a well-known business focused bank. I personally don't think it matters much in the beginning and you can always transfer later if you have a reason.

When you open the account, you can "seed" it with your personal money. This is known as your "basis" in the company. Anytime you transfer money from your personal account to your business account, it *increases* your basis by the amount you deposit. Likewise, when you transfer money from your business account to your personal account, it *decreases* your basis. Knowing your basis is important for tax and ownership purposes so keep good records of your transfers in both directions.

If you have business partners, you should each deposit an amount that's equivalent to your equity share. If you want to start with $1,000 and you own 80% of the company and your partner owns 20%, you would deposit $800 and your partner would deposit $200.

You also need a credit card dedicated to the business (my business partner and I each donated a credit card to the cause). This card will ONLY be used for business related purchases. In the beginning, it's ok to dedicate a personal credit card to the business, but you'll eventually want to get a credit card in the company's name.

Keeping your business finances separate from your personal finances is critical. If you get audited by the IRS, the auditor will NOT be happy if she has to rifle through your personal accounts to figure out your business expenses. And trust me, you do NOT want to irritate an auditor!

Tracking Expenses

One way to make an auditor happy is by keeping a good record of your expenses. There are several tools out there to help in this process. Some are free and some will cost you. You need to use something, and a shoebox doesn't count.

We used QuickBooks at QuoteCatcher. That's one of the most popular platforms for small businesses. My accountant prefers PeachTree because she feels that it's more powerful.

You also have some online options. Mint.com is designed for personal finances, but you can customize the categories to track business finances. It doesn't have invoicing features and it lacks some business accounting functionality, but if you don't need to worry about that, Mint might work well for you…and it's free.

Outright, Expensify, FreshBooks and Shoeboxed are online accounting and expense tracking tools that work together to create a very comprehensive business accounting and bookkeeping package. Most have free entry level accounts and charge for more advanced features. Outright calls themselves the "Mint for small business." The other tools offer similar and complimentary functionality.

If you're old-school, you can use an Excel Spreadsheet to keep track of your expenses and if you're REALLY old-school, you can use a ledger notebook. Believe it or not, office stores still sell them!

Whatever method you choose, just promise me you'll use something other than a shoebox (or at least in addition to).

> ## Did you know…
>
> If you have to use your personal credit card to make a purchase because you left your business credit card at home, expense it just like you would if you worked for someone else. That means you need to create an expense report, write yourself a check out of the business account, and store the expense report with your business documents. If you use a website like Expensify, it's a lot easier to manage this process and you won't need to print off and file anything.

Taxes

Yes, you need to pay Uncle Sam if you make money, but there's an upside. With business taxes, you pay everyone else first and then you pay taxes on what's left. With your personal taxes, however, you pay the taxes first and then you pay everyone else with what's left. That's why I will always have a business.

If you keep good records, doing your taxes will be much easier, but you should still hire a professional CPA to do them for you. Calculating your personal taxes is hard, but business taxes are MUCH more difficult. Businesses have so many deductions and loopholes that it's impossible for a non-professional to capture all of them. My accountant saves me more money in taxes every year than she charges to do them.

Unless you're an accountant, there's no need to subject yourself to that brain damage. Your time is much better spent working on your business. Do what you do best and pay someone else to do the rest.

Pricing

"What is a cynic? A man who knows the price of everything and the value of nothing."

~Oscar Wilde

The last thing I want to cover on the topic of finances is setting a price for your products and services. Choosing a price for what you're selling is one of the hardest decisions you have to make. If you did your competitive research, you should be able to refer back to your Competitor Intel Log for a baseline.

Researching your established competition is the easiest way to baseline your pricing, but trying to undercut them may not be the best approach. If you get into a pricing war, they'll win because they have the margins to lower their prices already. They may even be able to take short-term losses if it means putting you out of business. If you're selling the exact same thing as your competition, instead of starting a pricing war, try offering something they don't, like better service or a free gift.

If you're selling a premium product, don't sell it at a discounted price. If you don't charge enough, people will mistake it for being low-end and you'll miss your target audience. If you're selling a low end product, don't sell it at a premium price. Word of mouth will kill you if you try this approach.

Many people forget to include their salary and overhead expenses like utilities when they're calculating their price. Don't under estimate your cost of doing business and set your price accordingly.

Be flexible with your pricing. Don't worry about what people paid yesterday if you want to lower it today. Wal-Mart lowers their prices every day and nobody asks for their money back. If they do, offer a discount on a future purchase or give them the difference back if they insist.

Don't be a cynic. Know the value of what you're selling and charge a price that reflects the value. Then rely on sales and marketing to overcome price-related obstacles, if you have any.

That's all I have to say about finances. See, it wasn't too painful. There's obviously a lot more you can do, such as creating financial reports and analyzing trends, but that's beyond the scope of this web startup book.

Manufacturers & Suppliers

If your plan is to buy wholesale and sell retail, you need to research manufacturers and suppliers while you're still in the Starting Your Startup phase. If you can't get products at a reasonable price, you may decide to head back to the drawing board.

Finding products to sell in your online store can be a challenge. You can make them yourself, which will provide the most profit margin but will severely limit the volume you can sell, unless you're able to mass produce them somehow.

A friend of mine makes specialized pet accessories and sells them on Etsy.com under her brand name, SooperTramp. She enjoys making her own products and her customers like the hand crafted nature of them. However, she can't mass produce them (yet), making her volume very limited. In the future, once her business starts generating enough revenue, she may be able to contract a manufacturer to mass produce them, which will remove the limit to her volume.

You can also buy your products from a supplier, but your margins will be much lower because the supplier has a markup from the manufacturer, which means your markup will need to be smaller to keep your products affordable. This is the best option if you can only afford small quantity orders in the beginning.

Buying directly from the manufacturer will get you the best deal, but you'll also have to buy a larger quantity. If you're selling a single product and can afford to place a large order, this may be your best option. However, if you're selling a whole line of products, you may not be able to afford a large volume of every product.

You can find manufacturers and suppliers online by searching for your keywords on any popular search engine. For example, if you're planning to sell fishing lures, you can search for "fishing lure suppliers" or "fishing lure manufacturers." Most companies have websites, or you'll at least find a directory of suppliers and manufacturers with contact information allowing you to call them directly.

Don't accept the posted price without at least trying to negotiate it. Some companies won't negotiate, especially for small orders, but some will. Every penny you save on the product purchase means more profit when you sell it.

That brings us to the end of the Starting Your Startup section. Several of the things you have to do during this phase aren't very fun, but you need to do them. Luckily, you'll only need to do some of them once, but others will need to be done on a regular basis. It's just part of doing business. Block off time and get them done.

The next section is the fun part. It's all about designing and Building Your Website. I'm sure that's the most interesting part for you so let's jump on in!

Starting Your Startup Checklist

Here's a list of things to do during this phase of the process:

- ☐ Find your focus – energy, product and service
- ☐ Define SMARTER goals
- ☐ KISS It!
- ☐ Decide on a location for Company HQ – home or office
- ☐ Decide on a legal entity – LLP, LLC, S Corp, C Corp
- ☐ Choose a business name
- ☐ Get a Tax ID
- ☐ Open a business checking account
- ☐ Get a credit card or dedicate a personal one solely for business use
- ☐ Prepare an NDA
- ☐ Write a Partnership Agreement and get it signed by all partners
- ☐ Decide on a fair equity split
- ☐ Choose a domain name
- ☐ Choose a color palette
- ☐ Create your logo
- ☐ Craft your tagline
- ☐ Set your pricing
- ☐ Get your financials in order
- ☐ Hire an accountant
- ☐ Research manufacturers and suppliers

"Done is better than perfect."

~Facebook Motto

Phase 3: Building Your Website

Once you've started your web business, you're ready for the next step: building your website. In this phase, I'm going to discuss the 10 things every website needs and a few things you might want if your budget and time allows. I'm also going to help you define some features and requirements for your website, as well as give you some pointers on how to interview and manage your development team. But before I dive into that, I want to mention…

The Importance of Quality

Gone are the days of slapping together a website without spending any money on nice images or a professional design. Back in the 90's, many popular sites didn't even have an image for their logo…their logo was just text! But all that has changed (unless you're Craigslist).

Websites are like cars. When Henry Ford first introduced the Model A, he said "Any customer can have a car painted any color that he wants so long as it's black." How well do you think a car company would do today if black was the only color option?

Like the first websites, the first cars were very utilitarian. They (barely) got people from point A to point B. But now, nearly a century later, cars are amazing feats of technology. They have tons of features and they come in countless colors. A car company would no longer compete if it sold cars like the Model A.

Websites are no different. Well, they're a little different. It took cars nearly 100 years to evolve as much as websites have in the past 15 years. The web is propelling itself forward at an unimaginable rate, and a website that looks like it was built in 1995 won't measure up to the tough competition that exists today.

Luckily for you, the cost of graphics has come down, and the clean, simplicity that is the norm for today's websites isn't hard to achieve. Look at Twitter and Facebook. The design of those sites doesn't get much simpler, yet they still look very professional.

In the new age of websites, less truly is more in terms of *quantity*, but *quality* has never been more important. Unless you're a professional graphic designer, either buy a template that you can plug into your website or pay a professional to do your graphic design for you.

10 Things Every Website Needs

Every website is different, but every website also has some things in common and this is the list of commonalities. These may be obvious to you, but it will help to know what developers call them so you can speak their language.

Registrar

The first thing every website needs is a registrar. I covered registrars in detail in the "Master of Your Domain" section in "Phase 2: Starting Your Startup." Review that section again if you need a refresher on how to search for and register your domain.

There's one important thing you need to know about registrars, and that's how to set the nameservers for your website. This is the most technical thing you need to learn, but it's not that hard so please stay with me for the next few paragraphs.

Most non-technical people don't know what a nameserver is…don't feel bad if you're one of them. I promise not be too technical here, but essentially a nameserver is the name of the webhost's server where your website's files are stored (webhosts are discussed in detail next).

A nameserver is like a postal zip code. A zip code tells the post office what town you live in so they know where to look for your street address. Likewise, a name server tells the servers and routers on the Internet which webhost you use so they know where to look for your website.

The nameserver addresses will be provided by your webhost when your hosting account is setup. If you register your domain through your webhost, the nameservers will be set by default. That means you won't need to worry about setting them yourself. However, if you choose a separate registrar to register your domain instead of using the webhost, you need to set the nameserver values on the registrar's website.

Your webhost will provide two nameservers, usually something like ns1.webhost.com and ns2.webhost.com, where the "webhost" is the website address for your webhost. These values need to be set on the registrar's nameserver administration screen, which will be associated with each domain name you have registered with them. Figure 4 below shows what the nameserver admin screen looks like on GoDaddy; all registrars will have a similar admin screen. It's a simple process to set your nameservers, but if you have questions, call your registrar and ask for help.

Nameservers

Nameservers: (Last update 6/7/2012)
NS1.BLUEHOST.COM   Set Nameservers
NS2.BLUEHOST.COM   Manage DS Records

Figure 4

Webhost

The second thing every website needs is a webhost such as BlueHost or HostGator. In simple terms, a webhost is a company with lots of servers (fast computers) that are connected to the Internet. These servers are used to store the files associated with your website, and they allow people to view your website through a browser like IE or Chrome.

There are a variety of different webhosts, offering a variety of different packages for a variety of different technologies. Some web developers will offer a hosting package along with their website development. This will often be your best deal and the easiest to implement for the developer. Just make sure the webhost is reputable and professional. You don't want your website hosted out of a developer's basement.

Did you know…

Many web developers re-sell hosting packages offered by large webhosting companies. They provide all the service and handle all the issues that arise with respect to the webhost, for a modest markup on the hosting fees.

However, some developers actually *attempt* to host websites for their customers on servers located in their house or office. Don't agree to that, EVER! When you talk to them about hosting, ask where the webhost is located.

Professional webhosting companies have large data centers with redundant servers, offsite backups and uninterrupted power sources (batteries and diesel generators). They also have multiple connections to the Internet so if anything breaks, your website will still be live on the web. If your website is hosted in your developer's basement and his power goes out or his Internet connection goes down, your website will, too. Not good!

If you're searching for your own webhost, the technology you choose to build your site will be the largest determining factor (choosing a technology is covered in the Development section). Some webhosts only support Microsoft technologies, while others only support Linux.

The next important thing to consider when choosing a webhost is user reviews. Go to Google and search for "webhost reviews" to find websites that post reviews and comparisons of multiple webhosts. You can even be more specific with your search terms to find exactly what you need. For example, "php webhost reviews" or "wordpress webhost reviews" or "Microsoft webhost reviews" or "LAMP webhost reviews."

Did you know…

LAMP, sometimes called the LAMP Stack, refers to a suite of technologies used to host websites. It's an acronym that stands for Linux (the operating system), Apache (the web server), MySQL (the database) and PHP (the web page scripting language). It has gained a lot of ground in recent years mainly due to its affordability and reliability.

Once you've chosen a few webhosts that support the technology you're going to use to build your website, compare their pricing plan packages. Most will offer multi-year packages, but just like with the domain names, stick to a one-year package to start to reduce upfront expenses. You can always buy a multi-year package to save some money next year once you have revenue flowing to help pay for it.

Most webhosts offer a "Level of Service" guarantee for bandwidth and storage capacity, but these are virtually identical at every webhost. Therefore, your main deciding factors should be positive user reviews and the price of the package. I usually pick the webhost with the best of both.

Shared Hosting

With Shared Hosting, your website's files will be stored on the same server as other websites. This has one major advantage and one major disadvantage.

The advantage is that the shared hosting package will be much cheaper. You can get one for as low as a few dollars per month. This can save you a lot of money if you're strapped for cash and you don't have much traffic on your site.

However, the disadvantage to a shared hosting plan is that you have no control over the other websites on your server. I've had my website taken down by a developer on another website who wrote a script that put the server in an infinite loop and used up all the server's memory. Most webhosts these days have safeguards in place to prevent this from happening, but it's still a risk.

In addition to this major performance disadvantage, the types of customization you can do at the server level will also be limited. For example, with Microsoft web applications, you may need to increase the default timeout of your website because you won't have much traffic in the beginning. When your website isn't hit within 30 minutes (and sometimes less), it's removed from the server's memory and the next person to visit your website will experience a long delay while it's reloaded into memory. On most shared servers, you can't increase this timeout period.

Did you know…

You can ensure your site is always loaded in memory by downloading "ping" software such as FreePing that will request your website's domain name every few minutes. You can find several free versions of ping software and configure as many domains as you have. You'll just need to load it on a computer or laptop that's always on. If the computer is shut down at night, the ping software won't run and your web applications will timeout. You can also pay a company like InternetSeer.com to ping your site ever few minutes, which means your computer won't need to be on all the time.

Virtual Servers

With a Virtual Server, you gain some advantages over shared hosting, along with an increased price. Like the shared hosting option, you'll still be sharing your server with other websites (although not as many), but your site will be partitioned onto its own isolated section of the server that's protected from the other sites.

You could still have performance limitations and you'll pay quite a bit more for this package, but your site will be able to support larger traffic volumes than a shared host, and with less risk of being impacted by other sites on the server.

Dedicated Servers

This is the most expensive option, but gives you complete control and complete isolation from other websites. With a dedicated server, your website will be all by itself, allowing you to do whatever you want to it (within reason).

Since you won't be sharing resources such as memory or CPU bandwidth, you'll get a lot better performance; however, you can expect to pay several hundred to several thousand dollars per month for it.

Once your site has grown substantially and the site's performance is being impacted by the bandwidth limits of the shared or virtual servers, you can migrate to a dedicated server. Ideally, your shared webhost will provide dedicated servers so you can easily migrate without much impact. If you need to move your website to a different webhost that specializes in dedicated servers, it's not too complicated. There are a few extra steps you need to take, but your developer and your new webhost will know what to do.

QuoteCatcher ran on a shared server for the first half of its existence. As the traffic volume increased, we purchased a higher volume shared plan that was able to support more bandwidth requirements. Eventually, we had to move the website to a dedicated server that cost about $700 per month. A large part of that cost went to Microsoft's licensing fees for SQL Server and Internet Information Services (IIS). If you go with the LAMP Stack, your fees for a dedicated server may be considerably lower.

Most websites will be just fine on a shared hosting plan in the beginning. If you're not sure what you need, go with that for now and reevaluate as your traffic volume increases.

Content Management System (CMS)

Every website needs a content management system or CMS. Fresh content is one of the most important components of search engine optimization (SEO), which I'll discuss in detail in "Phase 4: Marketing Your Website." Google and other search engines rank sites that have constantly updated content higher than sites that haven't been updated in a while. Therefore, your website needs a CMS that will allow you to post fresh content on a regular basis.

A CMS is a piece of software that allows you to update your site's content without using a developer. Most CMS tools allow you to update content on existing pages, create new pages with links to them, post articles, blogs, images, testimonials and more.

WordPress is one example of a CMS. It started as a simple blog tool, but has since evolved into a full-fledged CMS platform. Thousands of large and small websites use WordPress, and thousands of 3rd party plug-ins have been created to provide almost every type of functionality your site will need.

Joomla!, Drupal and Ruby On Rails are also popular CMS tools. Most CMS tools are part of a larger development framework that can be used to build common website features, such as ecommerce, memberships, banner ads, etc., through plug-ins.

If you hire a developer to build your site, he'll have a preferred CMS package. Since most CMS tools offer similar functionality, I suggest using what your developer recommends because it will save development time and money.

> **Did you know…**
>
> Some developers have built their own CMS platforms. This is called a proprietary solution and something you need to avoid. Require your developer to use a popular CMS tool so if he gets hit by a bus or you decide to part ways for whatever reason, you can easily hire a replacement developer.
>
> Popular CMS platforms like WordPress and Drupal have tens of thousands of developers worldwide that can pick up where your old developer left off. However, no one will know his proprietary system, meaning you may need to rebuild your entire website if he goes the way of the dodo.

Content

There are some standard pages that I'll discuss shortly, but you also need content for your informational pages, articles and blog posts.

If writing isn't your strong suit, you can hire people to write for you or at least hire a copy editor to proofread what you write. You can find editors and writers on Craigslist and sites like Fiverr and Guru.

You want your site to look professional and it doesn't cost that much to make sure it does. Misspellings and grammar errors tarnish your credibility and they're easy to avoid.

Written content isn't the only type of content you need to consider. Video and audio are also forms of content that can add depth and appeal to your website. You can link to video and audio created by other people and posted online, or you can create your own.

Content is king! High quality, fresh content is an important ingredient for user satisfaction and SEO. The more content you have and the more often it's updated, the better your site will be ranked in search engines and the happier your customers will be. Fresh content won't make you an overnight millionaire, but it's critical to the long-term success of your website.

Images

Like written text, video, and audio, images are a type of content that can be used to give your website depth and appeal. There are two types of images to use on your site: graphics and photos.

Graphics

Graphics are digitally created images, such as logos, buttons and animated characters. These images never existed in the real world; they were created in a graphics program by a graphic artist. You can buy some graphics on image sites like BigStockPhoto.com, ShutterStock.com or iStockPhoto.com, but if they don't have what you need, hire a professional graphic artist to create them for you.

You can find graphic designers advertising on CraigsList. Ask for references and a portfolio of past work. You can also use sites like 99Designs or Fiverr to get designs from several different designers.

Photos

The next type of images your site needs are photos. Getting quality photos for your site doesn't mean you need to hire a professional photographer, although you certainly could. The web has many stock photo websites that sell images for nearly every conceivable need. The prices for these images vary by content, size, photographer, model and exclusivity.

Did you know...

If you only need a small, web-sized image, you can expect to pay $2 to $20 for non-exclusive rights. Exclusive rights, meaning no one else can use the photo, will cost considerably more, perhaps several hundred dollars.

The most important aspect of images is quality. You want graphics and photos done by professionals who have the equipment and software needed to create high quality images. If you're not a professional, don't try to do it yourself. There are far too many inexpensive options available to you.

Standard Pages

Every website needs several standard pages for legal purposes. Most users will never read your legal pages (unless you do something wrong to anger them), but it's important to have them, nonetheless. There are also a few content pages that are pretty standard, like the Home Page, About Us and Contact Us.

Terms & Conditions

Also called Terms of Use, this page outlines the purpose of the website and lists all disclaimers. It states that by using the site, it implies acceptance of the Terms & Conditions. It's best to have a competent lawyer create this for you, but if you're on a tight budget, you can find a sample on the web and modify it to meet your needs.

Privacy Policy

Also called a Privacy Statement, this page details how your website will handle user data such as names, emails and phone numbers. If you'll be sharing any of the data, either in detail or in aggregate, you need to spell it out here. People hate spam so your Privacy Policy needs to make them feel comfortable that their information will be safe with you. Again, it's best to have a lawyer write this, but you can find samples that will work with a few modifications.

FTC Disclosure

This is a relatively new requirement from the Federal Trade Commission instituted in December 2009. They're now requiring websites to define how they generate revenue from any content that is posted on the site. Think of this as an ethics statement intended to reveal any ulterior motives you might have for posting content on your website.

For example, if you review products on your site, you need to disclose if you are paid in any way by the product manufacturer, supplier, distributor, advertiser, affiliate, etc., for writing a review. You also need to disclose if you own stock in a company you're discussing.

The FTC believes this will help content writers be more honest and transparent by making their intentions known to their readers. The FTC also believes readers will benefit by being more aware of the motivations writers have for posting content. If a writer makes money from positive reviews of a product, a reader has the right to know it when gauging the credibility of the review.

The FTC Disclosure is mainly intended for blogs or other review oriented websites, but it doesn't hurt to have one even if your site's focus is on selling your own products or services. If you post any type of content that discusses any type of activity that will or has the potential to generate revenue for you or your business, you are required to include this page on your site or be subjected to fines and penalties.

You can find samples all over the web to get an idea of what to include. Write this one yourself to make it seem more personal and credible, but you may want to have a lawyer review it once it's complete.

About Us

The About Us (or About Me or About) page isn't required, but some users will look for it when they're deciding to buy from you. Use this page to tell people about your business and your website.

Since you normally won't meet website users in person, this page can make them feel like they know you better, especially if you have a unique history or a story to tell. Consider posting a video of yourself telling your story on your About Us page. That makes it seem more personal.

Contact Us

This page should contain one or more of the following customer service items: contact us form to submit a request, live chat link, phone number, mailing address, and/or email address. It's best to provide as much contact information as possible so your users have a variety of ways to reach you.

> ### Did you know...
>
> Many large companies don't have a contact form, or it's buried deep in the site making it next to impossible to find it. They have millions of users and it would be hard to respond to all the requests if they made it easy. Instead, they want you to answer your own question by making you read information. One of the benefits of being a small startup is that you can provide this type of personalized service that the larger companies don't.

Frequently Asked Questions

Also commonly called the FAQ or Help, this page is very useful to website visitors and can even reduce the amount of customer service inquiries you receive, which will save you time and money.

You can start with a few anticipated questions, and then add to the list over time as you start to see patterns of questions. Post a link to the FAQ page on your contact us form and ask users to review it before submitting their question.

17 Usability Guidelines

How did Google capture such a large part of Yahoo!'s market share so quickly? How did Facebook nearly put MySpace out of business in two short years? There's one main reason: usability.

Google revolutionized the search engine market by launching a site with a textbox and a search button. Prior to Google, most search engines were complex directories modeled after the *then* familiar phonebook. You had to drill down and down and down through a hierarchy of categories to find the web address for something you were looking for, only to discover that you went down the wrong tree and had to back up or completely start over.

But Google had a different idea. Why make people *find* what they're looking for? Why not just allow them to put a word or phrase describing it and show them the most relevant results? They made the process of finding things on the web so user friendly that they crushed AltaVista and nearly put Yahoo! under.

Facebook attacked MySpace in a slightly different way. When MySpace first gained popularity, people loved the ability to customize their "home" or profile page. They could change the layout, purchase themes to jazz it up, and share countless photos and videos with their friends. It was great!

But all that flexibility and customization allowed MySpace users to go too far. Some users changed their layouts so much and used such wild graphics that their friends had a hard time finding even the most basic information, and reading what they posted on their profiles was sometimes impossible. I had friends who posted multiple videos on their feed, which caused their profile page to time out when I tried to open it. The MySpace servers simply couldn't handle the demands placed on them by their users. In response to the slow servers and usability issues, a lot of people (like me) stopped using it. Enter Facebook.

Facebook came on the scene at the perfect time. MySpace users were becoming increasingly frustrated with the user experience, and Facebook provided a simple alternative. It didn't allow extreme customization of the main profile pages, keeping the server demands to a minimum and allowing people to easily find the information they wanted. It also didn't automatically load videos when a page was opened, further reducing bandwidth requirements and speeding page loads.

Furthermore, Facebook provided pertinent profile updates in a single feed, which was the main page people used. This simple feature allowed users to keep tabs on their friends without opening each individual profile.

Facebook also didn't require users to login every time they visited the site. MySpace required users to login on every new visit to force people to look at the ads on their login page, but Facebook realized the hassle of logging into a site that you use several times a day and opted to provide a functioning "remember me" option.

These simple usability enhancements, offered at the perfect time, crushed the once king of social media. When Facebook entered the scene, MySpace had well over 50% of the social networking traffic. Facebook now claims over 60% while MySpace claims less than 1%! In the meantime, MySpace is scrambling to reinvent itself as a purely music and video portal. This is the best and maybe only strategy it has to save the website, but it might be too little and too late.

MySpace had a company worth several hundred million dollars and they were on track to be worth well over a billion. However, because of a few irritating usability issues (and a couple other shortcomings), they lost their edge. Then Facebook came along and stole their prosperity.

The lesson here is: don't be a MySpace. Work hard to provide the most user friendly experience to your visitors so they'll keep coming back to your site and won't leave you for a competitor who does the same thing, only better.

How do you improve the usability of your site? This book is intended to give you a *broad* view of starting a web based business. In my effort to minimize confusion and to keep the book to a manageable length, my goal isn't to go *deep* in any single subject. I'm going to give you enough information to get started and create a very usable website, but if you want more information, check out one of the usability books that are available in the library or bookstore. I've also recommended a couple in the "Resources" section at the end of this book.

With that disclaimer out of the way, here are the 17 most common usability guidelines….

Page Load Time

The first usability guideline is to test all your pages in production for performance. Every page should load in less than 2 seconds (ideally less than 1 second) or you'll lose impatient users.

Fast page loads are especially important when you're doing paid advertising. The last thing you want to do is pay for a click on an ad only to have the user hit the back button before your page is displayed.

If you have to sacrifice a feature to improve load time, do it. Chances are, the feature won't win as many users as the slow load time will lose. Think MySpace vs. Facebook. Less is more.

Proofread

The next usability guideline is to ensure your content is free of typos, misspellings and grammatical errors. The fastest way to lose credibility and reduce your user base is to have sloppy content. If writing isn't your strong suit, hire a copyeditor and/or copywriter.

Readable Content

The next usability guideline is to use callouts and headings to break up the flow of the content and to help users zero in on the content they're looking for. Also, use multiple pages when the content won't fit on a single page without scrolling. This will also help your SEO, which I'll describe later.

Pick a font size that's big enough to read by young and old eyes. You may have young, 20-something eyes, but the majority of your website's users may not.

Choose a font color that contrasts with the background color. As I stated earlier, the best format is black (or dark) text on a white (or a shade of white) background. It's what most people are used to reading and it's easiest on the eyes. But if you're intent on adding some more pizzazz to your site, whatever colors you choose need to be easy to read and easy on the eyes. Some of your users may even be color blind…be sensitive to their eyes when you're choosing colors.

Avoid Dead Blogs

Blogs are the "hip" thing to do on any website, but users will notice if you haven't posted to your blog in two months or a year, and they'll think the site isn't active or current, which tarnishes your credibility and usability.

Unless you're committed to adding blog posts daily or weekly, don't start a blog. Instead, post articles that will add content to your site but won't make it look dead if you go a month or two without posting a new one. The only thing worse than *no* blog is a *dead* blog.

Simple Messages

When a user visits your home page for the first time, your message needs to be simple to understand and convey the purpose of your site in 5 seconds or less. Video is a great way to convey a simple message and capture the attention of your users.

Use language that's appropriate to your audience. If doctors comprise your target market, it's ok to use clinical terms that they'll understand and relate to. However, if your target market includes anyone between 18 and 60, you'll need to use language equivalent to an 8th grade reading level.

Simple Navigation

Make it easy for your users to find things on your site. Put the most important links in the top and/or side navs (e.g. Home, Products, Services, Contact Us, etc.), and put the less important ones in the footer (e.g. Privacy Policy, Terms & Conditions, FTC Discloser, Employee Login, etc.). I'll cover navigation in great detail in the next section.

Meta and HTML Tags

These are tags on your pages and images that tell search engines what the content is about. Meta tags aren't visible to users…they're behind the scenes on every web page and used only by search engines. The content they contain, however, IS visible to users. I'll explain how in the next few paragraphs.

Every page should have both a Title and Description meta tag. The Title Tag is what browser's use in the title bar and it's also the link name when someone bookmarks a page. A good Title Tag will begin with your website or company name, followed by a description of the content on the page. For example, Amazon's home page Title Tag is, "Amazon.com: Online Shopping for Electronics, Apparel, Computers, Books, DVDs and more." As you can see from this Google search result, the Title Meta Tag was used for the listing title.

Amazon.com: Online Shopping for Electronics, Apparel, Computers ...
www.amazon.com/
Online retailer of books, movies, music and games along with electronics, toys, apparel, sports, tools, groceries and general home and garden items. Region 1 ...

The Description tag is what many search engines use as the brief content below a page link. Each of these tags should be relevant to the page's content and different on each page. If you don't include a meta description, or if the search engine determines that the description isn't relevant to the rest of the content on the page, it will choose content from somewhere on the page instead.

"H" tags, or Heading Tags, are used for content headings. The most important H tag is the H1 tag, which should be at the top of your content and should be a relevant title to the content on the page.

You can also use H2 and H3 tags for sub-headings. They're a good way to delineate content areas on your page, making the content more readable and easier to skim. In addition, search engines use these tags to classify the content on your pages, making keyword relevancy crucial. I'll cover this in more detail in the SEO section of "Phase 4: Marketing Your Website."

"Alt" tags, or Alternate Text Tags, are the meta tags for images. If, for whatever reason, an image can't be loaded, this text is what the user will see in place of the image. Search engines use Alt tags to determine the image's content or topic, which helps them rank your image and your site in image search results.

Consistent Page Layout

Don't make your users learn a different content layout on every page. Keep your entire site as consistent as possible. You may want a different layout on admin or account pages, but strive to keep everything as similar as possible, especially on all your content pages. I'll discuss page layout in more detail later.

Contact Us

Include an easy to find link to your contact us page on every page of your site. Put this link in both the header and footer navigation.

You can also include a simple contact us form on each page. Many sites put a form with name, email and comment boxes on the right side navigation near the top allowing users to contact them without navigating to a different page. If your website is primarily used to generate sales leads, this is a great approach.

Check Hyperlinks

Clicking a link that goes to the wrong page or no page at all is very frustrating to users and gives your site an amateur feel. Test all your links to verify that they work as expected. You can also use a tool like BrokenLinkCheck.com to automate the process.

Also, your links need to be highlighted in some way. I once visited a website with hyperlinks that were a slightly lighter color than the regular content. The only way to see a link was to hover over the text to see the "hand" icon. Make your links obvious to your reader by selecting a contrasting color to the rest of your content, and underline them when it doesn't distract from the overall design of the site.

Avoid Popups

I'm not referring to the popup windows that improve usability on forms; I'm referring to the annoying email opt-in and advertising popups that load when you visit (or leave) a page. You need to build some rapport with a user before he'll part with his contact info and 5

The Web Startup Roadmap

seconds isn't enough time to do that.

Website owners are attempting to maximize the user interaction by either capturing the users' email so they can keep in touch, or by force feeding ads to improve their bottom line. Neither is acceptable and both are usability irritations.

If you provide valuable content on your site and an easy way to opt-in to your email campaigns, your users will want to sign up without forcing it on them. Ads have their place and blasted in the face of your users isn't one of them.

Avoid Flash-Only Sites

Flash is a web development technology that makes websites look more like video than static content. Some graphic designers only know Flash and they'll try to convince you that your site will be totally awesome if you build it entirely using Flash animation. Don't believe them.

First off, Flash sites are generally slower than non-Flash sites. I'm sure you've noticed the "loading" graphic counting up to 100% when you go to these sites. It's inconvenient to wait for a site to load and many people won't.

Second, you'll be punished by search engines because they can't index Flash content as easily as HTML. While some search engines are making an attempt to index Flash content, many don't, and those that do aren't very good at it. Also, since Flash-only sites load more slowly, the page ranking is punished for the slow load time.

Third, many Flash-only sites try to be too clever, which I've already shown is a bad idea. Your visitors want a simple, easy to use website. If you try to wow them too much with fancy graphics and too much animation, you run the risk of losing them.

Finally, some browsers don't support Flash animation anymore. Apple products like the iPad and iPhone can't play Flash, and Internet Explorer 10 on Windows 8 only supports very restricted Flash functionality. If you want animation on your website, create an animated video, upload it to YouTube and embed it on your site. That's the best way to ensure cross-browser compatibility.

Search Box

If you have a large amount of content on your site, provide a search box so people can find what they're looking for. You won't need this feature early on before you have much content, but keep it in mind once you've added tons of articles and blog posts.

Fix Bugs

Bugs are those little irritating anomalies that occur when a user tries to do something on your site, but something goes wrong and they're shown an error message instead. I once encountered so many bugs on a banking site that I switched banks, despite the hassle of changing all the automatic bill pays. Don't underestimate the power of a bug.

Test every feature on your site. That includes buying products, checking out, registering, changing your password, etc. Everywhere there's a button, test it using multiple different scenarios and types of browsers.

Cross-Browser Compatibility

At a minimum, test all the features in your site using the top four browsers, which are Internet Explorer, Google Chrome, Mozilla Firefox and Safari. You can also test it on Opera, but if you're on a tight budget, they claim less than 4% of the browser market share as of October 2012.

Test With JavaScript Disabled

This is a lower priority since the vast majority of users will have JavaScript enabled, but if you're concerned about making your site available to everyone, you need to test this. You can disable JavaScript in any browser's options/security settings. Turn it off, close and reopen your browser, and start testing. Your site should still function or at least fail gracefully.

Ajax

This is a relatively new technology (within the last few years) that allows users to perform actions without reloading the entire page. Facebook uses this technology when you post a status update. Next time you post one, notice that the entire page doesn't reload; instead, just the status list is updated. This technology provides a much faster, smoother experience to your users. Ask your developer to use it where it makes sense.

That brings us to the end of the 17 usability guidelines. Having a usable website is key to your success. Pay attention to other popular websites and do what they do. Limit your desire to be creative and unique, and focus on how your website visitors already use the web to make their experience more pleasant and less frustrating.

Get input from your developers. Many developers have been building sites for years, and they know what works and what doesn't. Don't accept their advice on face value, though. They may suggest something because it's easier for them to develop and not because it's better for your users. I'll discuss how to manage developers in more detail later.

Ask your family and friends to review the site and provide their feedback, as well. Create a questionnaire and ask them to fill it out, but word the questions to get unbiased answers.

You can also get several people in a room and treat them like a focus group. I've found this to be particularly effective because bouncing ideas off each other can help get the creative juices flowing. Record the session on video or audio and review it later.

Navigation

Navigation refers to the links that help people find things on your website. A website's navigation is similar to a table of contents for a book. If you want to find a section in a book, you don't have to read the entire book to find it. Instead, the table of contents helps you navigate directly to the section you want to read.

In this section, I'm going to discuss the 7 types of navigation bars (or nav bars) that you have at your disposal. You've may have seen all of these and know what they are, but it will help to know what developers call them so you can speak the same language.

Top Nav

The top nav is a horizontal nav bar at the top of the page or between the header and the content. This is where you put links to the most commonly used pages on your website.

Google uses their top nav for links to the following things: Search, Images, Maps, Play, YouTube, News, Gmail, Drive, Calendar and More. These are links to all the major sections or features that are core to Google's business and user base.

Account Nav

On most sites, the account nav is in the upper right-hand corner. This nav is used by members, or users who have registered on the site, and it contains links to account maintenance pages, login/logout, and any other links that are specific to the website's members.

Since the upper right corner is the standard location for account navs across most sites, it's good to put yours in the upper right corner, too, making it easy for your users to find it. Following industry standards is a usability issue. If you try to be too clever and violate common standards, your users will get irritated looking for things that aren't where they're supposed to be.

Left Nav

Some sites have too many important pages and the links won't all fit in a horizontal nav. Horizontal real estate (another way of saying screen space) is very limited because pages are a fixed width. Vertical real estate, however, is endless. If your most important links won't all fit horizontally, use a left side nav instead.

Amazon is a good example of this type of navigation. They have too many departments to list horizontally, so they use a left side nav bar that can be displayed vertically.

Right Nav

When the navigation isn't as important as the content on each page, you can use a right nav bar instead of a left nav.

Twitter does this, as well as the website Fiverr.com. Both sites want users to look at the content on the landing page before the navigation, so they placed the nav bar on the right.

Bottom or Footer Nav

The links placed in the bottom nav are usually for legally required pages, such as the Privacy Statement, Terms & Conditions, FTC Disclosure, etc. However, you can also provide links to the *most* commonly used pages, such as the Home page and Contact Us, and also to the *least* commonly used pages, such as About Us, Jobs and Help. The bottom nav is also the place for copyright statements.

> **Did you know...**
>
> You don't have to do anything special to copyright your content. Just put a copyright statement such as "© 2001 – 2013 Your Company, All Rights Reserved" in the footer of your website. If it appears on all pages, your content will be legally protected.

Facebook has a standard bottom nav bar, containing their copyright statement and links that are not commonly used by most users: About, Advertising, Developers, Careers, Privacy, Terms and Help.

Thanks to WordPress, the size of bottom navs has grown considerably over the past few years. Some sites, like eBay, have enormous bottom nav bars with sections and vertical lists of links to pages within the site, other companies owned by eBay, and all of the country specific eBay sites.

Google took the exact opposite approach. They have only four links in their bottom nav: Advertising Programs, Business Solutions,

About Google and Privacy.

What you choose to include in your bottom nav is up to you, but it's useful to consider these standards when making your decisions.

Breadcrumbs Nav

Breadcrumbs are useful when a user drills down into categories of products or content. For example, Amazon uses a breadcrumb nav to show users where they are in the tree of products they're viewing. If you go to the Books section and click on Romance, then Time Travel, you'll see a breadcrumbs nav near the top that looks something like this: Books > Romance > Time Travel. eBay also uses breadcrumbs for their categories.

If your site has several levels of product or content categories, using breadcrumb navs can be a very effective way of showing your website users where they are in the hierarchy, and it gives them an easy way to navigate back up to higher levels.

Hover Menus

The last of the 7 types of navigation is the hover menu. When a user hovers their mouse over a link in a hover menu, a box opens below, above or to the side of the link with additional links to sub-sections or categories. These menus are used to conserve real estate on the screen when there are far too many links to show in a single list.

Amazon uses a hover menu for the "Shop by Department" option located under their logo. This is a 2-layer hover menu. Hovering over the "Shop by Department" tab displays a list of their main departments, and hovering over a department shows a list of the highest level categories for the department. eBay also uses a category/sub-category hover menu.

Personally, I'm not a big fan of hover menus for three reasons. First, some of them are very hard to use. If you don't move your mouse exactly over the right spot, the hover menu disappears or you end up in a different sub-menu. That makes for a very frustrating user experience.

Second, not all hover menus are SEO friendly. The "hover" action of your mouse that causes the menu to display on your screen uses JavaScript code to generate the menu. Depending on how the JavaScript is written, some search engines may not be able to read or follow the links in the menu. I'm going to discuss SEO and how it works in much more detail later, but suffice it to say, if a search engine can't read or follow links on your site, your pages won't get indexed or appear in search results. And that's very bad.

Finally, some hover menus aren't cross-browser compatible because each browser has its own little JavaScript idiosyncrasies. That means it might work great on Google Chrome or Firefox, but not so much in IE or Opera. If one of your website's visitors is using a quirky browser, their impression of your site and their ability to use it won't be very good. If you decide to use a hover menu, test it thoroughly in all browsers.

Don't try to reinvent the wheel with your navigation. The web industry has some good standards that people are accustomed to seeing and using. Find some popular sites that you like, and mimic their navigation plan.

Navigation is one of the most important usability features on your website. If you have a good navigation structure that enables your users to find what they're looking for very quickly, they'll be much happier and more likely to come back.

Page Layout

You have some flexibility when you design your page layout. If you buy a template or theme from a website such as ThemeForest or Elegant Themes, the layout is already designed for you so you won't need to worry about it. However, if you're building a site from scratch, this is something you'll need to do.

If you've never done web design before, hire a professional to help you. There are some industry standards you should follow, some usability issues to avoid and some technical limitations you might not understand...but your developer will. Rely on their expertise to help guide you through the process.

However, just because you hired a professional, doesn't mean you're off the hook. For them to know what you want, you need to give them direction. The best way to do this is by using examples. Find websites that you like and show them to your designer. Explain what you like and don't like about them. You're not building the first website on the web so take advantage of the other websites that blazed the trail before you.

While you do have a lot of flexibility with your design, most websites follow a similar page layout pattern. Below is a diagram of the most common webpage layout design:

Logo	Header	Account Nav
Top Nav		
Left Nav	Main Content	Right Nav
Footer		

This diagram is often called a "wire frame" in the web design business. When you're talking to a designer about your website, it helps to have a wire frame as reference. You can create it using a Word table or Excel, draw it on a piece of paper, or draw it on a whiteboard and snap a photo.

When you're creating your wire frame, you can add, remove and adjust the layout sections. If you don't need a right nav, don't include that in your design. If you want your top nav above the logo, show it there. This wire frame is only intended to be an example of the most common webpage layout, so have your way with it and turn it into whatever you want.

There are only a few things you should keep where they are: your logo, the account nav and the footer. Like I mentioned before in the Account Nav section, the upper right corner is where people are expecting to find it. Likewise, the upper left corner is where they expect to see your logo. Don't make people hunt for basic things. Follow the industry standard.

Customer Service

The last of the 10 things every website needs is Customer Service. Most large sites don't have a contact us form anymore (or they bury it deep in the site) because they would be inundated with requests. However, as a small website owner, you want your customers to have as many ways to reach you as possible, and the Contact Us form is the most popular way of doing that.

Post your email address and phone number if you're ok with customers emailing or calling you. If you don't have 24x7 phone support, posting your operating hours helps set your clients' expectations about when you're available.

Live chat is another great customer service tool. At QuoteCatcher, we used Live2Support.com and it made our customer service reps much more efficient. Some of our customers preferred live chat over email or calling, and since there's a lag between posts, it allowed our reps to help more than one customer at a time.

Only use live chat if you're available during most of your standard operating hours, though. When you're "logged off" of the live chat, an "offline" message will appear in place of the "chat now" button. If it says offline more than chat now, your customers won't be very happy.

One of the major benefits of being the little guy is that you can afford to offer better customer service. That's one of your best competitive advantages over more established and larger competitors, so make the most of it by providing several ways for your customers to contact you. Exchanging emails or speaking to you might be their deciding factor in buying from you.

That brings us to the end of the "10 Things Every Website Needs." Here's a list for review:

- ❑ Registrar
- ❑ Webhost
- ❑ Content Management System (CMS)
- ❑ Content
- ❑ Images
- ❑ Standard Pages
- ❑ Usability Guidelines
- ❑ Navigation
- ❑ Page Layout
- ❑ Customer Service

In the next section, I'm going to cover a few things you might want or need for your website in addition to these ten.

8 Optional Things Your Website Might Need

In the last section, you learned about the things that are common to every website. In this section, you're going to learn about some other things that you *might* consider for your website.

SSL Certificate

An SSL Certificate is used to encrypt data transmissions sent from your website. How the process of encrypting and decrypting data works is extremely complicated, so I'm not going to explain the technical details here.

For a non-technical analogy, think of SSL as a lockbox and your SSL Certificate is the key that locks and unlocks it. When sensitive data like passwords or credit card numbers are entered on your website and sent over the Internet, the letters and numbers are scrambled and changed in a random way, and only your key can put them back in the right order on the other end.

SSL Certificates are purchased from SSL Certificate Authorities like GeoTrust, Thawte, Verisign, GoDaddy, etc. Most certificates are purchased for one or more years, and then renewed when they expire. You can expect to pay anywhere from $13 to several hundred dollars for a standard SSL certificate, depending on who you buy it from and what extra features you tack on.

In order to qualify for a certificate, you have to submit all the details of your business and provide proof that you have permission to buy a certificate on its behalf. It takes a few days to go through the verification process with most Authorities, so allow extra time for it.

Once your certificate is issued, you'll receive a text file with a bunch of letters and numbers in it. That's your "certificate" and it's unique to your website. The certificate is then installed on your web application server. Your developer or webhost will know how to install it. Once your certificate is installed, any pages that start with "https://" (e.g. https://www.domain.com/) will be encrypted both when sending and receiving data.

If you have a login screen with a password field, or if you accept credit card information, you need an SSL Certificate to protect your users from fraud.

Did you know...

The reason we have to go to all this trouble with SSL is because the world is full of bad people who sniff the Internet for information they can use to steal identities and money. If we don't encrypt sensitive data, these bad people have ways of intercepting it as it travels between your user's computer, your web servers, and whatever the end destination is (e.g. banks, credit card processors, etc.).

Site Map

A site map is a special page on your website that's mainly used by search engines to index your pages. Simply put, it's a single page that contains links to all your other pages. Most websites place a link to their site map in the footer nav, since it's not a popular tool for users.

Robots.txt

"Robots" are software tools created by search engines that constantly crawl the web looking for content. The "Robots.txt" file is used to tell the robots where they can look and, more importantly, where they *can't* look for content.

For example, if you have an admin section on your site and a user must be logged in to view it, a search engine has no business looking at those pages because they won't see anything (because they won't be logged in). By placing a special line in your Robots.txt file (e.g. DISALLOW: /Admin/), robots will know to skip that directory.

Your developer will know how to setup your Robots.txt file, but if you'd like to learn more about how it works, check out RobotsTxt.org for more information.

Web 2.0

There is a lot of confusion about what Web 2.0 means. It's a buzzword that you'll hear a lot and it's easy to misunderstand. In a nutshell, Web 2.0 refers to a type of website with features that allow its users to interact and participate in a community, and/or post content on the website. Think Wikipedia, Facebook, Twitter, StumbleUpon, Del.icio.us, Flickr, Amazon, etc. Blog sites that allow users to submit comments are also considered Web 2.0, but they usually lack the depth of true community sites.

Did you know...

Most of the confusion with regards to the Web 2.0 name stems from the historical use of version numbers like 2.0 for software upgrades. Web 2.0 doesn't refer to any technical upgrades to the web. Instead, it simply refers to our new way of interacting with it.

Web 2.0 has rapidly become the new standard for websites and those that lack any type of community feel will miss out on the value it brings. I recently did a search on Google for "designer jeans." Near the top of the search page was a website called UpscaleJeans.com, which is an affiliate site that lists all types of designer jeans offered for sale on eBay.

The site has great positioning on Google and does a nice job of aggregating all the designer jeans into one spot, but it lacks any type of member or community feel. As I was surfing the site, something felt wrong, but I couldn't quite put my finger on it. Then I realized that the site felt dead, even though the listings were updated in real time. There are no user comments, no member interaction, no site owner comments, nothing. It's purely a two dimensional website that lacks the three dimensional feel of a Web 2.0 site.

The main value of providing a community for your site is that people feel like they belong to something bigger than themselves and it makes them feel like your business is alive and thriving.

Think of it as the difference between a brochure and a salesperson. The brochure might get your message across, but it's also a lot easier to throw in the trash. However, a salesperson provides an extra dimension to the sales process and is much less likely to be ignored.

Having a community on your site is like having hundreds or thousands of salespeople who buy what you sell and recommend your products and services to their friends. This is the beauty of Web 2.0 and why it's so important for your website.

In the beginning, you may not have the revenue to support spending extra money on Web 2.0 features. In addition, Web 2.0 features are only truly valuable if you have users on your site, which you won't have in the early stages of your web business. However, remember these features for future site enhancements, and design your initial site with them in mind.

Mobile Access

According to StatCounter, almost 10% of all webpage hits in January 2012 were from mobile devices, and 25% of all mobile web users in the US are mobile only. We have over 200 million mobile web users in the US which means nearly 50 million Americans only access the web using a mobile device. That's an awfully big segment to ignore so you may want to provide some sort of mobile access to your website.

Mobile Friendly

Your first and easiest option for mobile access is making your website "mobile friendly." If your developer knows what he's doing, this isn't very hard to accomplish. Much of it can be done by changing the style sheets that control how your site looks. Your website can be setup to detect what type of device is looking at it and send back the appropriate styling so it looks right on that device. Mention this requirement to your developer before he starts coding so he can build the site accordingly.

Mobile Website

Depending on how complicated you want your mobile access to be, your second option is to create a separate "mobile website." When a mobile device loads the home page of your full website, it's redirected to your mobile website that's designed specifically to display on smaller screens.

If you've noticed on some websites that the "www" is replaced with "m" when you're looking at it on your mobile device (e.g. m.facebook.com), that means you're looking at a mobile website. Sometimes you'll see a "/mobile/" or "/m/" after the domain name (e.g. www.domain.com/mobile/). This is also a mobile website; the only difference is how it's configured. If you decide to go the mobile website route, you need to decide whether you want to use "m.domain.com" or "www.domain.com/m/" for your mobile URL.

> **Did you know...**
>
> Using "m.domain.com" is obviously much cleaner and shorter, but it comes with one major downside if your website needs SSL and you're on a tight budget. SSL, as I've already discussed, is used to encrypt data transmissions. If both your primary website and your mobile website need secure login and/or payment functionality, they both need to be secured with an SSL Certificate.
>
> The problem with using "m.domain.com" is that it will require what's called a "Wildcard SSL Certificate," which costs substantially more than a standard SSL Certificate, depending on the "extras" you choose. A standard SSL Cert will only secure your primary domain (e.g. www.domain.com), while a Wildcard Cert allows you to secure multiple "Subject Alternative Names" (e.g. www.domain.com, m.domain.com, shop.domain.com, mail.domain.com, register.domain.com, etc.). If you don't use m.domain.com, but instead use www.domain.com/mobile/ as your mobile website address, you can use the same standard SSL Cert and save yourself some money.

Mobile App

Your third option for providing mobile access to your website is by building a "mobile app." A mobile app is a whole project of its own and can be costly to develop for all 3 platforms (Apple, Android and Windows). Mobile apps are typically used for special functionality like banking tools or Facebook's status updates. They're not normally used to provide access to all of the features on the full website.

Making your website mobile friendly will be much cheaper than building a mobile app, especially if you tell your developer it needs to be mobile friendly before he starts writing code. If your target audience is under 40, you need to be mobile friendly at a minimum.

Gamification

Gamification is the process of bringing game mechanics and design to non-game things like websites, apps and even real life. Even though the term has only been used for the past few years, the concept has been around for a long time.

When I was 16 years old way back in the 1980's, I won a prize from a Coke bottle cap. McDonalds has offered their Monopoly game almost as long. There's nothing inherently game-like about drinking a Coke or eating french-fries, but they gamified it, nonetheless.

Today, many popular websites use gamification features, and there's no better example than Foursquare. If you're not familiar with Foursquare, I encourage you to create an account right now and play around with it. Their implementation of gamification features is next-to-none. For those of you who are unfamiliar with it, here's how it works….

Foursquare is a location-based social networking check-in website. If you're a member of Foursquare and you go someplace, you can "check-in" to that location. In response to checking in at various places, such as stores, restaurants, theatres, parks, your house, etc., you earn "badges" for your activity. For example, once you've checked into Foursquare 50 times, you get a "50 Check-ins" badge. If you check into the same place three times in one week, you get a "Local" badge. And if you check into the same place more than anyone else, you get to be the "Mayor" of that location.

Some businesses have learned how to use Foursquare to increase sales by giving discounts to customers who check-in frequently. Some places give discounts and free stuff to their mayors, which encourages them to keep coming back (and spending more money). Since only one person can be a mayor at a time, it's common for people to compete for "Mayorship" in order to reap the rewards of that illustrious position and to avoid being "Ousted" as mayor. That competition leads to more visits, more loyalty and more sales.

> ### Did you know...
>
> Foursquare gamified an act all of us do every day (going places), but they also created their own language. The words in quotes above are used by members in reference to their activities related to the site. In Communication Studies, we call this "in-group communication" and it's a powerful tool for fostering identity and creating loyalty.

Some businesses even sponsor their own badges. Macy's sponsored a "Macy's Parade" badge for the 2011 Thanksgiving's parade. If a Foursquare member checked in at the parade and received the badge, they were entitled to a discount off an in-store purchase. Smart, net-savvy business owners know the value of gamification, even if they don't know it's called that.

Foursquare isn't the only gamification website. In fact, several companies now provide gamification platforms and sell them to other websites allowing them to use the same concepts that have made Foursquare successful.

Session M is a platform used by companies such as Volvo to encourage people to take some form of action related to their brand. For example, by watching a Volvo commercial, you earn "mPoints" that can be used for prizes and special offers.

Badgeville is another gamification platform that has brought the gaming concept to corporate America by allowing employees to earn badges for doing various activities, such as exercising, taking training classes or turning off the lights to save energy. Employees can be assigned missions, earn points and achievements, participate in contests, level-up, and see their name on the leaderboard. This form of friendly competition has been shown to dramatically increase productivity and desired behavior.

Gamification can be used in all sorts of ways, and the beauty of it is in the simplicity of its 3-step process:

Step 1:   Assign a quest or *action* (go someplace or do something)
Step 2:   Give a *reward* once the action is completed (badges, points, achievements, prizes, etc.)
Step 3:   Provide a public means of *recognition* (leaderboard or public notices)

Many popular video games employ this same action-reward-recognition methodology, and that's what makes them addictive, which is an excellent segue into our next topic.

The Website Addiction Loop

Why does Facebook have a billion users? The answer is simple: it's addictive. Facebook and many other websites have intrinsic elements built into them that make them addictive to us in a very predictable way. I've labeled this process The Website Addiction Loop, and although it can be applied to other forms of addiction, my focus is on websites.

The Website Addiction Loop diagram in Figure 5 shows the process from start-to-finish. Follow along on the diagram as I explain each step in the loop. To help illustrate the loop, I'll use Facebook as an example.

Figure 5

1. **Awareness** – this is the first step and it occurs when we hear about the website for the first time. Usually, a friend tells us or we hear about it on the news or a link from another website. When I heard about Facebook in the news and from friends, I wasn't allowed to join it yet. They still had the .edu email TLD requirement and I wasn't a student so I had to wait several months to sign up.
2. **Motivation** – once we're aware of the website, we become motivated to see what all the commotion is about. Motivation resulting from awareness is a combination of curiosity and a need to belong. If we don't stay on top of new developments, we run the risk of being ridiculed by our friends for living under a rock. I was motivated to join Facebook because my friends were on it and I didn't want to be left out.
3. **Action** – once we're sufficiently motivated, we feel compelled to take action by going to the website and participating. Participation can come in many forms such as registering, reading, liking things, posting comments, buying something, etc. The first actions I took on Facebook were to register, setup my profile, find friends and send messages. That has evolved into posting status updates, pictures, and comments on other people's posts.
4. **Variable and Fixed Rewards** – if a website is designed with addictive elements, this is where they appear. A Fixed Reward occurs when the user expects it to occur, such as earning a badge on Foursquare. An action is taken and an award is given, every time. A Variable Reward, however, occurs at random and it's MUCH more addictive. When we post a status update or a photo on Facebook, we get an immediate Fixed Reward: the knowledge that other people are seeing what we're posting. That happens every time we make a post. We also get Variable Rewards (sometimes) from two different sources: the news feed and responses

to our posts. When you're reading your newsfeed containing all the things your friends have posted, most of the statuses are boring, but a few are either interesting or funny. I check my feed once per day, and I almost always learn something and laugh at something. The second source of variable rewards comes from responses to our posts. If we post something that's interesting enough, we'll get comments and likes. People crave this form of reward, also known as "attention" (another motivation).

5. **Positive Feelings** – whether the reward is variable or fixed, it makes us feel good. We get that feeling of excitement, like winning on a slot machine (and those aren't addictive at all!). On addictive websites, the positive feeling is usually tied to some need that's being fulfilled, which leads us back to….

6. **Motivation** – when we first enter the Addiction Loop, our motivations are different than after we've been around the loop once or twice, or a few times. On subsequent rounds of the loop, we have some additional motivations, such as a need for attention, need for affirmation, need for recognition, need for a sense of belonging, need for money, cure for boredom, curiosity about what we're missing, and most importantly, a need to experience the positive feeling we get as a reward for participating.

7. **Negative Feelings** – the only way to break the loop is if we experience negative feelings in response to the reward mechanism. This occurs when the rewards don't resonate with us, but it also happens when we realize we're addicted and decide it's bad for us. The negative feelings associated with addiction are often enough to make us "give up" and stop participating (at least for a while).

The Addiction Loop is a powerful tool that can be used for good or evil. Some people say there is no good form of addiction, but if you can create a website that helps people eat healthier, exercise more, be more productive or generally lead better lives, I don't see the harm (as long as you're not rewarding unethical or illegal behavior).

Ecommerce

If you're going to sell things on your website, you need an ecommerce solution. There are countless options for selling products on the web, either from your own website or on someone else's.

Hosted Stores

If you'd like to test the waters before investing in a full blown ecommerce website, start by using eBay, Craigslist, Amazon WebStore, Etsy, or any number of other web store sites. This will give you a good taste of what it takes to run a web business, while minimizing your overhead expenses.

Since these sites handle your credit card processing and some advertising, you can focus your energy on finding products to sell and shipping them. Amazon even has a fulfillment center that can package and ship your products for you. Of course, all these services come with fees, but they're a "pay as you go" model making it relatively inexpensive to get started.

Pay Now Buttons

If you want to build your own ecommerce website, you need to decide how you're going to sell your products. If you're only selling one or two things, you can use a PayPal or Google Checkout button.

The best thing about these services is how easy they are to setup. All you have to do is copy a little piece of code they provide and paste it on your product page and you're ready to accept payments (you'll need an account with them, of course).

The downside of these services is that when a user makes a purchase on your site, they are taken to the processor's website to do it. It's not a big deal, but it's also not a seamless experience for your user. You'll also pay slightly higher transaction fees for these services, although they claim to save you money in the long run by not charging setup or monthly fees.

If you're just starting out and aren't sure what to do, use PayPal or Google Checkout. You can always replace them with a built-in payment processing solution down the road to save a little on transaction fees or provide a more seamless experience for your users.

Catalog & Shopping Cart

If you have several items for sale, you're going to need a product catalog and a shopping cart. A catalog will allow you to organize your products into categories that will make the products easy to search and find.

A shopping cart allows your users to store the items they want to buy so they can be bundled into a single order. This allows the buyer to purchase all the items with a single credit card transaction and it allows you to ship everything at the same time.

You can buy ecommerce software packages that contain everything you need to sell merchandise and accept payments. Two of the most popular packages are Shopify and 1ShoppingCart. If you're going to hire a developer, he's already familiar with one or two ecommerce solutions that work well with the technology you've chosen. Do a Google search on the package he's recommending and read the reviews, but you should be safe going with his recommendation.

One thing you don't want to do is pay for a custom or proprietary solution. This will cost you a lot more and will also make it difficult to transition the development to someone else if your developer decides he wants to live with the monks in Tibet for a year. Besides, there are far too many inexpensive, off-the-shelf solutions that offer amazing features that would cost thousands of dollars to custom build. Don't let your developer talk you into a custom solution unless your feature set absolutely requires it.

> ### Did you know...
>
> "Off-the-shelf" is a term used in software development when referring to software that isn't custom built. Instead, it's software that has been developed by a company or group of developers and licensed for use to many different companies or people. It often has customizable features (think WordPress), but a feature for one means a feature for all, and a change to one means a change to all.
>
> Off-the-shelf software benefits from economies of scale since it can be sold countless times, but only requires development once. Custom software, on the other hand, must be built new (or mostly new) each time and for each client. Sometimes this is necessary to achieve the desired functionality, but it's much less efficient and much more expensive.

Don't talk yourself into a custom solution with outrageous requirements unless you have prior experience building websites and understand the risks. Chances are there's a reason why it's not available in an off-the-shelf ecommerce package. Your usability goal is familiarity and sticking with a popular ecommerce package will make your site easier to use.

Once your website is generating revenue, you can always go back and enhance or replace your ecommerce system with a custom solution, so don't think you're stuck with it forever. But if you're on a tight budget and want to get something up quickly, off-the-shelf is the best way to go.

Accepting Credit Cards

One of the most confusing aspects of a custom ecommerce website is how credit cards are accepted. I'm not going to explain the technical details of the seven step settlement process that occurs after someone presses the buy button on your website...that's just too much brain damage and it's not important that you understand it. What you DO need to understand are the three things required to make it work: a Payment Gateway, a Payment Processor, and a Merchant Account.

Payment Gateway

The first thing you need is a Payment Gateway. This is a piece of software that connects your website, your payment processor and your merchant account. When a purchase is made on your site, your shopping cart software will send the payment information to the payment gateway, which will then connect to the payment processing networks and transfer the money from your buyer's credit card to your bank account.

The buyer's card will be charged immediately, but it takes a few days to get the money from the buyer's credit card to your bank account so don't expect to see the funds when the purchase occurs. Examples of popular payment gateways are Authorize.Net, PayPal Payflow Pro, Google, Stripe, and many more.

Did you know...

Stripe is a new type of payment gateway that doesn't require a merchant account or a payment processor. If you go with them, you'll have a lot less work to do. The only caveat is they don't work with all shopping cart solutions yet.

Payment Processor

You need a Payment Processor if you want to accept credit cards. A Payment Processor is the link between the Payment Gateway and the various credit card issuers like Visa, MasterCard, American Express, Discover, etc. Some examples of Payment Processors are FreeCreditCardProcessing.com, PayPal Merchant Services, MerchantWarehouse, MerchantExpress, and many more.

When the Payment Gateway sends a purchase request with the

credit card information to the Payment Processor, the processor contacts the appropriate credit card issuer to first run a fraud check and then to verify that the customer has enough funds to make the purchase. If everything looks good, the processor returns a "success" message to the Payment Gateway and the sale is logged.

Merchant Account

The final piece of the puzzle is a Merchant Account, which is a special type of bank account that can accept credit card payments. Check with your business bank about this option. They may have an entire payment processing solution that you can use; however, compare their prices to other providers because their processing services may be a lot more expensive than other solutions.

Processing fees vary widely for these services. You normally won't have a fee for the merchant bank account, but you will for the payment gateway and the payment processor. There is typically a setup fee that's no more than $100, although you can ask them to waive this fee, and since there's a lot of competition, they usually will. There may also be a monthly fee of $10 or more. You'll also pay a per transaction fee that's around 25 cents plus a percentage per transaction fee that should be less than 3%. It's important to price shop for these to get the best deal. Over time, these fees add up.

That brings us to the end of the "8 Optional Things Your Website Might Need" section. Let's do a quick review:

- ❑ SSL Certificate
- ❑ Site Map
- ❑ Robots.txt
- ❑ Web 2.0
- ❑ Mobile Access
- ❑ Gamification
- ❑ The Website Addiction Loop
- ❑ Ecommerce

In the next section, I'm going to help you write all this down in a document that you can give to a web developer.

Defining Requirements

"Make everything as simple as possible, but not simpler."

~Albert Einstein

In the next part of the "Building Your Website" section, I'm going to talk in depth about how to find and manage your development team, but before you can do that, you need to know what you want them to build.

If you're going to build a house or a building, you work with an architect to create the blueprints. Luckily, web design isn't as complicated as designing a house, meaning you don't have to pay an expensive architect to do it. You can create the blueprints yourself by writing down everything you want your website to do in a Requirements Document.

Back in the elevator pitch section, I said you should focus on the benefits and stay away from listing features. It's just the opposite in the requirements document where you want to focus on the features, not benefits. Sometimes it's useful to provide a little information about the benefit of a feature to help the developer understand why you're asking for it, but it's not necessary.

Did you know…

It's better to develop your website in "phases" rather than trying to launch all of your feature ideas in the first release. Cutting back on the code required for the initial launch will allow you to

> launch more quickly, which will enable you to start getting traffic and prove your concept sooner. You may also discover new or better ways of doing things that will affect the design of new features. Build the MVP (Minimum Viable Product) and save the bells and whistles for later.

When you're defining the requirements for your website, break each section into Phase 1 and Phase 2 (or more) feature-sets. Put "must haves," or features required for launch, in Phase 1 and "nice to haves" in subsequent phases. This will cut down on both development time and cost for the first release.

Before you start talking to developers, you need at least a basic requirements document in hand. There are many different ways to write requirements documents, but for simplicity's sake, I'm only going to share the way I prefer doing it as both a developer and a development manager. I've also included a Requirements Document template in the downloadable materials.

Section 1: Purpose

The first section (after the title page and table of contents) is to describe the purpose of the requirements document. Talk about the "Scope" of the document here. For example:

```
This document describes the functional
requirements for XYZ website. It's intended to
establish a baseline record of the site's
features broken into phases. The requirements
in this document will be used to validate the
accuracy and completeness of the software
that's delivered.
```

In addition to the document's scope, also define the document's limitations. For example:

```
This document does not define the technical
requirements, except at a very high level.
Technical requirements, such as database and
software design, is the responsibility of the
developer and must be done in a way that
supports the functional requirements.
```

Section 2: Definitions

In the Definitions section, explain acronyms, jargon and special terms used by you or your industry that the developer may not understand.

For example, at QuoteCatcher, we had two different types of users: Buyers and Sellers. Buyers were people looking for services, such as web design or marketing. Sellers were vendors who provided the services that our Buyers were seeking. A developer might have different definitions for these terms than we did as the business owners so defining terms like these for a developer can help prevent confusion.

If you're developing a process, define all the statuses that refer to each step in the process. You can even draw diagrams to show the process flow, but the diagram itself should go in the section that defines the requirements for the process, instead of the Definitions section.

Section 3: Assumptions

Explaining your assumptions up-front can spark dialog that will remove confusion down the road. If you're making an assumption about ANYTHING, put it in this section and ask your developers if they understand it. Things you might want to include in this section are:

- Development platform you expect them to use
- Who will own 3rd party software licenses for plug-ins, etc.
- Cross-browser compatibility expectations

- Ownership of code once the website is delivered
- Ongoing support for bug fixes
- Etc.

Many years ago during my consulting days, I took over management of a project late in the development cycle. The project was only a couple of weeks from delivery and all I did was help the team put the finishing touches on it. When we delivered the project to the client, we discovered it wouldn't work on their servers because we wrote the software for Windows and they were running Novel!

Referring back to the requirements document that the client signed, it clearly stated in the assumptions section that we were building the software for the Windows Server platform. In that case, defining the assumptions protected the developer because it was the client's mistake. However, defining assumptions could just as easily protect the you from the developer.

Section 4: Site-wide Features

This section is used to describe all site-wide features such as navigation, layout, colors, security, CMS and any other features that apply to every page on the website. Define each feature in its own sub-section as follows.

Graphic Design

In this section, explain your vision for how the main page on your website should look and feel in terms of layout and colors. If you're planning to buy a template, this section only needs to state where the template will come from and the title of it.

If you're going with custom graphic design instead of a template, you'll need to do quite a bit of additional work. You can mockup the layout using a word table, draw a picture on a piece of paper (or a napkin) and scan it, or draw it on the whiteboard and snap a photo.

Paste the picture in your document and explain the purpose of each section. If some pages have a different layout, such as product or blog pages, do the same thing in the section of the document that describes them.

The next thing to define in this section are the primary colors of the website. You learned about how to choose colors in the section on "Identity," so refer back to that if you need a refresher. The important thing to remember from that section is that you want one primary color and one to three complimentary colors. Define each color and explain where each should be used in your layout (e.g. navigation, background, header, content, etc.).

When you're talking about colors with your graphic designer, be as specific as possible. "Blue" or "red" won't cut it because there's a dozen or more shades of each. The best way to avoid confusion is to use the hexadecimal color codes for the colors you want. Here's a good source to help you through this process: ComputerHope.com/htmcolor.htm.

However, if your intent is to give the graphic designer general guidance so they can create a design recommendation for you, it's ok to be a little vague, but you should still be as specific as possible. Instead of saying "blue" or "red," you might say "light dusty blue" or "deep dark red."

Providing examples is a great way to help graphic designers see your vision. Do some research and find some websites that you like. Then give the links to your designer and explain what you like and don't like about them.

If you're working with a separate graphic designer to create the visual design of your website, and they're not affiliated with your web developer, you can pull this section out of the requirements document and use it as your graphic design requirements document.

Content Management

Most web development platforms come with a Content Management System (CMS) by default. If your website is built using WordPress, Drupal or any of the other open source development platforms that I discussed earlier, you don't need to be too specific in this section because those platforms will do everything you want and more right out of the box.

However, if you're paying for a custom built website, define how you want to be able to update the content. At a minimum, you want to be able to update all the site's text, graphics and videos. Ideally, you should be able to create new pages and modify the navigation, without needing a developer.

Navigation

In the navigation section of the requirements document, define what the navigation should look like, how it should function, and the links that should be included in each nav bar. Do this for all nav bars that are common across the website, such as the top nav and footer nav. For example:

```
The Top Nav will contain the following links:
Products, Services, Testimonials, About Us,
Contact Us, and FAQ.

The Footer Nav will contain the following
links:

Terms & Conditions, Privacy Policy, FTC
Disclosure, About Us, Contact Us, and FAQ.

A page will be created for each link, defined
in the "Pages" section.
```

Input Field Validation

If your site has input forms that your customers use to submit information, such as a Contact Us form, comments, payment screens, etc., the data they enter needs to be validated for accuracy and completeness. In this site-wide feature section, explain how that validation should look to the user. For example:

```
Forms that require validation should all look
and function the same way. Required fields
should be noted with an asterisks and
```

```
highlighted in some way if they're left blank
when the form is submitted.
```

Search Box

If you want the ability to search the content on your website, you need a search box, usually placed in the header or the right-side nav section. Explain where you want the search box and what content it will search (all content, blog posts, product listings, etc.). Also explain how you expect the results to be displayed.

Security

If users can create accounts on your website allowing them to login when they return, you need a security system. This system will manage account creation, login, password reset, and account administration.

It's also used to manage roles, which grant access to different parts of the site and different features depending on the level of permissions assigned to the roles. For example, basic users may have access to their past purchases or special content, while paying members may have access to more specialized content or additional discounts.

You can even have multiple layers of administrative permissions. For example, a blog poster may only be able to post and edit blogs, and respond to comments, while a super admin can add pages and update all content on the site.

If your site needs a security system, define how it should work, what roles you need and what permissions should be assigned to each role.

Section 5: Components

In this section of the requirements document, define your components and explain how they should work. A component refers to a set of functionality such as a Catalog and Shopping Cart, a Blog, Customer Relationship Management (CRM), custom tools, etc.

Dedicate a sub-section to each component and define it in as much detail as possible, including webpages, process definitions, button functionality, backend process expectations, etc.

Section 6: Pages

Every link in your navigation bars needs a corresponding page (unless the link is to another website). In this section, define each page individually. If the page is only for content, all you need to do is document the name of the page and say it's for content. However, if it's more involved than that, explain the special functionality and how you expect it to work.

If you were building a house, you'd define the things that go into each room. A website is a lot like a house so think of each webpage as a "room" in your website. Write down what the page is for, any special functionality, what buttons do and anything else you can think of that will help your developer build it.

Section 7: Appendices

Use appendices for reference items such as process flow diagrams, screen shots, tables, lists, etc. that don't relate to the design of a specific component or page.

Your requirements document is more important than your business plan, at least in the beginning. By clearly defining what you want your website to look like and do, your web developer and graphic designer will be much better positioned to provide an accurate quote and build it the way you want it to be built.

The requirements document also protects you and your developer if requirements are missed or misunderstood. The document is your blueprint and if everyone works off the same blueprint, there's much less room for confusion, mistakes, time delays and cost overruns.

> ### Did you know…
>
> The more educated you appear, the less chance you have of being exploited. Some people say that working with a web developer is like working with an auto mechanic. If you don't understand the technology, you have to put all your trust in the person providing the service. Most people won't take advantage of your lack of knowledge, but some will. By writing a detailed requirements document, you give yourself the appearance of understanding (even if you don't) and that will encourage the techies to be more honest with you.

Website Development

Building your website is the biggest challenge you'll face during the startup phase of your new online company. If you outsource the software development to a developer or consulting company, you'll face many obstacles relating to requirements, scope and deadlines. If you decide to build it yourself using an off-the-shelf development framework, you'll face a different set of obstacles relating to the technology learning curve, quality and motivation.

In this section, I'll cover all the challenges and obstacles you'll face when building your website. I'll help you determine if it's something you can do yourself, or if you should hire a professional to build the site for you.

If you decide to outsource the development, I'll show you how to interview and manage the developers so they build what YOU want, WHEN you want it. Managing developers is like herding cats and knowing how to handle them is crucial to the successful, on-time delivery of your website.

DIY Web Design

With the user friendly development frameworks available today,

DIY or Do-It-Yourself website design is a real possibility. This is a tough call to make and only you can make it.

If you do it successfully, you'll save yourself a lot of money by using your own sweat equity to launch your online company. That's exactly how I launched all my companies and why I was able to start them with only $500 out of my own pocket. However, I have a software and website development background making it a no brainer for me. You may not have the same luxury, but that doesn't mean you can't do it.

Wizards

If you have no web development experience or only a little basic HTML experience and your website is a basic content or ecommerce site, you can use a wizard-based platform like ones offered by Shopify, ePages.com, 1and1.com, Web.com, GoDaddy, etc.

With these types of tools, you'll select a template, a series of setup options and click the "Build" button to automatically create your website. Wizard created sites like these only work well for very simple websites that have no custom functionality. It's also not possible to port the website to another webhost or to customize the configuration in any way. If you decide you want to move the website or add custom features, you'll have to start from scratch.

Open Source Frameworks

If the limitations of wizard websites don't appeal to you, the next DIY option is to build your own website using more comprehensive development packages such as WordPress, Drupal, Joomla! or Ruby On Rails. These types of tools are called open source development frameworks and they allow you to build just about any type of website you need.

You can buy a template or use a free one to make your website look professional. There are also thousands of plug-ins that you can use (most for free) to add additional functionality to your website. If you need more custom functionality now or in the future, you can pay a developer to write it for you on your existing website.

Another benefit of these open source platforms is that the licensing is free for development. You'll only pay a small licensing fee as part of your webhosting package once the site is launched. These frameworks are the most inexpensive way to do-it-yourself.

While these frameworks will work for just about any type of site, they each have their own strong suits. WordPress is ideal for content sites and blogs. You can buy plugins from 3rd parties that will allow you to plug additional functionality into your site, such as ecommerce and memberships, but it takes a little development to integrate them and it can get costly if you need to buy several plugins to make your site work.

Both Drupal and Ruby On Rails are much more comprehensive development frameworks that come with just about any type of functionality you might need. In addition to the out-of-the-box features, you can integrate 3rd party plugins just like with WordPress. These tools require a lot more code writing, but they make it easy to do.

In order to use any of these tools, you'll need to do some software development…there's just no way around it. They all support templates that you can customize to fit your needs, but eventually, you'll have to pop open the hood and get some grease under your fingernails.

These are great tools for building websites and I recommend them to most people; however, if you're new to web design and have little to no experience setting up a website, building a site using any of these tools is going to be a challenge, despite how easy they say it is. I've built several WordPress sites for my own use and the templates never quite look like I want them to. That means I have to write code to customize them, something most people won't know how to do.

If you have a logical mind, the ability to focus, and a lot of patience, the DIY frameworks are not hard to learn. But if you're the least bit ADD or have difficulty with basic math and logical reasoning, expect a struggle.

Another challenge to building your own site is making it look professional. As I discussed earlier, you can't launch a barebones, basic HTML site with poor quality graphics and expect people to use it. Your site can be very simple but it needs to look professional. Even if you decide to develop the site yourself and you don't want to buy a template, outsource the graphic design so it looks like a topnotch website that will instill confidence in your users.

For most people, do-it-yourself software development is not a viable option so don't feel bad if it's not your cup of tea. Accept your limitations and hire a professional before you waste weeks or months trying to build your own website.

Designer vs. Developer

If you decide the DIY approach isn't for you, you need to hire a professional designer and/or developer. In website development, there's an important distinction between a designer and a developer.

Designers care about aesthetics. They want things to look attractive and professional. Their goal is to appeal to emotions, which is what motivates most people to buy what you're selling. Developers, on the other hand, care about functionality. They want the site to function like it's supposed to, which will make your customers happy with the experience of using your website.

It's hard to find one person that's good at both because each set of tasks uses a different side of the brain. Designers are creative; developers are logical. Some web designers can create basic websites using tools like WordPress, but for custom coding, you need a developer. And please don't ask your developer to do graphic design. I've never seen a good coder who's equally as good at graphic design.

Local vs. Offshore

With the availability of cheap software developers from the Philippines, India, Pakistan, Russia and other emerging countries, I'm often asked if outsourcing software development overseas is a good idea. Like most things in life, there's no black and white answer. I've managed software teams based in India, so I have firsthand experience with the pros and cons of overseas outsourcing.

> **Did you know…**
>
> A project that costs $5,000 to develop offshore could cost $25,000 or more to develop in the US. Outsourcing overseas is a politically sensitive topic right now, but if it means the difference between following your dream and giving up, it's something you need to at least consider.

It's true. The rates for software developers are drastically lower overseas. You can expect to pay in the ballpark of $5 to $20 per hour for experienced developers in other countries, whereas developers with similar experience in the US will cost anywhere from $35 to $150 per hour. That's a huge difference, making overseas outsourcing very appealing. However, there are obstacles you'll need to overcome.

First, the time difference is in the neighborhood of 12 hours, depending on the region where the developers live. This means nearly all correspondence will happen via email. If you want to talk on Skype, you'll need to stay up late at night to meet with them, although some developers take on that burden by working during their night.

Because of the time difference, overseas developers won't be able to contact you during their workday to ask you questions. They might have a quick, thirty second question that will allow them to do 3 hours of work, but instead of asking you and moving on, they email it and wait until tomorrow to hear back from you. This delay can add significantly to the amount of time required to finish the project.

Second, you'll need to deal with language barriers. Some developers speak English very well, but many have thick accents that are hard to understand. If you have a hard time understanding them, they'll have a hard time understanding you, too. This translates into misunderstood requests and requirements.

Third, in addition to language barriers, you may also face cultural barriers that can affect timelines and productivity. For example, one of my project teams based in India was unable reach the office on more than one occasion due to national celebrations that gridlocked all the roads. We're not used to that here in the US with our relatively small population, but in a country with over one billion people, it's a real issue.

In addition, some cultures have clearly defined caste roles that make it difficult to communicate openly between superior and subordinate. This means that developers will be less likely to challenge or question their boss (you), which can lead to misunderstandings. They can also be more reluctant to offer suggestions, especially if they conflict with a superior's idea.

Also, if you're a woman, you may face even larger challenges. In many cultures around the world, women are simply not considered equal to men. If you're trying to manage a development team with this mindset, you've got your work cut out for you.

The final cultural barrier may be the worst, at least for your business. If your developer needs to deliver bad news, you may not hear it due to a cultural bias to "save face." Most American developers have no problem delivering bad news because we usually blame it on our superiors for setting unrealistic deadlines. However, in cultures that value social hierarchies, developers won't blame the boss for fear of violating social norms, and they don't want to take the blame themselves for fear of repercussions and losing face. Therefore, the bad news is sugar coated, oftentimes to the point of sounding like good news! This means you'll need to become very adept at reading between the lines and not be afraid to ask tough questions and continue drilling until you get to the bottom.

Finally, since you won't be located in the same office or even the same country, you'll face additional management obstacles that you won't face by hiring a local developer. Oversight and tracking are much more difficult when you can't sit down with the project team and look at each other over the table.

Even with Skype, you lose a lot of nonverbal communication compared to being in the same room. And due to the large geographical distance, sometimes you'll experience a technical lag of two seconds or more, which can make discussions tedious and frustrating.

Perhaps the biggest management challenge is keeping your team focused and motivated. It's very difficult to create a team atmosphere when you can't grab lunch together or play soccer after work. You'll be viewed as the outsider; the American who calls a few times a week to give orders and ask tough questions.

With all these obstacles for overseas development, you may be wondering why you wouldn't choose a US-based developer. Domestic developers do have several positive attributes. You'll speak the same language and have no difficulty understanding each other. If you live in the same city, you can sit in front of the same computer to review requirements and demonstrations. And since you're in the same time zone or close to it, you won't have those pesky late night meetings. That's all good news…so why go overseas?

Unfortunately, our way of life here in the US costs a lot more than in emerging countries, which means you'll pay dearly for US-based developers. If you're on a tight budget, you may not be able to afford a local developer and outsourcing overseas may be your only option. There are numerous obstacles to overcome with overseas developers, but if you succeed, you can get a quality product for far less than US-based developers will cost.

If you do opt to outsource overseas, consider using a local project manager (PM). Many overseas development shops work with US-based PM's to act as a liaison with the client. Since the PM has a relationship with the developers, you'll eliminate many of the obstacles I discussed above.

The PM will be the one staying up late at night on most occasions to communicate with the developers. And since they work together regularly, language and cultural barriers are less likely to be an issue. The only downside of using a PM is the cost.

While PM's typically charge less than developers, you'll still be paying $35 to $50 per hour for their services. However, if your project requires a development team with more than two developers, hiring a local PM could greatly increase the chances that your software will be delivered on-time and within budget.

Fixed Price vs. Hourly

If you can swing it, fixed price projects are more desirable than hourly. Fixed price means that the project will not exceed the cost quoted before development begins. This is the best option for you because it will force the development team to focus and get the job done as quickly as possible. Expect to pay a percentage (no more than 50%) up front and the remainder upon completion or in installments when milestones are reached.

The development team will want a caveat included in the contract regarding scope creep and requirements changes. If you decide to make changes during development, it will have an impact on the original quote. Changes such as these are generally handled with an addendum or separate "change of scope" price quote.

Hourly contracts mean you'll pay each team member based on the hours they work. The team members will keep track of their hours and submit an invoice to you at an agreed upon interval, usually weekly, every other week or monthly.

For small projects or minor changes to existing websites, paying hourly is just fine. For large projects, the challenge with hourly contracts is getting the development team to record their hours accurately, especially if they're working remotely. You could be paying for long lunches, days off and time spent on other projects without knowing it. That's why fixed price quotes are ideal.

If your development team is reputable and competent (and your requirements document is thorough), they shouldn't have a problem providing a fixed price quote. Nearly all the projects I've worked on during my years of software consulting were fixed price. It keeps everyone honest and focused.

Scope Creep

Scope creep is the bane of all software development, and it's something that you, as the client, have complete control over. But before we jump into that, let's first talk about what "scope" is.

Scope refers to the list of features and functionality that you want your website to contain, and it comes in a variety of sizes. There's the entire project scope, which refers to everything you currently have in mind for the present and future of your website. There's also phase scope, which refers to everything you want developed for the current release. And there's feature scope, which refers to everything you want a specific feature to perform in the current phase.

The term "not in scope" is something you'll hear often in software development, and it means you're not sticking to what you've asked for, and what absolutely needs to be done in order to launch the site.

Being the entrepreneurial visionary that you are, you're going to be constantly tempted to add new functionality or change existing functionality during the software development life cycle. This is called "scope creep" and it will spell certain doom for your project if it gets out of control.

There will always be changes and modifications that need to be made, but keeping them to a minimum will help ensure your project gets finished on time and within budget. Software development is an iterative process and you can always make changes later, after the site is launched.

Did you know...

"You should use iterative development only on projects that you want to succeed." ~Martin Fowler, "UML Distilled"

Iterative software development drastically improves the quality of your project and the likelihood it will be completed on time and on budget. The term "iterative" simply means that the software is written in small chunks with frequent client reviews, rather than delivering the entire project at the end of

> development. It provides opportunities for feedback and corrective action along the way, before it's too costly to change.

During my many years of web consulting, I've had several clients who couldn't stay in scope. Every day and sometimes multiple times a day, they requested changes or enhancements to software that was in the middle of development. In the worst cases, change requests were made one day, only to be reversed the very next day. Many of these projects were never finished. Their scope creep was out of control and some clients ran out of money before their site was launched. Others simply gave up because they felt like it would never be finished.

In cases like this, it's often the developers and the project team that get the blame for missed deadlines and buggy code, when in reality it is the client's inability to control their impulses and perfectionism. They think they have to launch a perfect site that requires no modifications…and that just isn't realistic. Every site will grow and change over time, but only if it gets launched and starts generating revenue, which is why staying in scope is so important.

When you're dreaming up features for your website, make a list of those that absolutely need to be present to launch the site, and those that you can live without for now. For example, if you're launching an ecommerce site to sell products, the site won't work without a catalog, shopping cart and payment processing. You may also require membership and registration, and perhaps a few other necessities.

What you *won't* need in order to launch an ecommerce site are in-depth reports on buying trends and spending patterns. Until you have people using the site and buying products, you have no need for these types of reports. The same can be said for product reviews. This is a nice-to-have feature that only adds value if you have customers to use it. Some website platforms come with many standard features out-of-the-box so this only applies to custom development.

Here's a list of features that *aren't* important for the <u>first launch</u>:

- Purchase reports (not to be confused with traffic analytics, which are important at launch)
- Product comments/reviews (you won't have any customers to submit them)
- Social media (you won't have any followers)
- Site search (you won't have any content)
- Discussion forum (you won't have any users to post on it)
- Advertising blocks (they won't generate any revenue without users, which you won't have)

In the interest of launching the website as quickly as possible, strip out EVERY feature that is not absolutely necessary for the first launch. This will form you MVP (Minimum Viable Product) containing only the things necessary for people to use your site and prove your business model.

The best way to keep track of what's important and what's a nice-to-have is to separate your requirements document into phases. This allows you to keep track of your brilliant ideas while maintaining scope. It also allows your developers to know where you're going with the future of the website, which can affect development decisions they make today.

You need to *prove* your website concept as quickly as possible allowing you to determine if it's worth your continued investment of time and money. The only way to do that is to launch it as quickly as possible so you can gauge interest and start generating revenue. This is the only way to know if your idea is going to work and it may also give you valuable insight into changes that need to be made to the software and even the entire business model.

By launching quickly, you may learn that an entire feature-set you had in mind is no longer needed or needs to be drastically changed in order to function the way your customers want it to. If you spend the extra time and money on this feature-set prior to launch, it may delay the initial launch, and it may also cost you more time and money to modify it to meet the actual needs down the road.

Fight the scope creep temptress as hard as you can and only make changes during development that are absolutely critical to the successful launch of the MVP. You can always go back and make changes or add new features later once the business model is proven and you have some revenue to pay for it.

Finding Talent

You've made your decision to hire a local or offshore designer and/or developer...now, where do you look?

Offshore Talent

If you're looking for offshore talent, start by checking out the following websites: Freelancer, Elance, Guru, and oDesk. You can post your project details on these sites and get several bids from different developers around the world. You'll be able to read customer reviews on each developer and choose the bid that's right for you.

I used Elance to find a designer to create the website for this book: TheWebStartupRoadmap.com. In response to the requirements I posted for the site, I received nineteen proposals over the course of two days. The prices ranged from $80 to $500 for a simple one page landing site. After reviewing all the proposals and exchanging emails with my favorites, I selected a designer/PM based in the United States who uses offshore developers to do the heavy lifting.

Another good option for finding offshore talent is to use the Craigslist country specific sites, such as "manila.en.craigslist.com.ph" to find local workers in the region of your choice. The Philippines is a good source because it was a US territory until the 1950's and much of the population speaks English fluently and with minimal accent. You can either post your project on Craigslist to get bids, or you can respond to some of the many ads posted by offshore developers.

Local Talent

If you decide to hire local talent, either in your city or somewhere else in the US, by far the best place to start the search is in your professional and social circles. Ask everyone you know for referrals. If someone had a bad experience with a developer, you'll know who NOT to choose. If someone had a good experience, you'll know you can trust their review.

Unfortunately, you may not know anyone who has built a website (hopefully my book will change that!). If that's the case, Craigslist is a good place to find local talent in your city. You can also do a Google search for "website design" and "web developers" to find a list of developers in your city and throughout the country.

Some people sponsor Meetup Groups that you can attend to network with developers. These meetings give you a chance to see how well you interact with each other, and how well they interact with other people.

Lastly, you can contact your local Chambers of Commerce, SCORE office, SBA, SBDC, or other organizations and ask if they have referrals. Once you have a potential developer or a list of them, it's time to start the interview process.

Interviewing

If you've never interviewed or hired anyone before, go to the library or bookstore and read up on the art of interviewing before you start the process of choosing your development team. You need to know what questions you *can* ask and the one's you legally *can't* ask. You also need to understand how to interpret the responses to questions and "read" the candidates to determine honesty and sincerity.

There's an old employment adage that states "hire slow and fire fast." Don't be in a big hurry to get your project started; at least not in such a hurry that you feel forced to choose the first prospect you meet. Take your time and make certain you're choosing the best candidate for the work that needs to be done.

Since you'll be hiring a software developer and potentially a project manager, I'm going to talk about the important things to consider for each. For designers and developers, the best way to gauge their work is to look at things they've already done. They should be able to provide you with a portfolio of projects, demonstrate how the websites work, and explain their role on the project and how they accomplished it. You also need to speak with the manager or owner who worked with them to develop the software they're using as a reference.

Since I like to do more than tell you *what* to do, I'm going to show you *how* I conduct interviews for web designers, web developers, project managers and references by providing lists of the questions I ask.

These questions are very specific and have a singular goal of helping you determine if the interviewee has the ability to create your website. You also need to ask them the touchy-feely questions to help you figure out if you'll actually work well together, but those are beyond the scope of this book. If you need some ideas for those types of questions, do a search on Google for "interview questions" or read a book dedicated to interviewing techniques. I've also included a few recommendations in the "Resources" section.

The next four sections contain questions and sample answers for each type of position. The question lists aren't exhaustive, and the answers are only intended to give you an idea of what you might hear. It's not important that you understand all the answers, but it is important that the interviewee has answers and delivers them confidently.

Being a startup entrepreneur, you don't have the time or money to waste on incompetent service providers. You want experienced people with a long track record and a string of good references.

Web Designers

Here's a list of questions I like to ask Web Designers, and some sample answers. Your web designer may also be your graphic designer, as I discussed earlier. If they're developing your logo and color palette along with your website, ask the following questions about both roles and ask for separate references for each.

1. **How long have you been doing web design/graphic design?**

    More than 3 years is a good answer.

2. **How many clients have you worked for?**

    More than 20 is a good answer.

3. **What software do you use?**

    Photoshop is the main tool for Graphic Designers. WordPress, Joomla!, Drupal, etc. are common tools for Web Designers.

4. **Can I see your portfolio?**

    Here's the link to my portfolio on my website.

5. **Do you mind if I call some of these for references?**

    Go ahead. Here are a few I'd recommend calling.

Web Developers

Here's a list of questions I like to ask Web Developers, and some sample answers.

1. **How long have you been doing software development?**

    More than 5 years is a good answer.

2. **How many projects have you worked on and what was your role on them?**

You want someone who's worked on multiple projects; at least 10. They should have been a developer on most of them, not a tester or manager.

3. **What coding standards do you follow?**

   They should be able to tell you what standard they use and explain why they use it, which should be appropriate for the development technology you've chosen. You might here things like Hungarian Notation, Positional Notation, Camel Case, the platform standard, etc.

4. **How do you document your code?**

   Good documentation is critical if you need to transition development to someone else. He should use comments and his code should be self-documenting, meaning he uses naming conventions and structures that are easy to understand.

5. **Have you missed deadlines before and why?**

   Almost every software developer has missed a deadline at some point so be leery of someone who says he hasn't. He should be able to explain why he missed the deadline and what he learned from it. Expect to hear things like scope creep, lack of resources, unrealistic deadlines, etc.

6. **How can you avoid missing deadlines?**

   This is a tough question, but my answer would be regular, open and honest communication about project statuses. Also, minimizing scope creep and realistic expectations would be good answers.

7. **If you don't fully understand a requirement, what would you do?**

You want a developer who will ask you to clarify requirements; *not* a developer who will build what they think is right and then ask if it's what you wanted. That can be a huge waste of time.

8. **If you have an idea for a fantastic new feature while you're in the middle of writing code that relates to it, what would you do?**

    You want a developer who will review new ideas with you before writing code for them. Many developers get caught up in "cool" features that may or may not be something you want, and then miss the deadline for the requirements you definitely need.

9. **If you have a coding problem that you're struggling to figure out, how would you resolve it?**

    Some developers will beat their head against a wall for an entire day or longer trying to figure something out. This can cost you extra money and result in a missed deadline.

    A good developer will start with Google to find discussion forums or websites that provide guidance on the issue. If that effort fails, he will ask someone he knows for ideas. This process shouldn't take more than a couple hours.

10. **Describe an experience you've had working on a development team. What was your role? How was the work divided?**

    This question can have a variety of answers. Your goal is to determine how well they work in a team environment. If you need more than one developer, being able to work effectively on a team is critical to the success of the project.

Project Managers

If you're hiring a project manager to manage the developers and/or designers, you can ask some of the technical questions above, especially if he's a technical PM. However, you'll also want to ask a few additional questions:

1. **Are you PMI certified?**

    PMI certification is offered by the Project Management Institute and the process for attaining it is grueling. If the project manager has gone through this process, you can rest assured that he at least understands the principals of project management (although that doesn't mean he knows how to apply them effectively).

2. **Do you use a project management application such as Microsoft Project?**

    The PM should be able to keep track of the project and show you progress at your request using some sort of tool. I've always used Microsoft Project, but there are a variety of tools to choose from, including Microsoft Excel. The important thing is that he uses something.

3. **How do you assign workload to developers?**

    The PM should follow the principals I cover later for managing developers. Every developer is different and each requires a specialized management style. The PM should break the project into small chunks and assign them based on experience and expertise.

4. **How do you track milestones and deadlines to ensure the project is on schedule?**

The PM should provide regular status reports. In the beginning, I would request daily reports. Once you're comfortable with the team's progress, you can change it to weekly if you want to. It's important that you stay current on the project, even if you have a PM managing it for you.

5. **If a developer isn't pulling his weight or he's missing deadlines, how would you handle it?**

   Again, refer to the section on managing developers for things to listen for while the PM is answering this question. You'll want the PM to keep you apprised of any issues relating to your project and its deadlines. This includes developer productivity and disciplinary issues.

6. **Do you have regular team meetings? How often? Do you use an agenda?**

   Communication is the key to successful software development. Several years ago, I inherited a project team from another project manager. Two of the developers had finished their tasks several weeks before and weren't working on anything. One developer was working on a part of the project that was cancelled 10 weeks earlier. The testers assigned to the project were recruited by another project manager to work on a different project, and the code for their own project wasn't being tested.

   All of these issues could have been avoided with regular status reports and team meetings. When I took over the team, I required daily status reports from every developer and instituted a weekly staff meeting to review what everyone was doing. These meetings proved very effective at creating a sense of team membership and also helped identify individual development challenges that the team helped to solve as a group. A good project manager will always know what his team is working on, and where they are in the process.

References

Designers, developers and project managers should be able to provide references for their projects, and you need to speak to them. Here's a list of questions to ask the references:

1. **What was their role and what did they do on your project?**

    Designer, developer, project manager, etc.

2. **Did you enjoy working with them?**

    Yes, they exceeded my expectations.

3. **Did they offer good ideas and suggestions?**

    Yes. They were very helpful but called before they coded.

4. **How were requirements clarified?**

    We had a kickoff meeting and they called or emailed when they were confused.

5. **How were deadlines handled and did they miss any?**

    They always kept me updated and missed deadlines were usually my fault (due to scope creep).

6. **Were they able to work without much guidance from you?**

    Yes, they seemed to know exactly what I wanted.

7. **Would you hire them again or recommend them to a friend?**

    Yes.

Please add your own questions to these lists. They're not intended to be exhaustive; only guidance on some of the important things you'll need to know about your new designer, developer and/or project manager.

Managing Your Team

Depending on the complexity of your idea, the cost of development will vary considerably. However, one thing will guarantee that it costs more than it should, and that's poor management.

I've managed developers on large and small teams throughout my career and I'm painfully familiar with the challenges you'll face. Managing developers is like herding cats. They have a mind of their own and if you're not looking, they'll do whatever they want whether you want them to or not. That's why you MUST monitor them through the entire process.

The worst thing you can do when managing your software developers is to make assumptions. Don't assume they understand the requirements. Don't assume they'll build what you want them to. Don't assume they're working on your project instead of someone else's. Don't assume their estimates for time and effort are accurate. Don't assume they'll meet your deadline. Don't assume all their suggestions are the best decisions for your business. Don't assume they even know what they're talking about. Don't assume anything. Period.

Now, don't get me wrong here. Web developers aren't out to be dishonest or deceitful (at least most of them aren't). They have many competing priorities, they're overly optimistic (or overly pessimistic), and they think they know what's best for you and your business.

The best developers are extremely logical and opinionated, which makes for great software, but poor business acumen. From a business perspective, the most logical course of action may not lead to the most revenue. Developers often don't see the big picture in this way. As the business owner, it's your job to make them understand that you're the boss and they need to follow your direction.

You may be working with a project manager who acts as a liaison between you and the developer(s). The same rules apply to them. Don't make any assumptions and let them know you're the boss. When you're discussing requirements, include the developers in the meeting so they can hear it straight from the horse's mouth. Don't rely on the project manager to convey your requirements accurately.

Documenting all of your requirements and separating them into phases is the best way to ensure everyone understands the features and functionality that need to be built, as well as keep them focused on the highest priority items. Work with the project manager and/or developers to make sure everyone understands and accepts the document. Once they agree to it, get them to sign it. This will protect you and them in the event that the project goes awry.

During the requirements phase, your developers will give you a Level of Effort, or LOE, for various components. The LOE is used to determine how long a feature will take to build, which affects how much it will cost. Software development is not an exact science and different people will take different amounts of time to do the same task. That's why it's best to buy as much functionality out-of-the-box as you can. But if the features you have in mind are truly custom, then you'll need to rely on your developer's abilities to deliver the software in a timely, cost effective manner.

Don't be shy with your developers. If they give you an LOE of three days for a feature, ask them to explain why it will take that long. They might speak in jargon that you don't fully understand, but it will help them think through the process in front of you, which can uncover mistakes.

If they quote three days but it only takes one, you may still pay for three. On the other hand, they may be underestimating (which happens a lot) and the feature may take much longer to build. This will lead to cost overruns and missed deadlines, making overly optimistic estimates just as bad as pessimistic ones.

When you're ready to start development, don't just pitch the requirements document over the wall to the developers and go on your merry way. You need to be actively involved in the management, even if you have a project manager.

Remember, don't make any assumptions. Every developer is different, but in the beginning, you need to treat them like they're all the same until they earn your trust. When I first take over a development team, I give each developer a small set of tasks, maybe one or two days' worth of work at a time. Before they get the next assignment, they have to show me that they've completed the current assignment first.

In your case, you'll want to provide a list of features in the order they should be built, and then tell them to choose one or two days' worth of work at a time. Some features will take longer than a day or two to build, so you'll need to be flexible. The idea is to "small chunk" the development making it easier for you to keep tabs on it and identify problem developers very early in the process.

When the feature(s) are finished, ask for a demonstration of the software they've written allowing you to verify that it's finished AND that it meets the requirements. Over time, you'll figure out which developers can handle more responsibility and less oversight. These developers will deliver their tasks in less time than expected and more accurately. Take this as a green light to give them larger chunks of work, which will reduce your management time. Gradually increase their list of tasks, though. Don't go overboard or you might overwhelm them.

While the star developers will make your life easier, the poor developers will make your life hell. They will consistently miss deadlines or deliver something that doesn't meet the requirements. They'll blame faulty estimates or misunderstood requirements. This can happen to any developer, but if it becomes a pattern, you know you've got a problem. If they're not working out, let them go or request that they be removed from the project team. This is your money. Don't be afraid to tell them what you want.

All the same management rules apply to web designers. When a designer is creating graphics for your site such as the logo and color scheme, ask to see the comps as soon as possible.

> ### Did you know...
>
> Comps, short for "comprehensives," is an industry term used to refer to a graphics proposal. In web design, this will include a mockup of your home page and possibly a couple of other pages, as well as the logo and miscellaneous graphic images throughout the site. Anything that's visual that you've requested for your site should be included in the comps.

Agree to a deadline with the graphic designer and hold them to it. It's ok to ask for status updates along the way, ideally at the half way point and again a day or two before the deadline. This lets the designer know you're serious about the deadline and will keep your project on the top of the stack. The squeaky wheel gets the grease.

This is a lot of information to absorb. You may want to read this section again, especially if management isn't your strong suit or you don't have much management experience. You need to strike a balance between a pushover and a total ogre, which is not easy to accomplish.

If you're too lenient, nothing will get finished; if you're too harsh, you'll alienate your development team. The best way to get your project completed successfully is to create a strongly cohesive team that works together synergistically to achieve the common goal, which is delivering your website on time and on budget.

Software development is the largest challenge you'll face up to this point in the startup process, and for that reason, it's also the most common reason many projects fail to launch. But if you stay focused, keep your project team focused and manage the entire process very closely, you'll greatly increase your chances of success.

> ### Did you know...
>
> Depending on who develops your website, you may not technically "own" it. You might just be leasing it for a monthly or annual fee. If you build your site using a wizard like 1&1 or Web.com, this is to be expected because the site only exists inside their wizard platform. However, if you pay to have a custom website built, you need to own the code.
>
> There's a difference between web hosting, which I discussed in detail above, and leasing a website. Hosting will require a monthly or annual fee, but your website should not. If you lease your website, that means you can't move it to a different web host or hire a new developer to maintain it. You won't have anything to move or maintain because you don't own it. You would have to completely rebuild it from scratch. Read the fine print in your contract and be certain that you own your site and its content.

Testing Your Software

Fact: Developers make terrible testers. Don't rely on your development team to test your software. If you've contracted a company to build your site, they should have dedicated testers on staff to perform quality assurance (QA) testing. These testers specialize in finding bugs and missed or misunderstood requirements. They'll test the software end-to-end to ensure it works to the specified requirements. In this situation, they'll work with the developers to fix errors before you begin your User Acceptance Testing (UAT).

If you don't have dedicated testers working on your project, that responsibility will fall on your shoulders. Recruit your friends and family to the testing team to get additional usability feedback from people who aren't as close to the project as you are.

There are entire books about testing software. Check out one or two of them if you've never done it before. The best way to test your software is to step through the requirements document and validate that each feature works as defined.

While testing, note all bugs, missed requirements, misunderstood requirements, changes, and enhancements you encounter, or conceive. In order to expedite the process of fixing/changing the software, log all pertinent information so the developer knows exactly where to go and what to fix in the software.

Here's a list of information to provide:

- Type of issue – bug, change, enhancement
- Location of issue – web page url, component, screen, etc.
- Original requirement reference, if applicable
- Steps to reproduce the bug – include the data you used and the order of the steps (include ALL steps from start to finish!)
- Description of the issue – include as much detail as possible
- Priority – high, medium, low

The fastest way to put a developer in the insane asylum is to send him an email saying, "The website is broken" or "I can't get feature X to work." Vague issue logs waste valuable developer time and cost you more money. Be as specific as possible so the developer has *no* questions about where to find an issue and what needs to be done to fix it.

When you're setting the priority, everything can't be "high" or the developer won't know what to work on first. Split the issues into relatively equal groups; you can always promote "lows" and "mediums" to "high" once the "highs" have been finished. If the development team doesn't provide issue tracking software, use your own list. This will allow you to keep track of the issues being worked on and where they fall in the queue.

If the development team *does* provide issue tracking software, then use it. Don't try to circumvent the process by sending an email directly to the developer about an issue. The issue will get lost in the shuffle and the developer has other, more important issues to work on that you've already assigned to him. If he drops everything to work on your special request, he could be stepping on another developer's toes, going against direct instructions from his project manager or missing deadlines for other issues he's working on.

Most developers are people pleasers so don't put them in situations where they have to choose between you and their duties. Follow the process defined by the project manager and the development team for reporting issues and your project will flow much more smoothly.

Did you know…

Don't send the final payment until the website passes your UAT. You want to stay on the top of the work queue until the site has been launched and is functioning to your specifications. The quickest way to get bumped to the bottom of the queue is to send the final payment before you're satisfied.

Deployment Time

Once you've thoroughly tested your website and you're satisfied with its functionality for the initial launch, it's time to deploy it into production at your webhosting provider. Your development team is responsible for copying the files and making sure the website loads properly when the domain name is typed into a browser, but you're responsible for the final round of production testing.

After the site is launched and visible on the web, verify that all functionality works, including registration, purchasing, SSL (secure pages), layout, graphics, links, etc. Pretend that you're a typical user and do what they do. Register for a new account. Buy a product and check your merchant account in a couple days for the deposit (use your own credit card for the purchase to test the credit card processing functionality). Go through the entire order fulfillment process to better understand the shipping practices. Post feedback. Submit the Contact Us form. Click links. Etc. Everything needs to work so you don't lose any of your first customers due to technical difficulties.

Since you're so close to the forest, it may be hard for you to see the trees; therefore, ask your friends and family to test the site as well. Offer to reimburse them for their credit card charges, or give them one of your credit cards to use for testing. If possible, have them test the site while you're watching over their shoulders. Resist the urge to help them, and write down any usability issues that may need to be corrected in the next release. Ask for their honest feedback on their experience. If your friends and family have trouble figuring things out, there's a good chance the average web user will, too.

Did you know...

Some new websites add the word "Beta" to their logo so users will know it's a new site and they'll have lower expectations and more patience as a result. This works well for early adopters who don't care and actually may use the site simply because it is new.

However, some users may be reluctant to use the site if they know it was recently launched, preferring to wait until all of the kinks have been ironed out. If you're selling products, you could lose a sizable number of your first customers because of this. Be careful and be certain you understand the impact of telling users you've just launched.

After you finish your final round of production testing, your new website is officially live on the web. Now what? Your job is far from over. In fact, it's really just beginning. The next section discusses everything you'll need to do to help people find your website and start using it. But take a few minutes and appreciate how far you've come. Building and launching a website is no small feat. Give yourself a little pat on the back before you jump into the next phase.

Building Your Website Checklist

Here's a list of things to do during the web development stage:

- ☐ Commit to building a quality website
- ☐ Review the 10 things every website needs: Registrar, Webhost, CMS, Content, Images, Standard Pages, Usability Guidelines, Navigation, Page Layout, and Customer Service
- ☐ Review the 8 optional things your website might need: SSL Certificate, Site Map, Robots.txt, Web 2.0, Mobile Access, Gamification, Website Addition Loop, and Ecommerce
- ☐ Create a detailed and thorough requirements document
- ☐ If DIY, pick a development framework and learn it
- ☐ Decide between local, domestic or offshore staff
- ☐ Start your talent search
- ☐ Prepare for the interviews
- ☐ Hire a graphic designer (or website design team)
- ☐ Hire a web developer (or website development team)
- ☐ Negotiate a fixed price contract if at all possible
- ☐ Manage the project team closely and avoid scope creep
- ☐ Request frequent reviews and demonstrations
- ☐ Write content for your standard legal pages: Terms & Conditions, Privacy Policy & FTC Disclosure
- ☐ Test the website and log bugs or missed requirements
- ☐ Perform final UAT once the website is ready to launch
- ☐ Launch the website into production
- ☐ Perform the final round of production testing
- ☐ Have your friends test the site and provide feedback

Phase 4: Marketing Your Website

Your website is finally built and you can see it on the web. Congratulations! Pat yourself on the back and do something special to celebrate your new website!

But it's no time to rest on your laurels. Just because you've launched a cool new website, that doesn't mean people will use it. If you build it, they won't come unless they know about it. It's time to transition from building your website to sales and marketing.

Before I get into the gritty details of all the marketing options you have for attracting traffic to your new website, you first need to understand how much you can afford to pay for a new customer.

Did you know…

The term "traffic" is often used to describe the volume of users that visit a website. Sometimes you'll hear online marketers and SEO professionals talk about "driving traffic" to your site. They're referring to their efforts to market your site so people know about it. I prefer to call this process "attracting traffic" because if you create a good website, post good content, offer a good service, and market it well enough, users will be drawn to it on their own and you won't have to "drive" them there.

Cost-Per-Acquisition (CPA)

It costs money to get new customers, in one way or another. Whether you're paying for advertising or giving affiliate commissions or paying sales staff, every customer has some cost associated with getting them to your website to make a purchase. The question you need to ask yourself is, "how much can I afford to pay for a new customer and still make a profit?" Calculating your cost-per-acquisition will help you find the answer to this very important question.

An example is the easiest way to explain this concept. Let's say you sell jeans on an ecommerce website and your average sale is $30. Since you're most likely buying wholesale and marking up the price, your cost of goods will be in the neighborhood of $15. That means you have $15 to spend on all your other expenses, such as website hosting, office space, phones, salaries, and also marketing. If you spend all of the $15 on marketing, you won't have anything left for your other expenses.

As a good rule of thumb, you should expect to spend one third to one half of your $15 on marketing and sales, meaning you can afford to pay somewhere between $5 and $8 to get a new customer in this scenario.

If you're paying $1 per click for an ad placed on the top of, or to the right of, Google's search results, and it takes 5 to 8 clicks on an ad to get an acquisition, you've got a winning marketing strategy…you'll be spending between $5 and $8 to get a new customer. However, if your cost-per-click (CPC, defined below) is $2 and it takes 20 clicks to get a sale, you'll be paying $40 for a new customer, which is more than your entire sale! That obviously won't work!

> **Did you know…**
>
> Cost-per-Acquisition goes by many names. You may also hear it referred to as Cost-per-Action and Cost-per-Conversion. They all mean the same thing: someone clicked a link to get to your website and then did what you wanted them to on your website. That could mean they bought something, registered to be a member or signed up for your newsletter. How you define an acquisition is up to you.

To make this mind-numbing math easier, I created a Cost-per-Acquisition Calculator shown in Figure 6 to help determine the maximum CPA and the maximum CPC benchmarks. Do a quick read-through so you're familiar with the terminology, and then I'll explain each line in detail afterward.

This example is specifically for pay-per-click advertising, but you can apply the same logic to all forms of marketing, as long as you have access to the cost and acquisition data.

> **Did you know…**
>
> A major component in reducing your CPA is to increase your conversion rate, or the percentage of people who take action when they visit your website. One effective way to increase your conversion rate is to use a "squeeze page." This is a type of page that has no exit except to take action by providing an email or making a purchase. In other words, it has no links to other pages. There's an art to writing squeeze pages and you can find great templates by searching for "squeeze page examples" on your favorite search engine.

Cost-per-Acquisition Calculator

$	30.00	Average Sale amount or new customer gross value
$	15.00	Cost of Goods
$	15.00	Remaining Revenue for other expenses (Average Sale – Cost of Goods)
	50%	Marketing Budget of Remaining Revenue
$	7.50	**Maximum Cost-per-Acquisition**: the maximum amount you can pay for a new customer (Remaining Revenue x Marketing Budget Percentage)
	2,000	Ad Views: number of times your ad is shown to potential customers
	2%	Click-Through-Rate: % of times your ad is clicked or a customer shows interest
	40	Number of Clicks (Ad Views x Click-Through-Rate)
	6%	Acquisition Rate: percentage of time a purchase is made from a click or contact
	2.4	Number of Acquisition (sales) per the number of clicks (Number of Clicks x Acquisition Rate)
$	72.00	Revenue from Acquisitions (Average Sale x Number of Acquisitions)
$	18.00	Total Cost of Acquisitions (Number of Acquisitions x Cost-per-Acquisition)
$	0.45	**Maximum Cost-per-Click:** the most you can pay for a click or contact based on the assumptions (Cost of Acquisitions / Number of Clicks)
	556	Number of clicks required to generate $1000 in revenue ($1000 x Number of Clicks / Revenue from Acquisitions)
$	250.00	Cost of clicks to generate $1000 in revenue (Number of Clicks to Make $1000 x Cost per Click)

Figure 6

The calculator is based on several assumptions that can be tweaked, however, both the Click-Through-Rate and the Acquisition Rate assumptions are typical, especially for a new website. Over time, as you tweak your ads, you'll increase both of these values, which means you'll be able to pay more per click. But I'm getting ahead of myself. Let's break this down line-by-line first.

1. **Average Sale Amount** – this is the amount of money your typical customer spends on your site.
2. **Cost of Goods** – this is the cost of buying or creating the things you're selling. This is easy to calculate if you're selling products. It's your purchase price from the supplier or the cost of materials if you're making them yourself.
3. **Remaining Revenue for Other Expenses** – this is the amount left over from the sale, after the cost of goods is subtracted out ($30 - $15).
4. **Marketing Budget of Remaining Revenue** – you choose this value. It's the percentage of remaining revenue you want to spend on marketing.
5. **Maximum Cost-per-Acquisition (CPA)** – this is your answer to the question, "how much can I afford to pay for a new customer?" It's calculated by multiplying the Remaining Revenue times your Marketing Budget percentage ($15 x 50%). If you spend more than this amount to make a $30 sale, you either need to increase your marketing budget percentage or you need to decrease the amount you're spending to attract customers.
6. **Ad Views** – this is the number of times your ad is shown. For example, in Google, Bing or Facebook ad listings, your ad would be shown 2,000 times (not necessarily to 2,000 different people) in response to a search or page view. Most ad sites provide Ad View stats. You can use the actual values once you have data. Until then, you can make an assumption.
7. **Click-Through-Rate (CTR)** - this is the percentage of time that your ad is clicked when it's viewed. 2% is a typical CTR.
8. **Number of Clicks** – if your ad is viewed 2,000 times and you have a 2% CTR, that means you'll receive 40 clicks (2,000 x 2%).
9. **Acquisition Rate** – this is another assumption that's typical

of what you should expect to see. At QuoteCatcher, our Acquisition Rate ranged from 2% to 12%, depending on several factors including the relevancy of the ad and the quality of the landing page.

10. **Number of Acquisitions (Sales)** – this is the actual number of sales you receive from your 2,000 Ad Views and your 40 Clicks. It's the Number of Clicks times the Acquisition Rate (40 x 6%).
11. **Revenue from Acquisitions** – this is the total amount of revenue generated from your sales. It's the Average Sale Amount times the Number of Acquisitions ($30 x 2.4).
12. **Total Cost of Acquisitions** – this is the total amount you spent to generate the Revenue from Acquisitions in number 11. It's the Number of Acquisitions times the CPA (2.4 x $7.50).
13. **Maximum Cost-per-Click (CPC)** – this is the most you can afford to pay for a click (assuming all of your assumptions are correct) if you want to stay under your CPA benchmark. It's calculated by dividing the Total Cost of Acquisitions by the Number of Clicks ($18 / 40).
14. **Number of Clicks Required to Generate $1,000** – this is just what it says. Based on your assumptions, for every $1,000 in revenue, this is the number of clicks you'll need. It's calculated using Algebra to solve for "x" (Mr. Koenig, my high school Algebra teacher, would be so proud!). Multiply $1,000 times the Number of Clicks and divide it by the Revenue from Acquisitions ($1,000 x 40 / $72).
15. **Cost of Clicks to Generate $1,000** – this is your marketing budget for every $1,000 in revenue. It's calculated by multiplying the Number of Clicks to Generate $1,000 times the CPC (556 x $.45).

If math isn't your thing, this might seem complicated, but you'll need to understand it if you're going to control your marketing expenses and generate a profit. One of the biggest mistakes new online companies make is not understanding how much they can afford to pay for a new customer, and therefore, they overpay for clicks.

You may be wondering how to figure out what your average customer value is, especially if you just launched your site and don't have any sales yet. You have a few options. First, you can do some research to figure out what the average sale or customer value is for similar websites, but this won't be easy to find since most companies closely guard their financial data.

Second, you can use the average sale price of everything you're selling, taking into account how many you expect to sell per visit to estimate the average sale amount. For example, if you're selling jeans that range in price from $20 to $100 and you expect people to purchase one pair per visit, you can average your sale to $60.

Finally, you can SWAG it (make a scientific wild ass guess). Until you have sales and history, you won't know your average customer value exactly. Be conservative and choose a value that will be good enough for now.

Did you know…

Over time, you may figure out that a certain percentage of your customers are repeat customers. Include the follow-on sales in the value of a new customer when calculating your CPA. For example, if 10% of your customers come back and spend another $30, this means your real value for a new customer is closer to $33 instead of $30 ($30 x 10% + $30).

The last three rows of the model will help you figure out how many clicks you'll need to hit your revenue goals. If you want to make $10,000 per month in revenue (total sales), you'll need at least 5,556 clicks (Number of Clicks to Generate $1,000 in Revenue x 10). This will help you determine your monthly and daily PPC budgets. But keep in mind that a low daily budget will likely result in your ads never, or seldom being shown. In the Cost-per-Acquisition Calculator example, the daily budget would only be $8 ($250 monthly budget / 30 days). A budget this low won't do very well on the major pay-per-click (PPC, defined below) channels like Google. Setting a budget that is both profitable and large enough to be shown is a delicate balancing act that you'll figure out with experience.

I have another piece of bad news for you. If you determine that 45 cents is the most you can pay for a click, Google isn't going to work for you unless you're targeting very low competition keywords with your ads. Most clicks go for well over $1 these days and if your bid isn't high enough, your ad will never be shown. I'll talk about this a lot more in the PPC advertising section below.

You may also decide that in the beginning, you're willing to take a loss in order to drive traffic. In other words, you'll pay more for new customers than they're worth. This is what many funded companies do, mainly because they can afford it and they're willing to gamble losses today for increased profits down the road. If your budget is tight, avoid this approach because you can easily run out of money long before the benefits are realized.

The explanations for the model above were for PPC traffic, but you can use the same calculations for any type of sales or marketing activities. Instead of clicks, you may substitute number of contacts. Conversions mean the same thing regardless of how they're accomplished and the customer value shouldn't change.

This model is crucial if you want to manage your sales and marketing costs effectively. Marketing is one of your largest expenses. Without proper management and understanding, you run the risk of it eating up all of your profits. You can't survive without sales and marketing, but you also can't survive if you spend too much to get customers leaving nothing for your salary and all your other expenses.

You have several options for sales and marketing, both online and offline. Even though your business may be 100% online, that doesn't mean you can't promote it out here in the real world if it makes sense. In the next few sections, I'm going to discuss several methods for promoting your business on and off the web.

Pay-Per-Click Advertising (PPC)

This might be the first thing that comes to mind for marketing a website. Since your site hasn't been around long, you won't have great organic positioning in search engines, making PPC a good way to get your business noticed early on. Unfortunately, though, the rules have changed quite a bit in the past few years, making it equally difficult to get your ads shown, especially on the big search engines like Google, Yahoo! and Bing. Let's look at an example to help explain why.

Let's say your website generates sales leads for auto insurance. Several years ago, you could set your bid amount and reliably choose your position in the list of ads, let's say number 3 in the list. Your ad would be shown every time a keyword that you bid on was searched, and close to that magic number 3 position, until your daily budget ran out.

However, now Google chooses when and where to display your ad based on several factors, such as click-through-rate, bid amount, daily budget, landing page ranking, etc. What does this mean for your new business that generates auto insurance leads?

First, because your site is new, you won't have any page ranking, especially compared to large insurance companies. That's your first "ding."

Second, you don't have a large budget for *high bids* or *large daily budgets* to compete with Geico, Progressive, All State and others who have deep pockets and can price you out of the competition. Ding numbers two and three.

Third, let's assume you've done your research and figured out exactly who your target market is and you've crafted a very specific ad that will only get clicked by your ideal customers. This approach used to be very effective at both minimizing your cost and maximizing the value to potential customers; however, since this leads to a low click-through-rate, you'll get penalized because the search engines don't make as much money (fewer clicks = less revenue), even though your conversion rate may be high. Ding number four.

If you have several "dings" for your website and/or ad, your ad will be shown less (perhaps not even enough to meet your daily budget); it will be shown at off times when people are less likely to be in buying mode (such as the middle of the night or on weekends); and it will be shown way down the list and often not on the first page.

The PPC deck has been stacked against you in favor of big business because the big guys can pay the search engines a lot more money than you can. It's not fair and it's contrary to the small business nature of our country's past, but stock holders don't care about ideologies; they want profits and they don't care who they step on to get them. But even though the system is flawed, it doesn't mean you can't still benefit from it.

Facebook also offers PPC ads that can be targeted to very specific demographics. Since Facebook knows gender, age, location, relationship status, interests (from pages that users follow), etc., ads can be targeted to very specific users. This means that if you want to sell designer cat accessories to single women over 35 who live in the greater Los Angeles metro area, you can use Facebook ads to do it.

It's my experience that Facebook ads cost much less than search engine ads, but I've also found the click-through-rate is much lower, which makes sense. When people go to a search engine to search for "designer cat accessories," they're in the market to buy them. However, if a cat lover goes to Facebook to see what her friends are doing, she's not in buying mode; she's in social mode. She may see the ad for cat accessories, but she might not be in the mood to click it now. Or she may be engrossed in what her friends are up to and she might not even notice the ad at all.

PPC on Facebook and other social networks is worth trying as part of your marketing strategy. It may work very well for you, but you may find, as I did, that it doesn't lead to new customers.

Place a couple ads on each of the major search engines (Google,

Bing and Yahoo!) and Facebook to see which one works the best. You can then focus your efforts on the one that generates the most value. Only time and testing will tell.

> ## Did you know...
>
> There's a very good book titled "The Ultimate Guide to Google AdWords" by Perry Marshal and Bryan Todd that covers several ways to improve ad performance and conversion rates through keyword selection, campaign design, A/B ad testing, and landing page relevancy.
>
> In addition, many of their suggestions can be applied to other advertising channels and even SEO landing pages. Whether you're managing your own ad campaigns or working with someone who does it for you, reading Marshal's and Todd's book will help you maximize the effectiveness of your PPC ad dollars.

There is also more than one way to skin the proverbial cat when it comes to PPC. Google gets the most traffic and generally higher quality traffic, but other search engines and websites can also generate traffic to your site with fewer hoops to jump through and more control over ad placement.

You can pay to place ads in directories, eNewsletters or directly on relevant websites that target your ideal customers. Since you'll have to research and find them yourself, it's not as easy as paying for clicks on a search engine, but it can be more effective and will give you more control over when and where your ad is shown.

Until your website has been around for a while and gets some SEO ranking and inbound links from other sites, PPC will be your main online means of driving traffic to your site. Don't underestimate your budget for this expense. You can expect to pay several hundred to several thousand dollars per month to get a reasonable volume of traffic. And you also need to keep a close eye on the CPA to make sure it works with your business model.

In the end, you may decide that PPC is just too costly or not effective for your website. If that happens, you're going to need other options.

Affiliate Marketing

Depending on what you're selling, affiliate marketing might be your best choice because you only pay the affiliate if you get a sale. With this type of marketing, other website owners place ads, articles and/or reviews for your website on their website or in their newsletters. If someone sees the information, clicks over to your site, and buys something, you pay the affiliate a portion of the sale or a flat fee, depending on the arrangement.

The nice thing about affiliate marketing is that you can choose the amount you'll pay the affiliate for a sale. Some affiliates will like the payout you offer, others won't, and the quality of your placement and volume of your clicks will depend on what you decide to pay them.

You can negotiate different payouts for different affiliates. Always start out as low as possible and gradually increase it if you're not getting any affiliates to sign up or if you're not getting the right type or quality of affiliates you want. Just like with everything else in life, you get what you pay for.

The typical payout ranges from 10% to as high as 100% of the sale price. Obviously, your Maximum Cost-per-Acquisition will determine how much you can afford to offer. If you're selling products that cost half of what you're selling them for, you can't possibly give away 70% of the sale price or you'll be losing money!

However, if you're selling an eBook that took time to write but has no inventory cost, you could easily give away 70% to the affiliate. After all, pocketing 30% of the sale price is better than 0% by not getting a sale.

> ### Did you know…
>
> Some people offer 100% of the sale price to the affiliate! How can they do that?! Are they crazy?! Nope. Not at all. Crazy like a fox, maybe. The reason they offer a 100% commission is because they know the real value of their customer comes from follow-on sales. Their goal is to get the customer's contact information allowing them to sell additional things to them later that cost more money. This only works if you're selling something with very little cost to you…eBooks, for example. You can't afford to give away 100% of the sale to an affiliate if you're selling a product like jeans or jewelry.

If you decide affiliate marketing is the way to go, you have several options for doing it. First, you can contact owners of websites where you want to place your links and ask them directly if they would like to be an affiliate.

The ideal affiliate website has good quality content that's relevant or complimentary to your business. Auto websites like Cars.com and AutoTrader.com do a lot of affiliate marketing. Most of the ads and some of the content are about topics such as insurance, financing, repair, maintenance, tires, etc. That's because the auto website target market is the same as these complimentary types of businesses.

If the affiliate website has a good SEO page ranking, it's even better because the inbound link they place on their website that points to your website will help your website's page ranking (as long as it's not a tracking URL).

> **Did you know...**
>
> A tracking URL is a special kind of link that some search engines and affiliates use to track clicks and conversions. Unfortunately, some tracking URLs don't contain your website's domain name, which means you lose the SEO benefit of having an inbound link pointing to your website.

Your second affiliate marketing option is to post your offer on websites such as CommissionJunction.com, ClickBank.com, SkimLinks.com, PayDotCom.com, or others. Some services specialize in certain types of product offerings so pay attention to that when you're choosing a provider.

For example, ClickBank focuses on digital products such as eBooks, music, reports, etc. that can be digitally downloaded. However, with CommissionJunction, you can list just about anything from physical products to sales leads. PayDotCom has even fewer restrictions.

A third option for affiliate marketing is to hire an affiliate marketing firm to setup and maintain your program. This can be an expensive option and you'll need a healthy budget for it. Don't forget to calculate those costs into your marketing budget and CPA analysis.

Finally, if your business relies on sales leads instead of products, you can contact website owners and ask to buy their excess or unwanted leads. At QuoteCatcher, we had over a dozen affiliates who sent leads to us. One in particular was a husband and wife duo who built websites. Their website was listed as the top search result on Google for several "website design" related terms. Since it was just the two of them, they couldn't possibly handle the volume of leads they got from their "request a quote" form so they cherry picked the few they wanted and we bought the rest to sell to other web design firms.

This arrangement worked great for both of us. We increased our inventory of leads that we could sell to our vendors with a fixed and predictable cost, and they gained an extra household salary without the extra mouth to feed (websites don't eat very much). Affiliate marketing is always a win-win if the payout structure is designed correctly.

If you're planning to do affiliate marketing with your website, take this into account during development. Most development frameworks come with some sort of affiliate marketing functionality out of the box, but if your solution doesn't, your options range from very easy to very hard.

If you're using a service such as CommissionJunction or ClickBank, all you'll need to do is put a couple code snippets on your site, usually on the thank you or confirmation page and sometimes on the landing page or in the site's header file. These services are easy to setup and they provide detailed instructions for where the code needs to be placed.

If you're going the homegrown route by signing up and managing affiliates yourself, you need a more robust solution. You have two options for this: You can buy an off-the-shelf solution and plug it into your website, or you can build it yourself. For QuoteCatcher, I built the software we used to manage affiliates, mainly because I could, and we didn't have the budget to buy an off-the-shelf solution in the early stages.

The nice thing about buying a solution is that it will probably contain everything you need (and some things you don't know you need). They come with affiliate registration and management, tracking and reporting, automatic payments, etc. Building it yourself will cost far more (unless you're a developer and you can build it yourself) and come with far fewer features than buying it.

As for choosing a solution, do your research. Check to see if it does everything you want it to do for a reasonable price (or at least a competitive price), and read reviews from people who already use it. It won't be easy to swap this system out once you're in full swing so you want to make the right decision the first time.

Affiliate marketing is the Holy Grail for some advertisers. If you have a product or service that sells well and you can afford to pay a sizable percentage of the sale price to the affiliate, you may not need PPC advertising at all.

Social Media Marketing

Social media marketing is used to describe a variety of different things. Although it has largely been associated with Facebook and Twitter, other websites such as MySpace, Reddit, Pinterest, StumbleUpon, LinkedIn, Yelp, Del.icio.us, HubPages, Squidoo, and many others also fit into this category. Any type of Web 2.0 site that allows you to share information about yourself (or your business) is considered a social media marketing channel.

If you're a member of Facebook, chances are you've "liked" or "followed" a profile or fan page for a celebrity or business. For instance, I'm a big fan of Robert Kiyosaki and the "Rich Dad Poor Dad" series, and I follow him on Facebook at www.facebook.com/RobertKiyosaki. He (or one of his assistants) regularly posts news, product offerings, information and inspirational messages to his wall and they appear on my Facebook live feed.

He uses this tool to create a community of like-minded people who are interested in the topic of money and financial freedom, and by no accident, they're also his target customer. By using Facebook to broadcast his messages, he creates the feeling of a personal relationship with his followers, which strengthens his customer loyalty and also attracts new customers when his followers "share" something he posts with all of their friends. Do you know what all this community and communication leads too? You got it: more sales of his books, games and training seminars. This is the value of social media marketing.

Twitter has become a very popular outlet for celebrities, social and political movements, and businesses. You can use it to post updates about your business or industry, or anything that might be interesting to your followers. You can also post sales and coupons, but you'll want to balance these posts with informational posts to create a perception that you actually care about your followers and aren't solely concerned with selling them something.

Twitter users created a special syntax to overcome the 140 character limit on their posts. It's important to use this syntax in your posts for a couple of reasons. First, it shows you're a true member of the Twitter community because you follow the "rules" the community has created. Second, the syntax allows people to setup searches that will return your posts in search results.

For example, let's say you sell skin care products on your site and you're offering a coupon for a well-known brand. You can post a tweet using the following syntax:

```
Save money on all your #skincare products at
MyDomain.com! #Olay #coupon
```

Many people have standard searches setup using tools like HootSuite or Tweetcaster to filter out posts that interest them. If a potential customer has a filter for #olay #coupon or #skincare, your tweet will appear in their live feed. Some people use this feature religiously to keep up on current events, information and sale opportunities.

For a list of all the Twitter syntax options, visit their Help page at support.twitter.com. Click on "Twitter Basics" and scroll down to the "Tweets and Messages" section.

LinkedIn is a professional network that's primarily used to maintain business networking contacts. However, it has recently been reinventing itself as much more than that. If you have a recruiting website or anything targeting business customers, LinkedIn is a great place for you to spend your time and marketing dollars.

Yelp is a consumer review website that has elements of a social network. It's similar to Amazon's product review feature, only it's for both online and real-world businesses. You can claim ownership of your business' page and post coupons, message customers and maintain your profile. At a minimum, keep an eye on Yelp for mentions of your business and quickly respond if someone posts a negative review.

Foursquare is a check-in service that's also very social. If your business is selling yourself (e.g. Information Marketer, Real Estate Agent, etc.), this is a great way to stay "top of mind" with your followers. By "checking in" at the various locations you visit as part of your business, your followers will see how active you are and know what interesting things you're doing. You can also connect your Foursquare account to your Facebook profile making your check-ins appear in your live feed, as well.

Pinterest, Reddit, StumbleUpon, Del.icio.us, Squidoo and HubPages are all sites that allow you to post links, information and articles that are relevant to your target audience. They each have a little different twist and some will work better for you than others.

You can create value by posting useful and relevant information for your target audience on social media websites. This value will naturally attract "followers" to your social media outlets; however, you can hurry the process along by advertising for followers directly on the social media sites using the PPC model described previously, and you can also manually mine for followers.

Mining for followers means that you manually search for people with similar interests and invite them to follow you. On Twitter and other sites, the act of following someone sends a notification and allows that person or business to follow you back. Most people have an "auto-follow" setting configured so they don't actually "see" your follow notice, but you gain a follower nonetheless. And the more followers you have, the more likely you are to be found by other people with similar interests.

> **Did you know…**
>
> Some software tools like TweetAdder and Tweepwise allow you to find and follow people and businesses automatically. These tools allow you to maximize the number of follow requests, but they lack the personal touch that comes with manually finding

> and following. You may end up following something you don't want associated with your business. It's also hard to target your niche market accurately with automated tools.

Social media is the latest craze in marketing and it can be very powerful, but it also comes with its share of problems. The biggest issue is that anyone can post anything about your business for the whole world to see. If you create an account on any of the social networking sites listed above, you're opening yourself up to potentially negative reviews. However, even if you don't create an account on these sites, negative reviews can still be posted about your business elsewhere in the social media world.

From a consumer perspective, online reviews are a good thing. It's a great incentive for businesses to up the ante on customer service and product pricing. It's also good for your business because you'll either provide good products and good services, or you'll suffer the wrath of disgruntled customers and you won't be in business very long.

It's the double edged sword of social media. You can attract lots of new customers with timely and relevant information, or you can lose lots of customers with one or two unkindly reviews. Whether you embrace it or avoid it, it's the new reality businesses must face, and time needs to be allotted for managing it.

Another problem with social media marketing is knowing what to post and finding the time to post things regularly. Just like a blog, there's only one thing worse than *no* social media presence, and that's a *dead* social media presence.

If you decide to go the social media route and create accounts on one or more social networks, you need to understand the level of effort you're committing to. Start off slowly with one social media site and grow your presence over time once you clearly define your strategy and determine what works.

If you create a fan page on Facebook, you need to post to it at least one or two times per week, every week, or your presence will appear dead. If a potential customer finds your page and nothing has been posted for two months, they may assume you're not in business anymore and go somewhere else.

The key to maintaining a successful social media presence is to post interesting and relevant updates frequently and consistently. Limit the number of "sales" oriented posts to prevent them from drowning out the informational ones.

Remember, managing a social media presence takes time and money, and both should be calculated into your cost of marketing. You need to understand your true costs of social media management to determine if it's time and money well spent for your business.

Setting Up Social Media Accounts

If you decide social media is right for your business, here's how to setup a few of the most popular ones.

Facebook

To create a Facebook Fan Page, go to: www.facebook.com/pages/. The process for setting up a page is simple, and Facebook does a good job of walking you through it. Choose a name for your page that either matches your business name exactly (if it's available) or one that's similar.

Did you know...

Facebook now allows "subscribers" to your personal profile and you can filter the posts that they see. However, there's currently a 1,000 subscriber maximum while a fan page has no max. Also, some of your friends might not want to see your professional posts. Therefore, you're better off using a fan page than your personal page for business marketing purposes.

After your account is created, upload relevant images for your profile and cover photos, and post a few updates to your live feed (refer to the next section for ideas about what to post). Then, search for other fan pages that have your same target audience and follow them. Make sure you're "using" Facebook as the page you just created by clicking the down-arrow in the upper right corner and selecting your new page from the "Use Facebook as" list.

Finally, the more followers you have, the easier it is to get more followers. Ask all your friends to "like" your new page to get the ball rolling. In fact, ask everyone you know and people you meet to follow your fan page. Put "like" boxes on your website and put the link to your fan page on your business cards and marketing materials.

Did you know…

You can pay for followers on sites like Fiverr, but DON'T DO IT! I created a fan page and bought a Fiverr gig to get followers as an experiment to see how it worked. What I got was 600 followers within 24 hours, exactly as advertised. However, as far as I could tell, every single "follower" was a fake account that looked somewhat real, but wasn't.

Facebook knows people are doing this and they're taking steps to disable the fake accounts. If your page has a substantial number of fake accounts as followers, there's a chance your page will be disabled as well. You can pay people to find *real* followers for you, but it will cost more than $5.

Twitter

To setup a Twitter account, visit Twitter.com and complete the signup boxes on the home page. The setup process is very easy on Twitter. It should only take a few minutes to get your basic profile up and running. At a minimum, upload a profile picture. You can customize your profile over time and possibly hire a professional graphic designer to help if your budget allows.

Once you have your twitter account created, submit your first few posts on relevant topics using the appropriate Twitter syntax described earlier. "Retweeting" is also a great way to share useful information you read, as well as create an index for your own use. After you've posted a few things, start searching for other people and businesses to follow. Just as with Facebook, seek out accounts that have your same target audience.

Your final step is to setup a Twitter search filter using a tool like TweetDeck allowing you to keep tabs on posts that mention your business or Twitter account. You can also monitor posts that are related to your field, and then follow whoever posted it. This is a great way to build your "follow*ing*" list, as well as your "follow*ers*" list.

LinkedIn

To setup an account on LinkedIn, visit LinkedIn.com and complete the signup boxes on the home page. You can spend hours creating your LinkedIn profile, but it only takes a few minutes to get the basic information entered. The more you include in your profile, the better. This is a professional website so don't include a lot of personal information.

LinkedIn has been adding lots of new and very interesting features over the past year. They've provided the ability to submit "recommendations" for quite some time, but they recently launched a new "endorsements" feature that I like. If you're promoting yourself, this is a great way to advertise your abilities.

If you're promoting a company, create a "Company" page by going to www.LinkedIn.com/companies and clicking the "Add a Company" link near the upper right corner. Follow the prompts to create your page and then post some updates. After your page is created, invite people to follow it and follow other people and businesses with similar target audiences.

Those are the big three social media outlets. Don't feel like you need to do all of them, though. Doing one very well is better than being mediocre on three or more. Pick the one(s) you like the best and that your target audience uses the most. Once you've mastered that and automated the process of posting as much as possible, then consider adding another.

Social Media Posting Ideas

The social media experts disagree on how often to post updates. Some say you should post at least once per week while others say you should post hourly. Personally, if someone posts hourly, I hide or un-follow them unless it's really interesting. Being un-followed is not good so be careful not to spam your feeds with useless posts. I think a good rule of thumb is to post once or twice a day, if you have something good to share.

Thinking of interesting things to post every day is easier than you might think . You can post all sorts of things as long as it's relevant to your target audience.

Here's a list of several types of information that make good posts:

1. Sharing articles, videos and images
2. Links to your blog posts
3. Motivational quotes
4. Lessons learned
5. Upcoming events (e.g. Teaching a seminar at XYZ.)
6. Recent experiences (e.g. Attended a book signing.)
7. Ask questions (e.g. What do you think about…?)
8. Promotional messages (e.g. Checkout my new book.)

Notice I listed promotional messages last. It's number 7 out of 7. That's not by accident. Some of my favorite social media fan pages never post promotional messages and some only post them occasionally. The ones that post all of the time get hidden by me and by everyone else. Use promotional messages sparingly…once per week or a couple times per month. The vast majority of your social media posts should be informational, educational, interesting, and most important of all, relevant to your target audience.

Responding to Negative Comments

Most of your customers are connected to the Web, and some are connected most of the time. That means they can post comments and feedback about your business from virtually anywhere.

If someone cares enough to provide feedback about an experience, it's usually because it was either really good or really bad. If you provide a bad service, you deserve to be called out, but just because someone posts a bad review doesn't mean you provided a bad service.

On the morning of July 4th, 2011, I went to a restaurant for breakfast with two friends. The place was almost empty and we were quietly talking when one of the customers became irate and began yelling at the waitresses. Personally, I thought the food and service were satisfactory; I had no complaints. But this customer, for whatever reason, was very dissatisfied and I doubt it had anything to do with the food or service. The incident escalated and I became a witness to an assault and had to write a police report documenting what I saw. I didn't see anything to justify his outrage. He was in a bad mood for some other reason and transferred his anger onto the business and its employees. If that man decided to go to Yelp and submit a review of his experience at that restaurant, I doubt it would be favorable and I know it would be unjustified. That bad review could have a seriously negative impact on their business, and they did nothing wrong.

At QuoteCatcher, we had a few unhappy clients over the years. Some clients had a hard time closing the leads we sent them, but it wasn't due to the quality of the leads, as they insisted. We know it wasn't the lead quality because when we received consistent complaints from a vendor, we called the other vendors who received the same lead (we sold each one to up to five vendors) and oftentimes, one of them closed the sale. The leads were fine in most cases, but the unhappy vendor just couldn't sell very well. They transferred their inability to sell onto our business and blamed the quality of our leads for their poor salesmanship. Did we deserve a bad review published online for everyone to see? I don't think we did. We did our best to ensure lead quality, but that didn't stop people from taking out their frustrations online, whether warranted or not.

Unfortunately, this will happen to you. A customer will be dissatisfied, and it may or may not be your fault. You won't have any control over their complaint, but you will have control over how you respond to it.

If you receive a complaint over the phone or email, be very thankful because you can handle it outside the public eye. I encourage you to do what you can to make them happy, even if they're a problem customer. You may eventually have to fire them as a client if they cost more in time and money than they generate in revenue, but you still want to part ways on good terms. Bend over backwards to turn their negative experience into a positive one.

Did you know...

At QuoteCatcher, we had to fire more than one client over the years. Clients that constantly complain and ask for refunds cost a lot of time and money. If they cost more than they're worth over time, you need to fire them.

When I told one of our clients "I don't think our service is working for you. I think it's time to part ways." his tone immediately changed and he talked me out of firing him that day. He eventually became one of our better clients. Sometimes the threat of being fired is enough to change the relationship.

If the complaint is posted online via a social networking site, such as your Facebook fan page or your Yelp profile, you'll be handling your unhappy customer in public. That means you'll need to be very careful about what you say and how you say it since everyone will see the interaction.

When bad reviews are posted online, the two worst things you can do are a) not respond and b) respond defensively. No response means you either aren't paying attention to your customers on the channels that they use, or you just don't care enough about them to respond. Obviously, neither is acceptable.

Responding defensively means you're allowing them to suck you into their rant. If that happens, you actually becoming a part of the bad review. Instead of defusing the situation, you're throwing fuel on the fire. You'll look very unprofessional and the complainer will be very happy by making you look like an idiot online for everyone to see.

To quote my mom, you need to be "sweet as pie" in your response to a negative review. Apologize profusely and tell them you'd love the opportunity to correct the mistake and earn back their business. Provide your direct phone number and ask them to call you to discuss their complaint.

Since their complaint was public, the resolution also needs to be public so other customers can see how you do business and that you honestly care about customer satisfaction. In addition, if you're being sweet as pie and the complainer continues to berate you and your business, they will lose all credibility and their negative post will carry little or no weight when other customers are reading it. They'll dismiss the reviewer as someone with an axe to grind or personal issues or mental instability. Regardless, you'll be off the hook and the negative review won't have a negative impact on your business.

Did you know…

You can offer negative reviewers a gift certificate or discount on a future purchase over the phone to make up for their bad experience (or bad attitude); however, don't offer one through the social media outlet or you may end up with a horde of complaints just to get the freebies.

The best way to deal with an angry customer (in most cases) is to be overly nice to them. Most people find it hard to be mean to someone who's being overly nice and their tone will usually soften over the course of the interaction. However, if you ignore them or you're aggressive in any way, the conflict will escalate and you'll lose that customer forever and potentially every other customer who reads the feedback thread, or who hears the story from the reviewer. Your goal isn't to win an argument; it's to win a customer. Do what you can to make them happy, or at least let everyone else know you did the best you could.

Email & eNewsletters

Email advertising may seem like a great way to market to new clients. All you need to do is buy a list, draft an email, and press the send button. But just like all other forms of advertising, it comes with drawbacks. You also need to clearly track and understand your CPA.

The best way to use email marketing, including eNewsletters, is to use your own client list. Buying a list of emails may seem like a faster way to grow your distribution list, but size is not the most important factor.

The most important aspect of any email list is the quality of the contacts. If you buy an email list from a provider such as InfoUSA or SalesGenie, you're buying a list of people who have checked promotional boxes on registration forms or completed surveys online. They may or may not be your true target market, but more importantly, they are also inundated with similar emails from everyone who has purchased their email address, and there's no way they can actually read all of them. And worse, they may not know where your email ad or newsletter came from, and report it as spam! Purchased email lists are low quality, cold contacts. In my opinion, they have very little real value.

Your own client database, which includes people who have purchased from you, as well as people who have registered directly on your site to receive correspondence, is a whole different story. These are hot contacts that already know and like you. Most will want to hear from you periodically, and those that don't can opt out of receiving your promotional emails.

Best of all, by sending promotional emails and eNewsletters to this list, you're staying top-of-mind making you the more likely choice when they need to purchase more of the products you sell.

Email marketing to your own list is by far the most effective use of this advertising channel. You won't need to pay for a list, but you'll still want to sign up for a service such as GetResponse, ConstantContact, MailChimp or AWeber to manage your email campaigns.

In the beginning, when you only have a handful of emails in your list, you may be able to manage it yourself and send emails using your personal email program. Just remember to put all the emails in the BCC (blind copy) field or send them to each individual separately. You don't want to provide your client list to everyone who receives the email by making the whole list visible in the "To" line.

Once your list grows to 50 or more, get a more robust service to help you manage all the intricacies of sending large numbers of emails.

The first benefit of using a service like GetResponse or MailChimp is that their servers are configured to send large numbers of emails efficiently. If you try to send an email to 1,000 recipients using most standard email applications, it may take a long time and there may also be limits to the number of emails you can send.

The second benefit of using an email service is that they know how to avoid spam filters. Their domains are on safe email lists and they can also filter out bad emails. Avoiding spam filters is critical to keeping your domain name clean.

The third and most valuable aspect to using an email service is the reporting. You can get detailed information about who received, opened and clicked links in your emails. You can even analyze which links were clicked more and what ads were the most effective. This is valuable business analytics that you just can't get from Outlook or Gmail.

Finally, these services help manage people who opt-in and opt-out of receiving your emails. The last thing you want is to have someone opt-out and continue receiving emails. That's a recipe for a spam notice and a complaint (or rant on a social network).

Most of these services have various pricing packages that will accommodate small lists in the beginning, and grow over time as your list grows. Do your research before you select a service and be certain you own the list and are able to export it. Down the road, you may decide to switch services and you'll want to transfer the list to them.

Postcards

Postcards can be an effective way to advertise a website, especially if you're selling off-line products or services. The key is to send the same postcard to each address at least three times, which is often overlooked or underestimated by first-time postcard advertisers.

In order to create awareness of your brand, you need to be seen more than once. That's why you receive the same mail ads for credit cards and satellite TV over and over. They know if you ever decide to sign up for their service, they'll be on the top of your mind (and your kitchen counter).

The key to an effective postcard ad is to get your point across quickly and to make it memorable. Avoid anything too controversial (unless your target audience appreciates that) and anything too clever or hard to understand. Keep your message simple and to the point.

Postcards are great for advertising specials or offering a discount. Use a different promotional code for each mailing to track which ones work the best. This requires that you have a promotional code tracking system built into your website, but it's critically important for helping you determine ad effectiveness, and also in calculating your ROI and CPA.

> **Did you know…**
>
> ROI stands for Return On Investment. Marketing is an investment. If it doesn't return more than it costs in terms of sales and revenue, it's not a good investment. This is called a bad ROI. If a marketing effort returns a reasonable profit margin, it has a good ROI. It's important to track your ROI to know if your marketing decisions are paying off.

You have several options for printing and mailing postcards. Local printers will do it, and they typically provide a higher quality product and service, but at a premium price. If you're on a tight budget, consider using one of the many websites that will handle the whole thing for you.

I've used both VistaPrint and PostcardServices in the past and had pleasant experiences with both. Their websites allow you to design and order your postcards entirely online using a credit card. You can buy mailing lists for targeted demographics and have them mail the postcards for you. You can even get help from one of their graphic designers for an extra fee. This is the most cost effective approach when you first launch your campaign.

Just be careful when going through the checkout process. You can easily get sucked into buying a bunch of additional services you don't actually need. Remember, you're going to need to send the same postcard to each address more than once and that's going to cost you. The postage for a small postcard is 29 cents; 44 cents for a large one. That doesn't cover the cost of printing or the mailing list. You can easily spend 45 cents or more to mail a single small postcard. Multiply that by 1,000 addresses and you get $450 for each mailing. The costs can quickly add up so keep your budget in mind and only buy what you need.

I said earlier not to buy email lists from services like InfoUSA and SalesGenie, however, they're great resources for physical mailing addresses. InfoUSA was the source for the majority of vendors we registered at QuoteCatcher.

Postcard advertising is an option that may work well for your business, but it can get expensive, making it even more important to track your CPA. If it costs too much to get a paying customer, either try a different ad or cancel your postcard campaign.

Telemarketing or Telesales

It's hard to telemarket to consumers these days (thank goodness). I remember when I was a kid, every night between 6 and 8 PM, the phone would ring non-stop with telemarketers trying to sell my parents everything under the sun. Now, with the no-call list, we don't have to worry about that anymore (unless it's election time). Businesses, however, don't have the same luxury.

If you're selling a service to a business, telemarketing may be your most effective strategy. At QuoteCatcher, we found that nothing was as effective as simply calling a business and talking to the manager of sales, or the owner.

Telemarketing is especially effective if you're selling something expensive. Our typical vendor purchased more than $200 in sales leads per month, and they wanted to talk to a real person before buying. We tried postcards and PPC ads targeting vendors, but found they simply didn't work for us. The only thing that did work was telemarketing. We had several telesales representatives making a hundred or more calls each day off a targeted telemarketing list.

If you don't like the idea of calling people you don't know, and trying to sell to them over the phone, you can easily outsource it to an individual or a call center. In the beginning, you may want to do it yourself to save money, but paying an expert to do it could have better results if you're not very good at it.

Cold calling is not easy and you'll need to get used to hearing "no" a lot. The old adage in sales is that every "no" is one step closer to "yes." If you're going to do your own telesales, develop thick skin and keep dialing those numbers. There's a "yes" in there somewhere…you just have to find it.

Networking & Shoe Leather Marketing

If you're selling a high end or an expensive product or service, getting out from behind your computer and talking to people in the real world may be a good marketing channel for you.

Networking events are held all the time in every major metropolitan area. Chambers of Commerce, leads groups, SBA, SCORE, business groups, etc. schedule events regularly where you can go for free and sometimes for a small fee to network with other people.

After you've just launched your website, going to these events to find your beta users might be very helpful. You'll meet them in person and develop a rapport with them. In exchange for their early adoption and feedback, you'll offer them free or discounted products or services. If they like what you offer, they may start spreading the word about your website to their friends and the viral dispersion will begin.

Shoe leather marketing is a term that refers to walking and knocking on doors. If you have a specific target audience such as owners of small clothing boutiques, walking into their store and asking for the owner or manager may lead to a new customer. Have a sales script prepared before you walk in and offer to come back at a time that's more convenient if they seem irritated or annoyed.

If you plan to go national with your website, person-to-person marketing isn't a long-term growth strategy, but it can be very useful when signing up your first clients.

Content Marketing

The last type of marketing I'm going to talk about is Content Marketing. There are a lot of people who make their living by using content marketing to sell the information products they've created, but you can also use the same tactics to market a non-info marketing business.

Information Marketing is the process used to sell information based products such as books, audio and video programs, coaching, training, etc. Some of the most popular info marketers are Tony Robbins, Robert Kiyosaki, Tony Horton (P90X) and Wayne Dyer. These guys and thousands of others help change people's lives by educating them in a better way of doing things. In the process, they sell millions of dollars' worth of educational materials and supplies.

Why do people spend such huge sums of money on the products offered by information marketers? The answer is simple and psychological: they're the experts. Experts have spent a large amount of time learning their trade, crafting educational programs and speaking in front of groups. Over time, they've become recognized as experts, or thought leaders, and more and more people seek them out for advice. It's a brilliant marketing strategy, and one you can apply to your business.

> **Did you know...**
>
> A "thought leader" refers to an expert in a field who has influence on others through informational and educational services. They're often recognized for having innovative ideas and seeing old problems through new lenses. They also know more than the average person about their field of expertise.

One of the best ways (maybe THE best way) to market anything, is to be the expert on it. You might be asking, "How do I become an expert?" It doesn't actually take much. The first step is to learn as much as you can about your topic and then create content, such as writing a book or posting videos on YouTube about your topic. You can also create a keynote speech and start giving it wherever people will listen (e.g. Rotary Clubs, Kiwanis Clubs, Associations, Organizations and Corporations). If you like teaching and your topic lends itself to that, create a workshop and offer it to educational organizations such as SCORE, SBDC and local colleges.

This is the process of establishing yourself as an expert. When people see you and hear what you have to say, you'll be the first person they think of when they need what you're selling. Content Marketing works extremely well for service oriented businesses, but it can work just as well for product businesses.

Now that I've covered several ways you can market your new website, it's time to discuss Search Engine Optimization, or SEO, as it's commonly called.

Search Engine Optimization (SEO)

Search engines such as Google, Yahoo! and Bing are constantly crawling the web and analyzing the content that people post. The content they crawl is then ranked according to several factors and when someone does a search for information, the best pages are displayed in the search results.

Since the most relevant and highest quality pages are shown at the top of the list, it greatly increases the website's exposure to potential users and customers. The goal of all websites is to appear as high as possible in the list of search results on search engines and this is accomplished through search engine optimization or SEO.

What They Look For and How to Make Them Happy

While no search engine reveals its proprietary algorithms for ranking websites, we can apply a little common sense to figure out what they value.

When a real person goes to a search engine and types in a keyword or phrase, the goal of the search engine is to display the most relevant results in descending order of relevancy. This means that the website pages most likely to satisfy the user's search terms are shown on the top of the list and every subsequent page is a little less likely to be what the user wants to see.

We know this is the goal of search engines because people would stop using them if they couldn't find what they wanted. Search result relevancy is the bread and butter for all search engines and they've spent years tweaking and fine tuning their ranking algorithms to improve the results.

How do search engines determine what's most relevant to a search term? Here's a list of the most common things they look for when ranking your website and its pages, and what you can do to improve your position in search results.

Keyword Richness

The content on your site is the most important component of SEO. If you provide relevant content relating to the topic of your website, people will want to read it and search engines will rank you well for it.

The key here is to write your content with important keywords in mind. If your website sells cameras and camera equipment, write content that contains the keywords people are searching for, such as "Nikon D90 reviews" or "Canon Battery Packs."

Use the Google Keyword Tool to determine the most common search terms for your topic before you write your content. This will help guide the words you choose so they'll be as relevant as possible to what people are searching for.

Make a list of your top keywords and keep them handy so you'll remember to use them. If you've written a phrase such as "Canon batteries" in an article but you know from your keyword research that people are more likely to search for "Canon battery packs," swap out the word "batteries" with "battery packs" (unless you're specifically targeting that term).

Don't get carried away, though. If you use your keywords TOO much, you'll be punished for "spamming" your site. For instance, this would be considered spamming: "We offer a complete line of Canon Battery Packs that will fit any Canon Battery Pack need you may have for Canon Battery Packs."

You get the idea. Use your common sense and write quality content that people will want to read and search engines will reward you for it with improved ranking.

Content Freshness

Websites that update their content regularly are valued over sites that don't. Search engines like websites that appear to be vibrant and alive, and the only way they can determine this is by how frequently the content changes.

Many websites now offer blogs as a way to keep content fresh. Blogs work very well for this purpose, as long as you post to them on a regular basis. But keep in mind, as I mentioned earlier, the only thing worse than no blog is a dead blog. If a search engine or a user sees that you haven't posted to your blog in a month or six months, it will tarnish the perceived value of your entire site. Before you launch a blog on your site, make sure you're willing to commit what it takes to keep it going.

One way to avoid the dead blog syndrome is to post articles instead of blog posts. Articles are typically more in-depth and less time sensitive than blog posts, meaning they go into more detail and the details are also more timeless.

Think of it as the difference between a newspaper and an encyclopedia. Newspaper articles written today may be completely outdated and inaccurate by this time next week due to the changing nature of current events. Encyclopedias, on the other hand, contain far more information on specific topics, but the information is less likely to drastically change, especially in the short-term.

Did you know...

You can post articles on websites such as EzineArticles.com, ExploreB2B.com, eHow.com and other free article submission websites. While these won't provide content directly on your website, they will provide an inbound link to your website (discussed shortly), while helping establish yourself as an expert in the field.

The nice thing about articles is that your site isn't punished for posting them on an irregular basis. Some websites haven't posted new content in years, yet they show up on the first page of search results. This is because the content they posted years ago is still highly relevant and people still want to read it today.

However, if you're launching a new site, you don't have the benefit of being around for years building credibility, so the best way to turbo-charge the process is to make your site look as lively as possible.

Special Tags

HTML is the language of websites, and it comes with several "tags" that tell search engines what the content on the page is all about. Using these tags will help organize your content, and will also help search engines rank it accurately.

As I discussed earlier in the Usability section, Meta Tags are placed in the markup of the page, but aren't visible to the user reading it. Meta Tags are important usability considerations for people who use your site, but they're just as important for SEO. The two most important Meta tags are the Title and Description.

The Title should be different on every page of your site and should contain relevant keywords to the main topic on the page. This title doesn't appear in the content of the page, but it will appear in the title bar of the browser window, which is visible to the user. Search engines use this tag (if it's relevant to the content on the page) to classify your site and its content.

The Description Meta tag is only visible to search engines and it should also contain relevant keywords to the topic of the page. This tag should be a brief one sentence synopsis of the content on the page. Like the Title tag, it should also be different on every page.

The Keyword Meta tag once carried a lot of weight, but people spammed so many of them with keywords that search engines no longer value them as much as they once did. In fact, Google states that they have stopped using the Keyword Meta tag completely in their ranking algorithm. You can still use it to list relevant keywords for your site, but don't spam it with a hundred terms and don't expect it to have a large impact on your ranking.

"H" Tags, or Heading Tags, are used in the content of the page to group the content and label it. Every page should have only one H1 tag, which should contain the title with relevant keywords for the content. You can further group content with H2, H3, H4, etc. tags to signify subsections of the content, as shown in Figure 7 below. Think of using H tags as a keyword rich outlining and grouping mechanism.

Heading 1

Lorem ipsum dolor sit amet, consectetu massa at tortor porttitor dignissim vel a

Heading 2

Lorem ipsum dolor sit amet, consectetu massa at tortor porttitor dignissim vel a

Heading 3

Lorem ipsum dolor sit amet, consectetu massa at tortor porttitor dignissim vel a

Figure 7

If you have a page that requires the use of sub-heading tags like H2, H3 or H4, break the content into additional pages. For some readers, too much content on a page may discourage them from reading it.

"Alt" tags are used to provide a label for images. Since most search engines can't look at an image and intrinsically know what it is, the alt tag gives them a way to index it. This is also the text that is displayed to the user if, for some reason, the image can't be displayed in the browser.

Search engines look at Meta tags, H tags and Alt tags as indicators of the most important aspects of the content. The keywords you use in these tags must relate to the content on the page, or they won't add any value. Don't think you can fool the system. This type of behavior falls under the "black hat" umbrella, which I'll discuss below.

Inbound Links

These are links on *other* websites that point back to *your* website. Search engines use these inbound links to gauge the value other website owners have given to your site.

If you have inbound links on highly ranked websites, it can greatly increase the ranking of your site. This is because highly ranked websites have already earned credibility with users and search engines, so if they like what you're posting, chances are it must be good quality and relevant to the search terms.

The challenge is getting these inbound links placed on other sites. When search engines first started ranking sites based on inbound links, website owners contacted other website owners and asked to be placed on their "links" page in exchange for a link back to their site. Back in my consulting days with PromoteWare, I created a module specifically for this purpose and even contacted hundreds of other website owners to do a link exchange for my own business.

However, gone are the days of link exchanges and link lists. They don't work anymore and search engines may even punish you for having them. This is because anyone can post a link, even if it's irrelevant, just to increase the number of inbound links they have. Search engines figured out that link exchanges in no way reflect content relevancy, so they changed their algorithm.

Now, the only way to guarantee an inbound link will be rewarded by search engines is if it's placed in relevant content on a relevant website. Websites that are highly ranked will definitely help your ranking. However, websites that aren't ranked well will probably have little or no influence on your position in search results.

There are SEO companies who will try to sell you their inbound linking services, but be wary of them. They will surf the web and post links back to your website in blogs and comments on highly ranked sites. The reason to be wary is because of the way they do it.

Many of these companies post meaningless content that adds no value to users. I'm sure you've seen these posts before, but maybe you didn't realize what they were. You're reading the comments on a popular blog site with a vibrant exchange of ideas, and right in the middle of the dialog, you see a post that looks something like this: "For more information on this topic, visit www.domain.com."

This counts as an inbound link, but it certainly doesn't add any real value to your website. Some blog software and blog writers now routinely scour their comments and remove these types of spam links, which defeats the purpose of paying someone to post them.

Posting comments to blogs with links back to your website is a great way to increase your inbound links, but only if you do it the right way. The most effective strategy is to take part in the discussion. Share your insights and experiences. Give advice. Answer questions. Ask questions. And provide a link back to your site in your signature line.

Unfortunately, you'll most likely have to do this yourself since SEO companies won't be able to add the same amount of value that you will. They haven't had your experiences and they aren't qualified to give advice. Sometimes, you just can't take the shortcut.

A good goal is to spend 2 to 4 hours per week working on this project. Add it to your list of things that you have to do every week and block out time for it. Find online communities and blogs that are relevant to your website and join the discussion. This exercise will not only help your inbound linking, it will also keep you current on developments related to your industry and you may even make some valuable connections in the process.

Bounce Rate

Bounce rate refers to how many people hit the back button when they visit your site, and how long they stay on your site. There will always be users who hit the back button for whatever reason, but if the percentage gets too high, the search engines will take that as evidence of poor quality or non-relevant content.

If, on the other hand, a large percentage of users visit your site, read the content, and click a few links to other pages, search engines are programmed to believe your site has value. And they're right.

Your website visitors obviously saw something they liked and they stuck around to get more of it. There is no better evidence that you have a quality site with relevant content than when users stay on your site and read for a while.

One way to increase the depth of visit (meaning how many links a user clicks on your site) is to divide your articles into pages. This has two benefits.

First, by breaking up your content, it's easier to read. Articles that go on forever and require scrolling in the browser window can be hard to read and may discourage some users who think the article is too long from reading it. Breaking the article into pages makes the content seem more accessible.

Second, dividing an article into multiple pages causes readers to click links to go to the next page. This increases the depth of visit and makes your site look more relevant to search engines.

The goal of all sites is to reduce bounce rate and increase the amount of time each user spends on the site. To *search engines*, more time on the site means the site is more valuable, which will make it rank higher in search results. To *you*, more time on the site means more opportunity to convert the visitor into a customer.

Website Performance

This refers to how fast pages load when a user or search engine robot visits your site. If a user clicks a link to your site and the page takes longer than 2 seconds to load, that user will click the back button before the page loads, and as we know from the discussion on bounce rate, that's bad.

People simply have no patience anymore for slow websites. We've all been spoiled with high speed Internet connections so if a site doesn't load immediately, we're off to find one that does.

Additionally, if a search engine robot hits a page and it takes more than a few seconds to load, the robot will flag the page as broken and potentially remove it from search results. Over time, this can greatly reduce the ranking of your entire site.

Your developer and web hosting provider are responsible for the nuts and bolts of making sure your site performs well, but it's up to you to make sure they do it. Routinely check several pages on your site at various times during the day and night, especially the home page. If it doesn't load in the blink of an eye, use a timer or stopwatch to see how long it takes for the page to be displayed. If it takes longer than 2 seconds, you need to get your developer and webhost working on it immediately.

Content Outsourcing

If you don't have the time or ability to write content to keep your site fresh and interesting, you have a few alternatives.

At QuoteCatcher, we hired independent content writers to author articles for the website on various topics. They typically charged by the article and used the keywords we requested. They often did research for the articles to ensure they were accurate and relevant.

The downside to outsourcing your content writing is that not all writers are created equal. It's best to find a writer who has specific industry experience relating to the topics he or she is writing about so the content will have more meat than fluff. The content needs to appeal to your readers, as well as search engines.

Let's say you have a website selling computer equipment and your target audience is technology professionals. This is a highly knowledgeable audience that won't be fooled by fluff. The writer may be able to fool search engines by providing relevant content with the appropriate keywords, but your real audience that spends money on your site will see through it and your site will suffer.

For your content to be considered valuable to your audience, it must be compelling. This is achieved by providing useful information, insights, experiences and advice that isn't easily found elsewhere. Your goal should be "ah hah" moments. If your users read an article and learn something new, they'll come back to your site more often and they'll also share the experience with their friends.

Another option for outsourcing your content is to use a service such as ConstantContent.com. This company provides an interface for writers to post content that they've written. You can then preview the content and purchase it for display on your site. Since this type of service attracts more specialized writers, you may get higher quality content; however, you'll pay more for it.

If you decide that you're the best person to write the content for your site, but grammar has never been your strong suit, hire an editor to clean it up for you. The quality of your content is very important so if you can't write smooth flowing, grammatically correct sentences, get some expert help. You can find editors advertising their services on CraigsList under the Services Offered section, as well as on websites like Elance.com and Freelancer.com.

Black Hat SEO

Black Hat SEO is a practice that is highly frowned upon and severely punished by search engines. It refers to any tactic intended to fool the search engine into ranking a site higher in search results than what it deserves.

If you do any type of black hat SEO and the search engines figure it out, you'll be black listed indefinitely, which means your website will be removed from their search results. Here are some common black hat practices to avoid.

Keyword Stuffing

This refers to placing long lists of keywords on your website pages. It's ok to have an index of your most relevant keywords that link to related content, but placing a list with hundreds or thousands of keywords on a page will get you black listed from search engines.

Keyword Spamming

This refers to the overuse of keywords in your content. If you have a paragraph with 100 words and 50 of those words are repetitive keywords, you run the risk of it being considered black hat. It also provides for a pretty bad user experience by making your content hard to read, which will also lead to a high bounce rate.

Invisible Text

Let's say the background color of your website is white. Placing keywords on the page with a white font color will make them invisible to the users, but not to search engines. The robots are sophisticated enough to know that you're trying to fool them by placing invisible text on the site and they don't like that.

Remember, the search engine's goal is to display the best websites with the most relevant content for the user. If the content is invisible, the user won't be able to read it so it doesn't add any value to the user experience.

Doorway Pages

These are pages designed specifically for search engines and won't be seen by the user. The search engine is tricked into ranking these pages due to the highly relevant content on the page shown to the search engine robot; however, when a user clicks the link, they're shown a different page that isn't nearly as relevant. It may take the search engine some time to figure this one out but when they do your site will be black listed.

In the early days of search engines, it was easy to fool them into ranking your site higher than it deserved to be. However, it's not so easy to fool them anymore and the punishment for trying to is severe. You might be tempted to cheat the system for your own personal gain, but it will cost you dearly in the long run. My advice is to avoid these tactics at all costs.

The Coveted Top Ranking

When I was a web consultant, clients would demand top search engine ranking for their website. In fact, many listed it as a primary requirement that their site be ranked in the top five or ten search results on Google for their main keywords. Unfortunately, it's just not that easy.

It takes time to move up the list. A brand new website can't compete with a site that's been around for years and is deemed highly credible by users and search engines. It can take three months or more just to appear anywhere in search results for your keywords. Even then, you'll probably be way down the list on page 10 or page 50. The only way to move up the list is to follow the SEO tips provided above, apply them consistently over time, and then wait.

If an SEO company promises you top ranking, be very suspicious and read the fine print carefully. They are most likely guaranteeing top ranking for keywords that won't benefit you very much, such as your domain name, company name, non-relevant keywords or extremely long-tail keywords.

Did you know…

"Long-tail keyword" is a term used in SEO to denote long search terms. For example, "Denver co auto body repair and paint" would be considered a long-tail term because it has multiple keywords strung together. Any search term with three or more words is considered long-tail.

It's relatively easy to get some long-tail terms ranked highly on search engines because few websites use them and few people search for them. If your site is one of the few using them, you won't have much competition. These long-tail terms are often what SEO companies promise to get ranked, but since the search volume is so low, it may not benefit you very much unless you're targeting a large number of them.

The most valuable keywords face stiff competition from an SEO perspective and the only way to dislodge the incumbents is to beat them at their own game, which takes time and consistent effort, but the payback can be tremendous. To the victor go the spoils and top ranking in search engines can be the difference between a thousand dollar month and a million dollar month.

That brings us to the end of the "Marketing Your Website" phase. My goal with this section was to expose you to a variety of different sales and marketing options without going into too much detail about any of them. As I've already stated, this book is meant to be a roadmap, not a city guide. If you want to dive deeper into any of the various marketing concepts I've mentioned, visit the "Sales and Marketing" section at your favorite bookstore or library. Each of these topics has multiple books written about them and they can help you fine-tune your marketing materials and sales pitch. I've also included several recommendations in the "Resources" section.

In the next section, I'm going to prepare you for business ownership. It can be a lot of fun, but it's not all cake and champagne. You have lots of work and long hours in your future. Come along with me for a little sneak peek….

Marketing Your Website Checklist

Here's a list of things to do to help people find your website:

- ❏ Calculate your maximum cost-per-acquisition (CPA)
- ❏ Identify your ideal advertising and marketing channels (PPC, Affiliates, Social Media, Email, Postcards, Telemarketing, Networking Events, Shoe Leather, Information Marketing, etc.)
- ❏ Write SEO valuable content for your website.
- ❏ Craft your marketing message
- ❏ Draft several ads to be placed on PPC channels
- ❏ Select one or two PPC websites to test your ads
- ❏ Perform A/B testing to determine ad effectiveness
- ❏ Adjust your ads and place them on additional PPC networks as time allows
- ❏ Create your affiliate marketing strategy
- ❏ Identify potential affiliates
- ❏ Contact affiliates about sending leads and/or traffic to your site
- ❏ Identify the most relevant social media network(s)
- ❏ Setup your social media accounts
- ❏ Post relevant content to your social media accounts regularly and consistently
- ❏ Advertise and mine for followers in your chosen social network(s)
- ❏ Analyze your social media presences to determine their ROI and effectiveness

"I do not believe a man can ever leave his business.
He ought to think of it by day and dream of it by night."

~Henry Ford

Phase 5: Running Your Business

Starting and owning a company can be the best and the worst thing that you've ever done. It requires hard work, intelligence and perseverance to run a successful company that turns a profit and stays in business. It's a job, only you're the boss and you're responsible for all the good things that happen, as well as all the bad things.

Entrepreneurship Unplugged

Owning a business is fun. You get to call the shots. You don't have an irrational boss breathing down your neck to meet a deadline. You decide when to go on vacation and you don't need approval from anyone to take it. You control your own pay, bonuses and raises. And if the business is successful, you get to reap the rewards. If you have what it takes to start and run a business, you have no excuse not to do it…but it's not all fun and games.

It's easy to romanticize owning a business. It's an American dream that's even older than owning a home or a car. People dream about the riches they'll acquire from their new venture (sometimes spending the money before they make any). But entrepreneurship isn't the bed of roses many people think it is.

Owning a company is hard. Although you will hopefully enjoy your work, the hours are seemingly endless. When I first started my company, it was common for me to work 60 to 80 hours per week. I worked all day and then went back to work when my family went to bed. I worked on weekends when they were outside playing or running errands. I worked all the time. And if you think you'll be the exception to the rule and you won't have to work a lot of hours, especially in the beginning, you're kidding yourself and you should seriously consider whether you have what it takes to run your own business.

In addition to long hours, you'll need to get very comfortable taking risks and dealing with uncertainty. When you're an employee, you might think your boss has all the answers and knows exactly what he's doing, but no one can predict the future. When your boss makes a decision, he's taking a calculated risk based on known facts and his understanding of them. When you're the boss…that's YOUR job.

You won't have anyone telling you what to do, which also means you'll have to make the decisions yourself. This can be difficult and you'll have a tendency to question yourself. That's ok, but don't let it paralyze you. Sometimes it's better to make the wrong decision more quickly so you can change it and adapt sooner. If you take a long time to analyze and decide, you may still make the wrong decision, but you'll have lost valuable time in the process.

You should also consider getting a mentor, such as a friend who has been in business before, or a SCORE mentor. You can bounce your ideas off of him or her and get feedback. Sometimes, it's just nice to have an outside, objective observer to validate your actions and decisions. But in the end, it's still your call and you'll need to become comfortable making it.

Once you've been in business for a while and you've started to realize some success, you may think it gets easier or less stressful. It's true that the issues you battle in the beginning, such as finding clients and making payroll, will get easier. But other, bigger problems will take their place.

When your small business becomes successful enough to get noticed, you may not be happy with everyone who notices it. You'll become a target for government audits; they'll want to ensure you're paying all your taxes and treating your employees correctly. You'll become a target for disgruntled employees; they'll want to sue you for worker's compensation or unemployment. You'll become a target for competitors; they'll want to steal your clients and sue you for patent infringement.

Once you have what other people want (success and money), they'll try to take it from you and you'll have to fight tooth and nail to keep it. I was told once that "you're not a CEO until you've been sued." It's a sad commentary on the state of our legal system, but it's the reality in which we live. The key is to budget for it, hire great lawyers to defend your business, and don't go down without a fight.

You may think I'm trying to discourage you from starting a business, but that couldn't be farther from the truth. I'm an entrepreneur at heart and I encourage anyone with an entrepreneurial spirit to chase their dream. But you need to start the chase with your eyes wide open and understand that you'll face enormous challenges along the way. Successful entrepreneurs embrace the challenges, make tough decisions and overcome obstacles. It's a fun and rewarding process that can have a substantial financial payout.

Reinvestment

Once you get past the startup phase and you start generating revenue, you'll need to decide how to use the profit. It's tempting to write yourself a big, fat bonus check, but consider reinvesting your extra funds into the growth of your business.

Some of your potential reinvestment options are to:

- Hire additional employees, especially sales people
- Buy updated equipment that will allow you and your employees to work faster
- Launch a new ad campaign or try a new advertising channel
- Purchase tickets to attend a tradeshow
- Buy a booth and lease a spot at a tradeshow

The Web Startup Roadmap

- Move into a bigger office
- Set up a more robust phone system with automated response features
- Increase the speed of your internet connection with a T1 or additional broadband lines
- Add new features to your website
- Automate time consuming tasks
- Add additional product lines or services
- Improve the graphics of your website
- Completely overhaul your website to make it easier to use
- Etc.

You have many options for reinvesting your profits, and a bonus to yourself may be one of them, especially if you've been making sacrifices for a long time. But you need to keep you goals in mind when deciding how much to withdraw. The more money you reinvest, the faster your business will grow and the more it will be worth.

The best way to keep the bonuses to a reasonable amount is to pick a percentage and define it in your business plan and/or partnership agreement. For example, after you pay your salary, 10% or 20% of all profits will be taken as a bonus distribution. By setting the limits before you have the profits, you'll be more likely to stick to it when you have a healthy balance in the bank account.

Having money in your business bank account is a great problem to have, but it can be very tempting to spend it on frivolous things because you "deserve it." After all, you've been toiling and sacrificing for such a long time, you deserve that new Jet Ski. But the sign of true maturity is delayed gratification. If you can hold out for a little longer and reinvest your profits, you may well end up with a much larger payday in a shorter amount of time.

Growth Phase

Once you're in full forward motion and the revenue is flowing, you've entered the growth phase. This phase is both fun and scary at the same time. It's extremely rewarding to know that your idea is worthwhile and people are willing to pay money for it. But it's scary because you'll be confronted with a whole new list of problems and obstacles to overcome.

Office Space

If you started small and you've been working out of your home by yourself, office space will be one of your first major decisions. If you're ready to hire an employee or two, you may not want them lying on your spare bed to work.

When it's time to take the leap and get office space, it'll be obvious to you. First, you'll have enough revenue to pay the lease and purchase office equipment. That's the first requirement. Second, you'll be out of space in your home office, making it difficult and inefficient to work. Third, you're ready to separate your work life from your home life because the interruptions are making you less effective and you also have a hard time disengaging when you're supposed to be spending time with your family. Finally, if you're hiring employees, that's a good indicator it's time to move out of the house and into an office.

Don't go overboard on your first office. You don't need to lease something that will accommodate all your future needs. Get just enough to cover what you need now, plus a little extra growing room.

You may also consider leasing a small place that has room for expansion, either into a larger office in the same building, or by knocking down a wall enabling you to expand into the office next door. If you continue to grow, being able to expand easily is nice, but you don't want to pay for it until you need it. Plus, your needs a year from now may be totally different than your needs today. Keep it simple and get exactly what you need right *now*.

A shared office or executive suite might work well for you so check with companies in your area that provide these types of services. Regus is a company that provides office solutions around the world. You can rent rooms by the hour, day or month. They also come with some of the benefits of being in a regular office, such as an administrative assistant to answer phones and a break room stocked with coffee. They handle all the infrastructure for you so you can focus on your business.

A new type of shared office solution has popped up in recent years. It's called a "pay-to-play" incubator. Most incubators have strict admission criteria, but these new pay-to-play incubators allow anyone to rent space for a monthly fee. Innovation Pavilion and Uncubed are two examples of pay-to-play incubators in the Denver metro.

The great thing about these types of office solutions is that you'll be surrounded by other like-minded startup entrepreneurs who are happy to give you feedback and advice. Plus, the energy is contagious…you may actually enjoy your office more than your home.

An office will be your first big commitment. Shop around and negotiate the best deal. Also consider the commute and how conducive the atmosphere is to hard work and creativity. The last thing you want is to lease an office that you hate to work in.

Another consideration when choosing a location is the availability of local talent. My first office was located in a small mountain community twenty minutes outside Denver. We had a hard time finding local talent to hire and no one wanted to drive up the hill for work. Locating your office near the people you want to hire will make your job finding employees much easier.

Remember to budget for office equipment. You'll need desks, chairs, phone lines, broadband Internet connections, a phone system and phones. You may want a coffee maker, a water cooler, shelving or desk lamps, too. Just be sure you really need the things you get and don't waste money on equipment that could be better spent on advertising or salaries.

The day you move out of the house and into an office will be one of the best days of your entrepreneurial career. You will definitely feel like you've accomplished something…and you have. It's ok to be proud, but keep your exuberance in check and don't bust the bank by leasing the coolest office in town. Stay modest and get only what you need to be successful.

Outsourcing

One way to delay moving out of the house is by outsourcing some of your work to contractors or companies that specialize in the skills you need.

For example, if you need telesales people to make calls, hire an independent phone rep who works out of her house or hire a call center. If you need help managing your ad campaigns, hire a PPC/SEO management company to do it for you. If you need someone to answer the phones and do customer service, consider hiring a call center to screen the calls and answer the basic questions.

Outsourcing may appear to be more expensive than hiring an employee, but it may actually be cheaper once you add in all the extra employment expenses, such as workman's comp insurance, unemployment insurance and employment taxes. In addition, you'll save time by not interviewing people, hiring, firing, handling sick days and vacations, etc. You may also gain access to better trained talent with a support infrastructure that makes them far better than an employee.

Employees

Outsourcing is a great way to fill bandwidth needs early in your business, and it can be very useful down the road, as well. However, there will come a time when you'll need to hire employees so you'll have more control over the job they do, when they work and what they work on.

Employees are a double-edged sword. When you find a good employee, you can mold them into what you want and better control how you want things done. Outsourced contractors report to their own company's boss first and you second. If they're told to work on a project for another client, they will…and sometimes you won't even know about it. That doesn't happen with an employee (if they're managed and incented properly).

The best thing about an employee is that you can train them how to do the job the way you want it done. I'm not saying you need to micromanage and dictate their every move. In fact, some employees have fantastic suggestions for improving workflows and customer interactions. If you maintain the proper balance between direction and autonomy with each employee, you'll maximize the output you get from them.

We utilized both contractors and employees at QuoteCatcher. Some employees were great and others were not. Some contractors were great and others were not. One of the bad aspects of employees is that it's hard to get rid of them if they're not working out. With a contractor, it's easy. Just terminate the contract. However, with an employee, you have a lot of hoops to jump through, and you could end up paying them unemployment even if they don't deserve it. Even though your unemployment insurance writes the check, your premiums will go up and the more unemployment you pay, the higher your premiums will go.

Firing an employee isn't an easy matter, either. You'll need clear documentation as to why you're letting them go. Speak to an employment attorney (since I'm not qualified to give legal advice) if you need to fire someone. Before you utter the words, get all of your ducks in a row or you could face a lawsuit. An attorney can save you FAR more than they cost by helping you avoid getting sued.

When you're under the gun to get help, you may rush into hiring someone just to fill the need. Don't do it. Hire slow and fire fast. If you make a rash decision and hire the wrong person, you could end up wasting far more time than if you do your diligence during the interview process.

When interviewing candidates for jobs, conduct an initial phone screen to weed out the people who just don't have what you need. Then have the candidate come into the office for a face-to-face interview. Then have them come back a few days later or the following week for a second interview with you and at least one other person (your wife/husband, a friend, mentor, other employee, etc.). Finally, do a background check and call all the references.

> **Did you know…**
>
> Don't skip the background check! I can't stress the importance of background checks enough. We were on the verge of hiring a very nice house-wife from a prominent suburban neighborhood in the Denver metro. She gave a fantastic interview and was qualified for the job. After we received the report from the background check, we were amazed to find out she had over a dozen charges and convictions for everything from theft to assault. Bottom line: you can't judge a book by its cover. Sometimes the cover looks great but the pages are all torn out.

There are entire books written on employees, interviewing and management practices, so I won't go into much detail here. Suffice it to say, if your business is growing (and that's the goal), you'll need to hire one or more employees at some point. It's fun to share your experience with other people, but keep a healthy distance and never underestimate their likelihood to take legal action if the relationship sours. Protect yourself and protect your company.

Contractor vs. FTE

Again, I'm not qualified to give legal advice, but I can speak from experience about the difference between a contractor and a full-time equivalent employee or FTE.

One of our first contractors performed customer service and account management duties for us. He worked in the office, used our equipment, worked the hours we dictated and we paid him using his personal name (not a business name). In most states, that makes him an employee, a fact our accountant neglected to mention. There is a list of qualifications that define the difference between employee and contractor, and you need to learn the list for your state and talk to an employment attorney before you hire a contractor.

The reason why this is important has to do with how the government earns revenue from your business. If you hire a contractor, you don't have to pay employment taxes, workman's comp insurance or unemployment insurance. You simply pay the contractor for the work they do, and they're responsible for paying their own taxes.

If you hire a contractor that your state or federal labor department deems an employee, you could be responsible for paying back taxes, back unemployment insurance and back workman's comp insurance, in addition to penalties and interest on the amount you owe. That's exactly what happened to us when the state labor department decided to conduct an audit of our employment history, and it ended up costing us thousands of dollars.

Many small businesses hire contractors who are legally classified as employees, and they never get audited and never have to pay for the mistake. However, if you're one of the unlucky few who get caught, you can save yourself a lot of time, money and stress by following the rules from the beginning. If you get caught at a bad time, it could literally put you out of business.

The Dreaded Audit

For reasons I'm not at liberty to discuss, we were audited by several government agencies...but we survived. We had some minor infractions, but overall, we were mostly clean.

The biggest cost, by far, was the drain on our time collecting information, organizing records, attending meetings and getting interviewed by auditors. When you're a small business owner, your most valuable asset is time and if you have to spend a large portion of it on non-revenue generating activities, such as talking to government officials, you're losing money.

Getting audited is an unfortunate reality for many businesses. Some companies never get audited, but if you're an online company with fast revenue growth and several employees, you become a target. Your best strategy for dealing with it is to hire a good attorney, keep all your records in order, and do your best to accommodate all the auditor's requests in a timely manner.

Although the auditors were very thorough, they didn't want to crush our business and were very forthcoming with information and advice on how to follow the regulations. All of the regulatory offices had free information and counselors to talk to. Don't be afraid to call them with your questions to make sure you're doing everything by the book.

You may be one of the lucky businesses that never gets audited, but if you do, just accept it as a cost of doing business, hire great lawyers, be courteous and respectful to your auditor, and try to get through the process as quickly as possible so you can get back to growing your business.

Exit Strategy

When you start a dotcom, you need to consider your potential exit strategies. An exit strategy refers to what the end destination is for your business. The three most common exit strategies are: close it, sell it, or go public with an IPO. Each one has its pros and cons.

Closing the Business

Closing is the least desired for most people. This usually means your business has failed to generate enough revenue to cover operating costs, or it never generated any intrinsic, marketable value that exists outside your personal involvement.

In order to be sold or taken public, your business will need a steady stream of revenue and something tangible that can be sold, such as a large client list, top SEO ranking, patents or other intellectual property.

Many people make the mistake of thinking that if they have a good idea and pay someone to build a website for it, they can immediately sell the website for a profit. Unfortunately, it doesn't work that way. Without an existing revenue stream or something that has tangible, quantifiable value, you're not likely to get enough from a sale to cover the cost of software development, assuming you can find anyone interested enough to buy it.

Anybody can build a website that does something similar to yours, and large companies (your typical business buyer) normally have in-house development staff that can do it cheaper than what you paid. Rather than pay you for a website that hasn't achieved critical mass or gained a foothold in the industry, they'll just roll their own.

> ## Did you know...
>
> "Roll their own" or "roll our own" is a term used in the tech world that refers to building the software in-house rather than using someone else's software. Most large companies have a sizable development staff and new code needs to fit into their existing code base. That means they often decide to "roll their own" instead of buying it.

Selling Your Business

Selling to a larger competitor is the approach we took with QuoteCatcher. This was the best solution for us because we hadn't generated nearly enough intrinsic value to go public, and we didn't want to go public anyway (for reasons I'll discuss in the next section).

Our intrinsic value was in our client list (vendors who purchased leads), our affiliate list (well-ranked websites that sent us leads to sell), our systems and technology, our expertise in the industry, and our reputation. Those were the assets that made our company valuable enough that a larger company was willing to pay seven figures for it.

Deciding to sell our company was not an easy decision to make. QuinStreet sought us out, but we turned them down the first time. When they came back six months later, we decided it was time to cash out and enjoy some of the fruits of our labor.

It was also becoming increasingly more difficult to compete with them since they were buying up all of our competitors and they were able to pay more for affiliate leads and advertising than we were. The writing was on the wall: either we sell or run the risk that they would eventually drive us out of business.

As part of the sale contract, my business partner and I were required to work for them for a period of time. I negotiated my contract down to six months, although I ended up staying eleven months while I managed a development team responsible for integrating several systems. My business partner agreed to stay a full year, which he did.

When I sell my next company, I won't be part of the purchase agreement. Not that I didn't enjoy working for QuinStreet; I just didn't enjoy traveling to California as often as I did. I also prefer working at my own company, or at least a smaller, more agile company that can move and change directions more rapidly.

If you get to the point of selling your web-based company, negotiate the best deal for yourself. You may be required to work for them for a period of time, but that length is usually flexible. You may also be able to negotiate a contract that makes you available for consultation for a set number of hours to terminate on a specific date.

Hire an attorney who specializes in selling businesses to negotiate on your behalf. They'll make sure your interests are protected and that nothing will get by without your approval.

Deciding to sell your company is the hardest decision you'll have to make. You've put years of hard work, blood, sweat and tears into your "baby" and now you're confronted with kicking it out of the nest and sending it to live somewhere else. It won't be an easy decision and you'll have to fight your emotions to make the right one, but try to weigh all the pros and cons and do your best to make a rational business decision. Even though you may not want to sell, it may be the best time and the right thing to do.

I spent such a large amount of my time working on QuoteCatcher and thinking about it, that it actually became part of my identity. After we sold it, I was lost for a while and somewhat afraid to start something else for fear of losing it, too. I've since overcome that (the money helped quite a bit).

The prospect of not having your business anymore may be daunting, but if you decide selling it is the best course of action, rest assured that you'll overcome the loss and emerge a better business person from the experience.

Going Public (IPO)

"Going public," also known as an IPO or Initial Public Offering, is the last exit strategy I'm going to discuss, and many web-based businesses take this approach.

Back in the 90's, this was the goal of all dotcoms. It was the big payday we all waited for. Parties were had in many a break room to celebrate the creation of overnight millionaires. It was a jubilant time when the ticker symbol hit the wire and traders started buying and selling shares of the company's stock. It is truly a big moment to launch an IPO and to own millions of dollars of stock and options, but it comes at a steep price if you're the founder.

I'm not speaking from first-hand experience here since I've never worked at a company when it went public, but I've seen the changes that occur as a result. If you think an IPO is your desired exit strategy, you need to understand what you're getting yourself into.

First, you'll have a board of directors to answer to, as well as thousands of stockholders. Missing a sales projection no longer affects only you and the sales staff; it affects thousands of people who own your stock. To avoid their wrath, you'll be confronted with questionable decisions and ethical dilemmas. The "right" thing and the "profitable" thing are not often the *same* thing. Your decisions carry a lot more weight and you'll feel constant pressure to do what's right for the bottom line and not necessarily what's right for your conscience or for humanity.

Second, if the company fails to meet expectations set by Wall Street, you can actually be fired from the company you founded. The board of directors can have a vote of no confidence and oust you from power. You'll still have your stock and money, but no one handles being fired very well, especially from their own company. This is exactly what happened to the founders of Cisco, and they're still bitter about it to this day!

Third, decisions you used to make in minutes, can take weeks or months. For major things like offering a new product or launching a new type of ad campaign, you'll likely need approval from the board. They'll want to be sure it's in line with your business and it's not too far out of the ordinary. The trial and error approach that led to your success no longer exists. Everything must be well thought out and clearly defined (and approved by the lawyers) before you can act.

> ## Did you know...
>
> Richard Branson was so discouraged by his publically traded company, Virgin, that he bought it back and took it private again after only two years on the stock market.

If taking a company public has so many negative factors, why would anyone want to do it? There are times when it's the only option and may actually be required to keep up with the growth of the company.

Selling shares of stock is a very effective way to raise capital for large expenses such as new distribution centers, national ad campaigns, research & development, overseas expansion, and acquisitions. When a company hits a certain size, it requires more money than banks, individual investors or venture capital firms can provide to sustain the growth. Selling stock generates far more capital to cover growth expenses than any other avenue.

Buying other companies is a very popular growth strategy for larger companies, especially with dotcoms because it's easy to increase revenue by sharing information and sales across website domains. This strategy has been used for years and it requires large sums of money to accomplish. If you plan to buy a company for $100 million or $1 billion or more, borrowing money from a bank or from individual investors isn't feasible. Stockholders, on the other hand, are more than willing to lend money in return for a share of the profits.

An IPO is also the desired form of payback for most early round investors, especially Venture Capital firms. This is because they own a large number of shares of the company's stock, typically priced at only a couple dollars per share, then when the stock goes public, their investment immediately grows exponentially.

To illustrate this concept, let's look at Google's IPO. When Google went public in 2004, the company offered 19.6 million of its 271 million shares to investors who could purchase them on the stock market for $85 per share. That sale generated roughly $1.67 billion in instant capital for the company to spend on growth. But more importantly, it made the other 263 million shares worth approximately $22 billion.

The owners of those shares were the founders of Google, its employees, some individual investors and two venture capital firms that invested $25 million in 1999. In 2004 when the company went public, after only 5 years, their $25 million investment was worth several billion dollars.

Did you know...

The two founders of Google tried to sell their fledgling company to Excite in 1999 for a measly $1 million. They wanted to be able to focus on their graduate studies at Stanford University. Luckily for them, Excite turned them down and within just a few years, they would become two of the youngest billionaires in the world. The moral of that story is that sometimes you may be convinced that selling is the right thing to do, but holding out a little longer may be the wisest move.

When speaking to people about their startup dotcom, I always ask them about their exit strategy. It may not seem important when you're first starting, but having the end in mind when you begin can help guide your decisions and motivate you to keep moving forward.

Running a successful business is hard work, but working for yourself is far better than sitting in a cube in a large office grinding out a paycheck week after week, year after year. Besides, working for someone else seldom leads to the good life, which is the likely end result if you start and run a successful business of your own. The good life is where you'll be when all your hard work pays off, and it's the topic of the next section.

The Good Life

"I've been poor and miserable. I've been rich and miserable. Rich and miserable is better."

~Burt Reynolds

Everyone has different reasons for starting their own company, but the main reason shared by most people is the same: to become wealthy doing something you enjoy. If you're one of the few with a profitable idea, a strong work ethic and the persistence to stick with it, you could achieve more than your wildest dreams.

Money can't make you happy, but it removes a lot of the little obstacles in life that make you very unhappy. By removing things that make you unhappy, in a way, money can buy you happiness. In fact, according to a survey conducted by the Pew Research Center in 2006, 50% of the respondents in family households earning over $150,000 per year rated themselves as "very happy," compared to only 23% of households earning less than $20,000 per year.

You may think money isn't important and that's not why you want to start a business. Your goal is to help people; not become a greedy, money hungry monster. I have two responses for this. The first is that the more money you make, the more good you can do with it. Warren Buffet and Bill Gates have donated billions of dollars to charities around the world. They've managed to live the good life AND make a huge difference in other, less fortunate people's lives. You can make a difference just like they have, but only if you have the financial resources to do it.

My second response for those of you who think money is evil or that it'll make you a bad person is that you need to change your mindset. If you think money is bad, you'll never *have* any because having it would make you a bad person and nobody wants to be a bad person (well, most people don't). Since money is the natural conclusion to owning a successful business, your attitude about money will almost certainly prevent you from being successful.

Money is not intrinsically evil and it won't make you an evil person if you have it. I personally know some great people who have a lot of money. They live the good life in every aspect of the term. They're generous to their family and friends, they donate to churches and charities, and they use their money sense to continuously generate more money, enabling them to continue their generosity.

If you struggle with this tainted view of money, you're going to have a hard time achieving the good life. Spend some time before you get started in your new business to do some self-reflection and self-examination. "The Millionaire Mind" by T. Harv Eker is a must read for you. It's the best place to start if you have negative beliefs about money. "The Secret" by Rhonda Byrne is another good resource to help you attract the things you want into your life.

I've found that a good motivational tool is to write down all the good things you'll do when you have the financial means to do them. Then look at each one and say whether it helps people (yourself included) or hurts people. I bet they all help people in one way or another. If that's the case, how can money be the root of all evil? The rational person will say, "money isn't evil...people are evil...and I'm not an evil person so it's ok for me to have money."

The "good life" is fun! I've seen and done things I never thought I'd do, like riding in a helicopter over an active volcano and scuba diving in a cave. Without money, the options you have for life's experiences are severely limited.

I'm not saying that starting your own business will lead you down the same path I've taken because there's no way I can guarantee your business will be successful. Only you have control of that. But if you do something you love and pour your heart into it, your chances of being successful are good. If you start now, you could be living the good life in no time at all.

Hopefully you've learned some things you didn't know from this book. You may decide after reading it not to start your own company right now. Maybe the timing isn't right. Maybe your idea didn't turn out to be as good as you thought it was after you did the research for your business plan. Maybe you underestimated how hard it will be and you realistically don't have the resources to do it right now.

Or, maybe you have even more resolve now than you did before. Maybe you had some questions and didn't know where to start, but now you do. Maybe you lacked the confidence before, but now you realize you have what it takes to be successful.

There is no right or wrong. Sometimes not acting is the best decision. My goal with this book is to help you understand everything that's required to start and run a thriving online company. If, for whatever reason, you decide not to do it, then I've hopefully helped you save some of your valuable time and money.

On the other hand, if this book confirmed what you already knew and provided the details about how you can do it, then I've hopefully helped you start down the path to a prosperous future in the dotcom world.

Starting and running a successful online business is one of the most rewarding things you will ever do. It's challenging and frustrating and exciting and fulfilling and lucrative and so many other things. For those of you who have the courage to take the risk, the good life awaits. The time to act is now! Get out there and go for it!

Please Review!

If you enjoyed reading my book and learned a few things, please review it on Amazon right now. More reviews means more people will see the book. This book may be the catalyst for someone to start the next big thing! Help them find it by submitting a review here:

JPStonestreet.com/AmazonReview

About the Author

JP Stonestreet has been in the software and Internet business since 1995. He has built applications and websites for large and small companies, as well as building several of his own. In 2008, he sold QuoteCatcher.com and PromoteWare.com to QuinStreet, Inc. in Foster City, CA and now focuses his energy on helping others follow their entrepreneurial dreams.

Learn more about JP on his website, JPStonestreet.com, on Facebook/JPStartupCoach, on LinkedIn/JPStonestreet, and on Twitter/JPStonestreet.

Resources

Business Plans

"Alpha Teach Yourself Business Plans in 24 Hours" by Michael Miller

"The One Page Business Plan for the Creative Entrepreneur" by Jim Horan

"Something Ventured" by Miralan Productions (2011 Documentary)

Web Design

"Don't Make Me Think: A Common Sense Approach to Web Usability, 2nd Edition" by Steve Krug

"Designing with the Mind in Mind: Simple Guide to Understanding User Interface Design Rules" by Jeff Johnson

"The Principles of Beautiful Web Design" by Jason Beaird

Interviewing & Outsourcing

"96 Great Interview Questions to Ask Before You Hire" by Paul Falcone

"Hiring the Best: Manager's Guide to Effective Interviewing and Recruiting, Fifth Edition" by Martin Yate

"Hire With Your Head: Using Performance-Based Hiring to Build

Great Teams" by Lou Adler

"Virtual Assistant Assistant: The Ultimate Guide to Finding, Hiring, and Working with Virtual Assistants" by Nick Loper

Sales

"Little Red Book of Selling: 12.5 Principles of Sales Greatness" by Jeffrey Gitomer

"Secrets of Closing the Sale" by Zig Ziglar

"SPIN Selling" by Neil Rackham

Marketing

"The Ultimate Guide to Google AdWords" by Perry Marshal and Bryan Todd

"Email Marketing That Sells: Your Guide to Building a Fired Up Email List!" by Robert Coorey

"Marketing With Pinterest - How to Drive Traffic, Sales and Results with Pinterest" by Shawn Manaher

"Brand Against the Machine: How to Build Your Brand, Cut Through the Marketing Noise, and Stand Out from the Competition" by John Morgan

"Likeable Social Media: How to Delight Your Customers, Create an Irresistible Brand, and Be Generally Amazing on Facebook (And Other Social Networks)" by Dave Kerpen

"Ultimate Guide to Facebook Advertising: How to Access 600 Million Customers in 10 Minutes" by Perry Marshall and Thomas Meloche

"Landing Page Optimization: The Definitive Guide to Testing and

Tuning for Conversions" by Tim Ash

"Inbound Marketing: Get Found Using Google, Social Media, and Blogs" by Brian Halligan, Dharmesh Shah and David Meerman Scott

"Content Rules: How to Create Killer Blogs, Podcasts, Videos, Ebooks, Webinars (and More) That Engage Customers and Ignite Your Business" by Ann Handley and C. C. Chapman

"The New Rules of Marketing & PR: How to Use Social Media, Online Video, Mobile Applications, Blogs, News Releases, and Viral Marketing to Reach Buyers Directly" by David Meerman Scott

"Real-Time Marketing and PR: How to Instantly Engage Your Market, Connect with Customers, and Create Products that Grow Your Business Now" by David Meerman Scott

"Facebook Marketing: Leveraging Facebook's Features for Your Marketing Campaigns (3rd Edition)" by Brian Carter

"The Presentation Secrets of Steve Jobs: How to Be Insanely Great in Front of Any Audience" by Carmine Gallo

SEO

"SEO Made Simple (Second Edition): Strategies For Dominating The World's Largest Search Engine" by Michael H. Fleischner

"Search Engine Optimization (SEO): An Hour a Day" by Jennifer Grappone

"Rich Dad Poor Dad: What The Rich Teach Their Kids About Money That the Poor and Middle Class Do Not!" by Robert T. Kiyosaki

Entrepreneurial

"Screw It Let's Do It" by Richard Branson

"Think Big and Kick Ass In Business and Life" by Donald J. Trump

"The Snowball: Warren Buffett and the Business of Life" by Alice Schroeder

"The 4-Hour Workweek: Escape 9-5, Live Anywhere, and Join the New Rich" by Timothy Ferriss

Inspirational & Motivational

"The Secret" by Rhonda Byrne

"Think and Grow Rich" by Napoleon Hill

"The Secrets of the Millionaire Mind" by T. Harv Eker

"Awaken the Giant Within: How to Take Immediate Control of Your Mental, Emotional, Physical and Financial Destiny!" by Anthony Robbins

Thought Provoking

"Blink: The Power of Thinking Without Thinking" by Malcolm Gladwell

"Outliers: The Story of Success" by Malcolm Gladwell

"The Tipping Point: How Little Things Can Make a Big Difference" by Malcolm Gladwell

"How to Win Friends and Influence People" by Dale Carnegie

"Socialnomics: How Social Media Transforms the Way We Live and Do Business" by Erik Qualman

"Talent Is Overrated: What Really Separates World-Class Performers from Everybody Else" by Geoff Colvin

Index

1-800-Flowers, 81

24 million dollar football, 15

Affiliate Marketing, 235
    CommissionJunction, ClickBank, SkimLinks, PayDotCom, 237
    Payouts, 235
Alliteration, 131
Angel Investors. *See* Seed Capital
API (Application Programmer Interface), 27
Attracting Traffic, 224
Audits, 281

Black Hat SEO, 266
    Doorway Pages, 267
    Invisible Text, 267
    Keyword Spamming, 266
    Keyword Stuffing, 266
Business Plan, 63
Business requirements filter, 31
Businesses
    City Info, 13
    Home-Showing.net, 18
    Informed Decisions, 15
    MeteredWorks, 17
    PromoteWare, 18, 21, 25, 53, 115
    QuoteCatcher, 20, 21, 25, 32, 33, 48, 54, 88, 97, 101, 102, 115, 120, 148, 169, 188, 229, 237, 247, 254, 279, 283, 284, 292
    Stonestreet Enterprises, 18
    TimeToParent, 19, 20, 51, 52, 53

Changing the World vs. Making Money, 50
Checklists
    Building Your Website, 223
    Marketing Your Website, 270
    Planning For Success, 83
    Starting Your Startup, 140
Color Palette, 124
Competition Is Good, 44
Competitive Advantage, 46
Competitive Research, 40
Competitor Intel, 41
    Document your findings, 42
    Search keywords, 42
Comps, comprehensives, 217
Content Management, 149
Contractor vs. FTE, 280
Contracts, 99
Copyright, 165

Cost-Per-Acquisition (CPA), 225
  Repeat customers, 230
Cost-per-Action. *See* Cost-Per-Acquisition (CPA)
Cost-per-Click (CPC), 229
Cost-per-Conversion. *See* Cost-Per-Acquisition (CPA)
Crowdfunding. *See* Seed Capital
Crowdinvesting. *See* Seed Capital
Crowdlending. *See* Seed Capital
CrunchBase, 44
Customer Service, 169

Define Your Idea
  Problem to solve, 38
Deployment, 221
  Beta, use or not, 222
Designer vs. Developer, 197
DIY Web Design. *See* Website Development
Driving traffic, 224

Ecommerce, 181
  Accepting Credit Cards, 184
  Catalog & Shopping Cart, 182
  Hosted Stores, 181
  Merchant Account, 185
  Pay Now Buttons, 182
  Payment Gateway, 184
  Payment Processor, 185
  Stripe, 184
Elevator Pitch, 70, 73
  30 Second Pitch, 75
  Follow-up Pitch, 72
  Four rules, 73, 74
  Greeting Pitch, 70
  Under 2 Minute Pitch, 75
Executive Suite, 276

Exit Strategies
  Closing, 282
  Going Public (IPO), 285
  Selling, 283
Expenses, 135

Finances, 133
  Business bank account, 134
  Pricing, 137
  Tax ID, 134
  Taxes, 136
  Tracking Expenses, 135
Finding Talent, 205
  Local, 206
  Offshore, 205
Fixed Price vs. Hourly, 201
Focus, 85
  Energy, 86
  Product, 87
  Service, 87
FTC Disclosure, 152

Gamification, 176
  3-step process, 178
  Foursquare, 176
Google's IPO, 287

Identity, 114
  Color Palette, 124
    Why the web is blue, 125
  Company Name vs. DomainName, 114
  Domain names, 116
    Benefits, 116
    Creative, 117
    Email, 123
    Guidelines, 116
    Opinions, 120

    Parking, 123
    Registering, 121
    Searching for, 118
Logo, 126
    Colors, 127
    Font, 129
    Mark, 127
    Text, 128
    Phone and Address, 131
    Tagline, 130
Images
    99Designs, 151
    BigStockPhoto, 151
    Fiverr, 151
    FotoSearch, 151
    iStockPhoto, 151
Incubators, 277
Innovation Pavilion, 277
Intellectual Property (IP), 61
Interviewing, 207
    Project Managers, 211
    References, 213
    Web Designers, 208
    Web Developers, 209
Iterative software development, 203

Job vs. Business, 61

KISS It, 91

LAMP Stack, 146
Legal CYA, 92
    Business entities, 98
    Contracts, 99
    NDA (Nondisclosure Agreement), 93
    Operating Agreement, 93
    Piercing the veil, 98
Licensing, 113
Local vs. Offshore, 198

Malcolm Gladwell, Outliers, 29
Managing Your Team, 214
Manufacturers & Suppliers, 138
Marketing
    Affiliate Marketing. *See* Affiliate Marketing
    Content Marketing, 255
    Email & eNewsletters, 250
    Networking & Shoe Leather, 255
    Pay-Per-Click Advertising (PPC). *See* Pay-Per-Click Advertising (PPC)
    Postcards, 252
    Social Media Marketing. *See* Social Media Marketing
    Telemarketing, 254
Meta Tags. *See* SEO: Special Tags
Microlenders. *See* Seed Capital
Mobile Access, 174
    Mobile App, 175
    Mobile Friendly, 174
    Mobile Website, 174
Monetization Plan, 48

Navigation, 163
    Account Nav, 164
    Bottom or Footer Nav, 165
    Breadcrumbs Nav, 166
    Hover Menus, 166
    Left Nav, 164
    Right Nav, 165
    Top Nav, 164
Need vs. Demand, 51
Notebook of ideas, 37

Off to the Races, 77
   Control your excitement, 77
   It's a family business, 78
   Peseverance, 81
   Ready, fire, aim, 80
   You're so lucky, 79
Off-the-Shelf Software, 183
Outsourcing, 198, 200, 265, 278

Page Layout, 167
Partnerships, 101
   Clearly defined leader, 103
   Equity Split, 109
   Homogeny is bad, 103
   Licensing, 113
   Life Insurance, 108
   Partnership Agreements, 104
   Termination Agreement, 112
Pay-Per-Click Advertising (PPC), 232
   Facebook, 233
   Problems with, 232
   Ultimate Guide to Google AdWords, The, 234
Pay-to-Play Incubators, 277
Piercing the Veil, 98
Privacy Policy, 152

Quotes
   Albert Einstein, 186
   Arthur Ashe, 84, 141
   Benjamin Franklin, 22
   Blaise Pascal, 70
   Burt Reynolds, 288
   Dennis Crowley, Foursquare Co-Founder, 53
   Francis Ford Coppola, 130
   Henry Ford, 271
   Napoleon Hill, 63
   Oscar Wilde, 137
   Sir Winston Churchill, 81
   Sonny in "The Godfather", 78
   Sun Tzu, 29

Registrar, 143
Regus, 276
Requirements, 186
   Appendices, 193
   Assumptions, 189
   Components, 193
   Definitions, 188
   Knowledge is power, 194
   Pages, 193
   Phases, 187
   Purpose, 188
   Site-wide Features, 189
      Content Management, 191
      Graphic Design, 190
      Input Field Validation, 192
      Navigation, 191
      Search Box, 192
      Security, 192
Richard Branson, Virgin, 286
Robots.txt, 172
Roll their own, 283
Running Your Business
   Audits, 281
   Contractor vs. FTE, 280
   Employee background checks, 280
   Employees, 278
   Entrepreneurship, 272
   Office Space, 276
   Outsourcing, 278
   Reinvestment options, 274

SAAS, 18
Scope Creep, 202
SCORE, 21, 66, 77, 206, 255, 256, 273
Search Engine Optimization. *See* SEO
Seed Capital, 53
   Bootstrapping, 54
   External funding, 55
      Angel investors, 59
      Bank loans, 56
      Crowdfunding, 57
      Crowdinvesting, 58
      Crowdlending, 57
      Friends and family, 55
      Microlenders, 56
      Venture capital, 59
SEO
   Black Hat. *See* Black Hat SEO
   Bounce Rate, 263
   Content Freshness, 259
   Content Outsourcing, 265
   Inbound Links, 262
   Keyword Richness, 258
   Long-tail Keywords, 268
   Top Ranking, 267
   Website Performance, 264
Site Map, 171
SMARTER Goals, 89
Social Media Marketing, 239
   Buying followers, 244
   Facebook, 239
   Foursquare, 241
   Keys to success, 242
   LinkedIn, 240
   Negative comments, 247
   Posting ideas, 246
   Problems with, 242
   Setting up accounts
      Facebook, 243
      LinkedIn, 245
      Twitter, 244
   Twitter, 239
   Yelp, 240
Squeeze Page, 226
SSL Certificate, 170
   GeoTrust, Thawte, Verisign, GoDaddy, 171
   Wildcard Cert, 175
Standard Pages, 152
   About Us, 153
   Contact Us, 154
   Frequently Asked Questions, 154
   FTC Disclosure, 152
   Privacy Policy, 152
   Terms & Conditions, 152
SWOT analysis, 43

Tax ID, 134
Terms & Conditions, 152
Testing Your Software, 218
   How to report an issue, 219
   Quality assurance (QA) testing, 219
   User Acceptance Testing (UAT), 219
Thought Leader, 256
Traits of successful startups
   Idea and execution, 25
   Small niche, 25
   Value proposition, 26
TweetAdder, Tweepwise, 241

Uncubed, 277

Usability, 154
   Ajax, 163
   Avoid Dead Blogs, 158
   Avoid Flash-Only Sites, 161
   Avoid Popups, 160
   Check Hyperlinks, 160
   Consistent Page Layout, 160
   Contact Us, 160
   Cross-Browser Compatibility, 162
   Fix Bugs, 162
   JavaScript Disabled, 162
   Meta and HTML Tags, 158
   Page Load Time, 157
   Proofread, 157
   Readable Content, 157
   Search Box, 162
   Simple Messages, 158
   Simple Navigation, 158

Venture Capital. *See* Seed Capital

Web 2.0, 172
Web Business Models, 32
   Brokerage, 33
   Content creators and aggregators, 34
   Ecommerce or eTailing, 32
   Games, 35
   Human connections, 33
   Software tools, 35
Web startup benefits
   Low startup costs, 24
   Risk/reward ratio, 24
Webhost, 144
   Dedicated Servers, 148
   Shared Hosting, 146
   Virtual Servers, 148
Website
   Quality, 142
Website Addiction Loop, 178
Website Development, 194
   Designer vs. Developer, 197
   DIY Web Design, 195
      Open Source Frameworks, 196
      Wizards, 195
   Features not needed in first release, 204
   Fixed Price vs. Hourly, 201
   Lease vs. Own Code, 218
   Local vs. Offshore, 198
   Scope Creep, 202
What should I do?, 29